HITLER'S NEW DISORDER

STEVAN K. PAVLOWITCH

Hitler's
New Disorder

The Second World War in Yugoslavia

Columbia University Press
New York

Columbia University Press
Publishers Since 1893
New York

Library of Congress Cataloging-in-Publication Data

Pavlowitch, Stevan K.
  Hitler's new disorder : the Second World War in Yugoslavia / Stevan K. Pavlowitch.
    p. cm.
  Includes bibliographical references and index.
  ISBN 978-0-231-70050-4 (cloth : alk. paper)
  1. Yugoslavia—History—Axis occupation, 1941–1945. 2. Germans—Yugoslavia—History—20th century. 3. Italians—Yugoslavia—History—20th century. 4. World War,
1939–1945—Yugoslavia. 5. Balkan Peninsula—History—20th century. 6. Yugoslavia—Politics and government—1918–1945. I. Title.
  DR1298.P379 2008
  940.53'497—dc22
                            2007044193

♾
Columbia University Press books are printed on permanent and durable acid-free paper.
This book is printed on paper with recycled content.
Printed in India

c 10 9 8 7 6 5 4 3 2 1

References to Internet Web sites (URLs) were accurate at the time of writing.
Neither the author nor Columbia University Press is responsible for URLs
that may have expired or changed since the manuscript was prepared.

CONTENTS

FOREWORD

A synthetic treatment of a complex topic it may be, but it has had a long gestation. This book has grown out of a special subject on the Second World War in Yugoslavia, taught for many years to undergraduates at the University of Southampton, and out of the parallel research undertaken for a study of Italy's involvement across the Adriatic in the same period, that I never found the time to write. It is the unsatisfactory answer to the innumerable questions I asked as the gap grew ever wider between what had happened at ground level (at the various ground levels) and how things were seen by people at the time, on the one hand, and the conventionally received rendering of history books both in communist Yugoslavia and in the (essentially British) West, on the other.

The second destruction of Yugoslavia by the Yugoslavs, with the wars of the Yugoslav succession in the 1990s, has now overtaken in public interest the first destruction by Hitler and Mussolini, and the wars of the early 1940s through which its reconstruction was achieved by the Communist Party of Yugoslavia. Most sources are available for the study of the Second World War period, even if some supposedly delicate intelligence sources are still withheld, and many documents have not survived. Comparisons and cross-examinations are possible. As the Balkans generally remained in the shadow of other fronts, my aim is to see what actually happened in overshadowed Yugoslavia. I do not generally look at British, American or Soviet policy, except through the prism of what the local actors believed Churchill, Roosevelt or Stalin did or did not want to happen there.

The view has long prevailed in communist Yugoslavia that the country had played an important role in the war, on the side of the 'anti-fascist coalition', through the action of its Peoples' Liberation Movement. That view held that there was really no civil war, as the world (including Yugoslavia) was simply divided into a fascist camp and an anti-fascist camp. A more sophisticated version was accepted in the West, mainly provided by literate British actors who had ended up supporting those who in Yugoslavia had come victoriously out of the war and reunited the country, which was what the Allies had wanted.

Questions were already being asked by historians in Yugoslavia and abroad at the time when the country began to slide into disintegration after Tito's death. Reasoned scholarly questioning too quickly gave way to emotional revisionism, in all directions. The state-directed and state-distorted approved version of the Second World War was taken over by collective, communal, local and personal memories. The fear of losing one's identity, the feeling of frustration towards the present and even of helplessness towards the future, opened the way to an obsession with the past. There are various markets to buy it all—the rehabilitation of all that was anti-communist in different sections, as well as the return of a nostalgic and fundamentalist communist partisan interpretation.

This is possible as the Second World War in Yugoslavia was indeed the juxtaposition of many such parts. Testimonies tell of loss of bearings, of irrational acts, of lives tossed about in the storm, of combatants seized by the frenzy of battle, of individual acts of compassion. Even so, we only hear the testimonies of those who survived. The historian needs to understand how all the players saw what was happening, and acted accordingly, without forgetting those who did not actually fight. Writing after the 1990s, after the second destruction and the wars of the Yugoslav succession, he must be careful not to get carried away by his knowledge of what has happened since, and fall into anachronistic explanations. He should be able to exchange feelings with the past, even with his own past. He should not be frightened by the fact that he may be destroying legends. This is a period when war and ruin opened up the wounds of societies that had not yet recovered from the First World War, and had not really been given the chance to reorganise, modernise and integrate in a stable new structure. Anarchic behaviour rose to the surface, with irrational evaluations of what was possible, and unreal (not to say surreal) perceptions of circumstances. One should acknowledge the existence of antagonisms that were not necessarily primeval, but that were easily rekindled. Saul Friedländer says, with regard to the Shoah: 'Admittedly, a detonator was needed. But also much deadwood and scrub for the fire to start.'[1] There was little solidarity between victims of different communities. Muslim militiamen dressed up as Serb chetniks or partisans, Croat ustashas as Muslims, Serb chetniks as partisans and vice versa, to provoke enmity or to divert reprisals to other yet similar villagers.

The historian should beware of numbers. Yugoslav reports use numbers as did medieval chroniclers or Old Testament prophets. Size counts. It improves one's victim status. Yugoslavia's population losses in the Second World War were huge, but the figure of 1,706,000 provided by the Yugoslav government in 1945 to the Inter-Allied Reparations Agency is a myth. Some Yugoslav scholars have since made valiant efforts to arrive at a more realistic figure. In particular, Bogoljub Kočović lets census figures speak for themselves, avoiding politically charged issues of how many died in specific operations, at specific times and in specific locations. He calculates 1,014,000 real war losses, with a minimum of 900,000 and a maximum of 1,150,000.[2] As for German Wehrmacht reports, the exact number of 'enemies' killed is so clinical that one almost expects them to come with decimals, as if to rationalise the efficiency of hostage executions and anti-insurgent operations. On the Italian side, allowances should

---

1   Saul Friedländer, 'La Shoah ou la solitude des Justes', in *Le Monde*, Paris, 7-8 January 2007.

2   Bogoljub Kočović, *Žrtve Drugog svetskog rata u Jugoslaviji*, London, 1985, with subsequent editions in Sarajevo and Belgrade. Latest edition, *Sahrana jednog mita. Žrtve Drugog svetskog rata u Jugoslaviji*, Belgrade, 2005. See also his *Etnički i demografski razvoj u Jugoslaviji od 1921. do 1991. g., po svim zvaničnim a u nekim slučajevima i korigovanim popisima*, Paris 1998. 'Everyone interested in the truth about wartime population losses remains indebted to him for his work', writes Jozo Tomasevich of Kočović's work (*War and Revolution in Yugoslavia, 1941–1945. Occupation and Collaboration*, Stanford, CA, 2001: 736).

be made for differences between orders given at the highest level of the Regio Esercito, orders issued at lowest level, executions actually carried out and executions reported.

Yugoslav extant original documents also need a careful examination. Some of those captured from rivals have been doctored, while other documents have been altered by their recipients. Many were left open-ended for completion in case of need. Even by going to genuine source material, it is not easy to crack the carapace of truths, half-truths, non-truths and errors which covers the period. Yet it remains essential to recreate the way things appeared to people at the time, and to overcome the complexity of their points of view. In spite of the fact that a narrated historical account is always an interpretation, I believe that a dispassionate history that accepts the intricacy of what it has unearthed is both possible and necessary.

In order to try and give a synthetic account, in less than 100,000 words, of the interconnected events that took place between 1941 and 1945 from the Alps to Macedonia, from the Adriatic coast to the Danubian plain, over what had been, somehow remained, and gradually again became, Yugoslavia, I have eschewed the full scholarly apparatus. The list of my sources appears in an appendix. I assume responsibility for an interpretation which is based on a comparison and a cross-examination of sources and on forty years of trying to understand what went on, with whatever objectivity post-modernism will allow me. Even after the effort, I remain with my doubts, always fearful of that character from Sanja Domazet's recent novel, *Ko plače* (Belgrade, 2006), who enters the house at night with the 'slow, confident steps of one who has never been tormented by doubts'. I have met him: he is heavy-footed and big-headed, he knows everything, and is ever ready to lecture historians.

I wish here in particular to thank the colleagues and friends listed below in alphabetical order, who pushed, read, questioned, criticised, corrected, answered questions, suggested and noted when they had better things to do, who were patient, who listened or did not listen, and who were helpfully around: Dejan Djokić, Bogoljub Kochovich

(Kočović), Zhivka Koleva, France Pavlowitch, Kosta Pavlowitch, Nenad Petrović, Andrea Reiter Drabkin Klaus Schmider and Desimir Tošić.

The participants (all men) whom I interviewed or with whom I corresponded were an invaluable source. Most of them are no longer alive. Three of them managed to tell me almost nothing by courteously ignoring my questions. One of them told me too much, and lied almost systematically. I am grateful to all of them. What I gathered from written sources, and from other participants, helped me to formulate my questions to them, and often to return with new questions. What they told me always enabled me to shed more light on written sources. I want to single out two of the leading participants in the events studied—Milovan Djilas and Zvonimir Vučković—who expressed no hatred in what they wrote and in what they told me. They are no longer alive. I hope they do not mind my dedicating this study to their memory.

Paris, 13-14 July 2007   St. K. P

ABBREVIATIONS

AVNOJ   *Antifašističko veće/vijeće narodnog oslobodjenja Jugoslavije* —Anti-Fascist Council of the Peoples' Liberation of Yugoslavia

HSS   *Hrvatska seljačka stranka*—Croat Peasant Party

JVO   *Jugoslovenska vojska u otadžbini*—Yugoslav Army in the Homeland

JMO   *Jugoslavenska muslimanska organizacija*—Yugoslav Muslim Organisation

JRZ   *Jugoslovenska radikalna zajednica*—Yugoslav Radical Union

KPJ   *Komunistička partija Jugoslavije*—Communist Party of Yugoslavia

MVAC   *Milizia volontari anticommunisti*—Volunteer Anti-Communist Militia

NDH   *Nezavisna Država Hrvatska*—Independent State of Croatia

NOB   *Narodnooslobodilačka borba*—Peoples' Liberation Struggle

NOP   *Narodnooslobodilački pokret*—Peoples' Liberation Movement

NOVJ   *Narodnooslobodilačka vojska Jugoslavije*—Peoples' Liberation Army of Yugoslavia

OF   *Osvobodilna fronta*—(Slovene) Liberation Front

OZNa   *Organizacija za zaštitu naroda*—Organisation for the Protection of the People

SAS   Special Air Service

SD   *Sicherheitsdienst*—(Nazi Party) Security Service

SDK   *Srpski dobrovoljački korpus*—Serbian Volunteer Corps

SDS   *Srpska državna straža*—Serbian State Guard

SKK   *Srpski kulturni klub*—Serb Cultural Club

SOE   Special Operations Executive

SLjS   *Slovenska ljudska stranka*—Slovene People's Party

SUK   *Srpski udarni korpus*—Serbian Shock Corps

SZ   *Slovenska zaveza*—Slovenian Alliance

LIST OF ILLUSTRATIONS

Between pages 150-1

1. Belgrade, 27 March 1941. Demonstrators with portraits of King Peter heading for central Belgrade. On that day a military coup proclaimed Peter II of age, thus bringing to an end the regency and the government that had adhered to the Tripartite Pact two days earlier. Hitler immediately gave orders for Yugoslavia to be destroyed 'with merciless brutality'.
© Author's Collection, from K. St. Pavlowitch Papers

2. Guerrillas leading German prisoners, somewhere in German-occupied Serbia in September 1941. Received in London by the Yugoslav government in exile, the photograph was captioned as 'Serbian chetniks leading German war prisoners' (specifically through the village of Koštunići, near Ravna Gora).
© Author's Collection, from K. St. Pavlowitch Papers.

3. The German military go into counter-action. This photograph, similarly received in London at the time and apparently taken by a hidden bystander, shows the rounding up of hostages in a town in Serbia in October 1941.
© Author's Collection, from K. St. Pavlowitch Papers.

4. Cazin, northwest Bosnia, July 1941. As the ustashas lost control of vast tracks of their Independent State of Croatia, Italian forces were slow to withdraw, and then returned to specific areas, to end the insurgency in the hinterland of Italy's new Dalmatian coastline. They launched a propaganda campaign to convince the population they had come as protectors.
© Author's Collection, received from General Umberto Salvatores.

5. Drvar, western Bosnia, September 1941. Most of the insurgents, who had risen against the ustashas, were not interested in taking on the Italians. However, in Drvar, a small industrial centre where the communists had set up a well-organised base, Italian troops moved in and took away captured insurgents. Tito would set up his head-quarters in Drvar in February 1944.
© Author's Collection, received from General Umberto Salvatores.

6. Belgrade, 14 January 1945. Demonstrators with portraits of Marshal Tito and 'Down with the King' banners heading for central Belgrade. Back in liberated Belgrade, Tito had made final arrangements in November 1944 with Šubašić, the last prime minister of the government in exile, for King Peter to delegate his prerogative to a regency, and for a joint government to organise the transition to a postwar régime.
© Vlado Strugar, *Jugoslavija u ratu, 1941-1945*, Belgrade, 1975:383.

General map of Yugoslavia, with pre-1941 borders,
physical features, regional and place names.

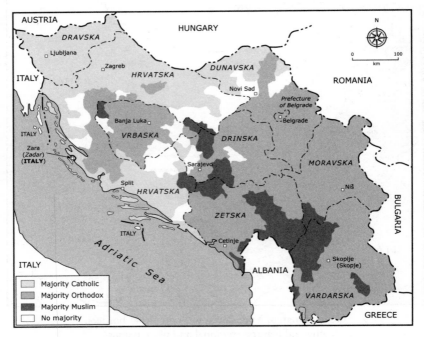

Prewar Yugoslavia, administrative and religious, showing banovinas
after 1939 creation of Banovina of Croatia (Hrvatska), and religious
distribution of population according to 1921 census.

Partitioned wartime Yugoslavia: the western regions
and the Independent State of Croatia.

Partitioned wartime Yugoslavia: the eastern
regions and German-controlled 'residual Serbia'—
between Hungary, Romania, Bulgaria, Albania,
Montenegro and the NDH.

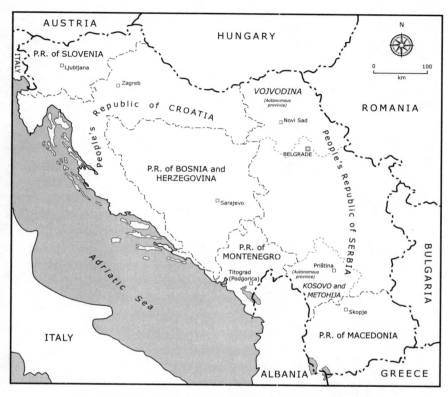

The KPJ's 'New Yugoslavia', showing the federated republics
(and Serbia's autonomous provinces) of the post –1945
Federative Peoples' Republic of Yugoslavia.

1

THE END OF THE KINGDOM
OF YUGOSLAVIA
AUGUST 1939–APRIL 1941

On 26 August 1939, the Yugoslav regency started a process of restructuring the state. Six days later, on 1 September, the German attack on Poland started the Second World War. Since its foundation in 1918, Yugoslavia had managed to protect its territorial integrity and its independence, by acting with and through the League of Nations, and by seeking the support of the victorious powers, until the Depression, the rise of Hitler's Reich, the decline of French power, and the Western Allies' scant sympathy for the country's economic problems led its rulers to neutrality, increasingly slanted towards Rome and Berlin. Yugoslavia, as a united state, was generally accepted, but not so the ideology of integral 'Yugoslavism', which was supposed to merge all the component identities. The parliamentary system, set up by the Constitution of 1921, had not been the result of a consensus between the state's different communities, and it was not able to establish such a consensus in the following years, when it operated under the ever more impatient and authoritarian guidance of King Alexander, before the monarch abrogated it in 1929. Even though Croat opinion in particular had been dissatisfied by that constitution, which had established centralist rule, the royal takeover did not solve the 'Croat question'. In 1931 Alexander granted a new constitution, under which the government was responsible to the monarch alone. He was assassinated in 1934, at the start of a state visit to France by a militant of the terrorist Internal Macedonian

Revolutionary Organisation acting for, and in cooperation with, the extremist Croat Ustasha (*ustaša*, insurgent) Movement.

Prince Paul, who headed the regency council for Alexander's underage successor, King Peter II, started looking for a way out within the framework of the Constitution of 1931. From 1935, his prime minister Milan Stojadinović, who had formed a new government party, the Yugoslav Radical Union (JRZ, *Jugoslovenska radikalna zajednica*), to coalesce all government supporters, had managed to bring in the Slovene People's Party (SLjS, *Slovenska ljudska stranka*) and the Yugoslav Muslim Organisation (JMO, *Jugoslavenska muslimanska organizacija)* which represented the majority of Slovene and Muslim electors respectively, but he had failed to get the cooperation of the majority Croat Peasant Party (HSS, *Hrvatska seljačka stranka*). Meanwhile the opposition parties, Serb and non-Serb, united under the HSS leader Vladko Maček, had agreed by the end of 1937 on democratic elections for a new constituent assembly, which would work out an institutional structure to satisfy a majority of Serbs, a majority of Croats and a majority of Slovenes. Under pressure of a united opposition strengthened by the results of the 1938 parliamentary elections, and even more so of foreign events (the Anschluss, the dismemberment of Czechoslovakia, the invasion of Albania, the Pact of Steel and rumours of an impending German-Soviet treaty), Prince Paul hurried to solve the Croat issue directly with Maček. He organised the resignation of Stojadinović, who was getting too authoritarian and too close to the Axis, and obtained a reconstructed JRZ cabinet under Dragiša Cvetković in February 1939.

By the end of April, Cvetković and Maček had come to terms on the principle of a Province (*Banovina*) of Croatia, to be set up with wide local powers. The HSS agreed to join a coalition government, which would implement the agreement and prepare a new organisation of the Yugoslav state. The reforms would be enacted by ordinances under article 116 of the existing Constitution, on the basis of the crown's reserved emergency powers. More time was needed before the Cvetković-Maček Agreement (*Sporazum*), as it was generally called, was finalised in a form acceptable to Prince Paul–'to ensure the participation of Croats in the life of the state and thus to safeguard the national interest'.[1]

'Yugoslavia is the best guarantee of the independence and progress of the Serbs, the Croats and Slovenes'. Such was the opening statement of the Sporazum, published on 26 August 1939. It joined into one new Banovina of Croatia two existing banovinas (administrative provinces) and some adjoining districts; it gave it extensive powers taken from the state, a governor (*ban*) appointed by the crown and a local executive responsible jointly to him and to an elected assembly or *Sabor*. The final demarcation of territory and competence remained to be settled in the overall reorganisation of the state. Elections would be held under a new electoral law; the HSS would join a new government, with Cvetkovič as prime minister and Maček as deputy premier. The Slovene and Muslim parties, which were already components of the governing JRZ, the Independent Democratic Party, which was the HSS's mainly Serb partner, and a few other Serb politicians, all endorsed the Sporazum and agreed to join the coalition.

On the same day, the new government was appointed and parliament was dissolved. The provisions of the Banovina of Croatia were enacted; more ordinances empowered the government to extend these provisions to other provinces, whose territories could be modified, and to change 'political' laws (associations, press, elections). The measures set the stage for what was in fact a wider constitutional reorganisation. Leading HSS politicians also argued that they were but the first steps in setting up an autonomous Croatia within the common state, for there were differences of approach within the Croat majority party. Its radical right rejected any deal with Belgrade, and Maček felt it urgent to counter its appeal before a European war broke out. The Cvetković–Maček Agreement was followed by a political relaxation, which provided all discontented elements with unprecedented opportunities for increased activities. The HSS was in

---

1 Preamble to the Ordinance on the Banovina of Croatia, *Službene novine Kraljevine Jugoslavije*, Belgrade, 26 August 1939: 1.

favour of quick elections; not so the parties in Serbia which wanted first to complete the territorial settlement. In the circumstances, only the ordinance for elections to the Croatian Sabor was issued, and the only elections to be held were for rural councils in Croatia.

Maček had negotiated as if he were the leader of the Croats. When Prince Paul went to Zagreb in January 1940 to sign the ordinance on elections to the Sabor, the event was organised by the HSS as a manifestation of Yugoslav unity and of confidence between the prince regent and the 'leader of the Croatian people'. The HSS, which had evolved into a Croatian national movement, complete with peasant unions, cultural societies and party militia, became the governing party in Croatia. Its rural and civic guards, tolerated by the authorities, were legalised to protect the constitutional rights of Croatia and to act as auxiliaries to the forces of law and order. On the choice of *ban*, Maček agreed to Prince Paul's nominee—Ivan Šubašić, a HSS politician who was close to the palace and had acted as intermediary.

In Croatia, the Maček line generally prevailed, but many, especially in the middle classes of the larger towns, wanted more autonomy. Emigré HSS politicians had returned, notably Juraj Krnjević who became general secretary of the party, and so had many ustashas. The Ustasha Croatian Revolutionary Movement had been formed abroad by Ante Pavelić, who called himself the *Poglavnik* (leader), when King Alexander had introduced his dictatorship. Its origins lay in the small nationalist party of Josip Frank who, having first supported the trend towards Yugoslav unification in 1918, went on later in the year to call for the preservation of the national and political individuality of a greater Croatia. Ante Pavelić had represented it in parliament in the 1920s. He had linked up with Croat former officers of the Austro-Hungarian army who had never accepted Yugoslavia and who had stayed on in Austria, and with other separatists, notably from Macedonia. He had formed groups for carrying out sabotage and terrorist actions, trained in camps in Italy and Hungary, from where they smuggled propaganda and weapons into Yugoslavia. After the assassination of King Alexander, most of these ustashas went to Italy where they were interned. The presence of 500 or so of them, including Pavelić, was used by the fascist government as a means of putting pressure on Yugoslavia.

The ustashas were unreservedly anti-Yugoslav. They advocated a large Croatian state in which only Croats by blood and ancestry would form the nation, and which would be modelled on the totalitarian systems of Italy and Germany. At home they were active mainly in Zagreb, and noticed through their political propaganda. The weekly *Hrvatski narod* grouped intellectuals of the radical right; it campaigned against any deal with the government in Belgrade, and against the leadership of the HSS. Eventually in the course of 1940, the Banovina authorities imprisoned a number of activists and closed down pro-ustasha publications, thus pushing their activity underground. In the meanwhile they had infiltrated nationalist and Catholic clerical circles, legal organisations and the HSS Guard. They exerted a certain attraction on the young, particularly at Zagreb University where they clashed with communist-organised students.

The traditional dislike of Germany limited the appeal of a Nazi-inspired ideology in Serbia, but anti-Semitic and anti-democratic ideas could be attached to local nationalist traditions. Reactions to Western models lingered on from the days of Russian-inspired Slavism. The extreme right found expression in Dimitrije Ljotić's Zbor (rally) movement. During a stay in Paris, Ljotić had been influenced by French right-wing nationalist ideas, notably Maurras's Action Française. However, he had entered politics in the Radical Party, and adhered to King Alexander's dictatorship. As minister of justice, he had submitted to the monarch a draft for the royal Constitution in 1931, and had resigned when it had been rejected. In 1935 he had formed Zbor, which garnered some 10,000 adherents, and 30,774 votes at the 1938 elections—not enough for a seat in parliament. Originally an integral Yugoslavist movement, Zbor had in the late 'thirties began to look more Serbian Orthodox, adding anti-Semitism to anti-parliamentarianism, with a certain following in intellectual youth and church circles. It had come out against the Sporazum and had attacked Prince Paul and the government for policies that allegedly led to communism. In November 1940, the movement was banned and many of its members were prosecuted.

Prohibited since 1921, the Communist Party of Yugoslavia (KPJ, *Komunistička partija Jugoslavije*), had continued to act through legal organisations, but had become weak and increasingly dependent on the Communist International—the Comintern—which, having called for the dissolution of Yugoslavia, was more interested in the revolutionary potential of separatist movements. Taken over by its left, which gave priority to the struggle against the Serbian bourgeois nationalist interpretation of Yugoslavia, it had moved its centre from Belgrade to Zagreb. Even after it had changed its position on Yugoslavia, the Comintern wondered whether the KPJ was worth keeping. Yugoslavia's communists had got themselves terribly entangled until Josip Broz, known as Tito, had appeared at the eleventh hour to give the party some cohesion. Trade-union organiser, party official, Comintern operator and conspirator, he had worked his way up, in and out of Yugoslavia. In the autumn of 1940, after much travelling, he was back in Zagreb as the Comintern's anointed, to take over and purge a party that had just passed muster as a section of the Communist International.

The KPJ thereafter achieved some success as a disciplined movement formed on a federalist basis under a team of able younger men for whom Tito, the executor in Yugoslavia of a line received from Moscow, was the ultimate arbiter. It had been turned into a Bolshevik-type party devoted to the Soviet Union, living in the expectation of the revolution and the dream world of the communist society of the future. Special emphasis was placed on youth; the communists were actually more successful among students than on shopfloors or in villages. A vast and diverse student population came together at universities —particularly that of Belgrade—whose autonomous status facilitated political activities. With the Nazi-Soviet Pact on the eve of the invasion of Poland, the KPJ adopted a virulent stance against Great Britain and France. This drove a wedge between young communists and pro-Western opposition student groups, and caused a leftist revival within the party. It also led the government to revert to some of its controls. The establishment of diplomatic relations with the USSR in June 1940 partly changed the atmosphere yet again, so that between the end of 1937 and the spring of 1941, membership of the KPJ grew from 1,500 to 8,000–a larger following than at any time since the early 'twenties (not counting the more numerous adherents to the Communist Youth movement).

Tito had not solved all problems. His ascent had been opposed by a leftist faction which, from 1939, made a comeback in Montenegro, where it had contacts with the local Federalists (who opposed centralist rule from Belgrade, and who were also known as 'Greens'), and from where it penetrated the party organisation in Kosovo. Macedonia had been a headache for the KPJ because of the vagaries of the Comintern line. Its organisation there was largely under the control of Serbs, but was divided on the ground between potentially antagonistic pro-Bulgarians, pro-Serbs and intermediary Macedonians, in spite of Tito's efforts to tighten control and to convince Serbs that Macedonians were a distinct nationality. In an effort to gain popularity in the region, he had taken the risk of bringing back from Paris Metodije Šatorov 'Šarlo' (Charlot, from the French name of Chaplin's film tramp), known for his Macedonian nationalist views and Bulgarian links, to place him at the head of a new regional committee. Šarlo forthwith inaugurated a campaign against Serbian hegemony and the presence of Serbs settled in Macedonia under the terms of the land reform.

Serb opinion was generally dissatisfied with the Sporazum. After a decade of non-democratic government apparently brought about by the 'Croat question', the Croats had obtained rights still withheld from the Serbs. Many in the opposition felt that Maček had dropped his allies in order to share power with the JRZ government. The Serbian opposition was not adequately represented in the new government. Slovene party leaders asked for a Banovina of Slovenia, even though the existing Drava Banovina corresponded to the area inhabited by Slovenes and was controlled by their majority party, which was part of the JRZ. So the demand was also raised for a Banovina of the Serb Lands, which would have taken in all the rest of Yugoslavia, but the Muslim party insisted on a distinct region of Bosnia-Herzegovina. After two decades of life in Yugoslavia, Serbs re-examined their ideas about the Serbian nation. Should they cede to the Yugoslav synthesis, as state ideology had directed them to do, many hoping that Serbian characteristics would prevail, or should they preserve their marks of individuality, as did Croats and Slovenes?

Discussions on the position of the Serbs in Yugoslavia were initiated not only by party leaders, but also by the independent intellectuals in the Serb Cultural Club (SKK, *Srpski kulturni klub*). Founded in 1937 as a 'think tank' of professionals, businessmen and intellectuals to work towards the integration of Serb culture within Yugoslavia, the SKK became the vocal expression of the Serb intelligentsia's loss of faith in 'Yugoslavism'. The Sporazum turned it into a pressure group to define and defend Serb interests in the state. If the cultural line continued under its chairman, the eminent historian and constitutional lawyer Slobodan Jovanović, younger members pushed for a reawakening of Serb nationalism. Their ambiguous motto was 'a strong Serb identity—a strong Yugoslavia'.

The Serb opposition also resented the new slant of foreign policy. Germany's aggression against Czechoslovakia and Italy's against Albania had created a shockwave. Between spring and autumn 1939, there had been an intensification of diplomatic activity in the Balkans. The Yugoslav government hoped to keep the country intact, and ward off threats for as long as possible, but it was caught between sympathy for the West and fear of the Axis. The invasion of Poland was followed by Yugoslavia's declaration of neutrality, but there was no unity of view in ruling circles about the nature of neutrality and how to practice it. Confidence was shaken by the inability of the West to make good the loss of Czechoslovak military supplies.

The swift collapse of Poland, followed by German-Soviet partition, added to the feeling of dejection. By the spring of 1940, Mussolini was itching to attack Yugoslavia. Approaches were thus made to the Soviet Union that led to the establishment of diplomatic relations in June 1940, in the hope of obtaining armaments. By then, France had fallen, Mussolini had entered the war on Germany's side, and there was not much Britain could do for Yugoslavia. The fall of France in June 1940 came as the greatest shock of all and gave rise to something approaching collective mourning in Serbia. Yugoslavia was in no way prepared for military conflict. It lacked financial means and technical knowledge. It no longer had even the illusion of any real outside support, and many Serb generals doubted whether Croats had the will to fight.

So far, Germany had been satisfied with Yugoslavia's neutrality, intent as it was on furthering its economic interests in the country. Hitler had restrained Mussolini; he did not want to provoke Stalin into any further moves. Insatiable demands were made for Yugoslav labour; it has been estimated that there could have been as many as 100,000 Yugoslavs working in the Reich by the spring of 1941.[2] Under trade agreements on the eve of the outbreak of war, Germany expected Yugoslavia to deliver most of its copper, zinc and lead, along with other raw material and agricultural produce, in exchange for unspecified deliveries of armaments, which it used as a means of pressure. The war, Germany's expansion and its victories made Yugoslavia increasingly dependent on the Reich. The government took emergency measures towards economic mobilisation, which caused a sharp rise in the cost of living in 1940. There were demonstrations against the government and its pro-German economic policy. The government and HSS press raised the issue of looking at the experi-

---

2   If one adds over 40,000 officially recruited to Germany since 1933 to 45,000 older immigrants, perhaps as many as 15,000 on tourist passports or otherwise not registered, and 31,000 in Austria, less than 32,000 returnees since the beginning of the war. Mira Kolar-Dimitrijević, 'Movement of Labour Force between the Third Reich and Yugoslavia, 1933-1941', in Pero Morača, ed., *The Third Reich and Yugoslavia, 1933-1945*, Belgrade, 1977: 361.

ence of totalitarian countries in regulating relations between labour and capital in order to overcome social antagonisms.

Warned off Yugoslavia, and provoked by the entry of German troops in Romania, Mussolini attacked Greece in October 1940. The Belgrade government was worried. Italy could not be allowed to take Salonika, which was Yugoslavia's lifeline. General Milan Nedić had been appointed minister of war in the coalition government. He later became uneasy about the Sporazum because of its impact on defence, and began to argue in favour of closer links with, and concessions to, Germany as a way of surviving the war and of minimising losses. The historian Ljubo Boban has surmised that he might have wanted to forestall Italy over Salonika with German approval,[3] allegedly to prevent the British from taking the Aegean port. He made a backdoor attempt to sound out the Germans. The result was that Italy 'accidentally' bombed Yugoslav territory. Nedić had to resign. The Germans then set out to use Salonika as a decoy to attract Yugoslavia.

Germany's diplomatic offensive to get Yugoslavia off its neutrality had started with Prince Paul's state visit to Berlin in June 1939, when Hitler had displayed the full extent of Germany's propaganda machine and military might to seduce, impress and intimidate. As he prepared to go to Mussolini's help in Greece, the Führer began to put pressure, but it was still in order to attract Yugoslavia, as he did not want to provoke a reaction of Anglo-Soviet solidarity. He again wanted to see Prince Paul, who sent his foreign minister, Aleksandar Cincar-Marković, in November 1940. Hitler told Cincar-Marković of his plans for a world coalition and of his wish that Yugoslavia should be a member. The advantages for Yugoslavia were Serbo-Croat peace, protection from Italy... and Salonika, but it would not receive any arms for as long as it remained neutral. As Italian reverses in Greece had temporarily reduced the danger, the Yugoslavs continued to play for time. Through their military intelligence, they had heard something of Hitler's plans concerning the Soviet Union.

---

3   Ljubo Boban, *Maček i politika Hrvatske seljačke stranke, 1928-1941*, II, Zagreb, 1974: 381.

Prince Paul tried to play Mussolini against Hitler. The Yugoslav government also managed to bury the hatchet with Hungary, with whom no agreement had ever been reached: in December 1940, the two countries signed a 'pact of lasting peace and eternal friendship'.

After the fall of France, sympathies and hopes had been transferred to Great Britain, but the latter was no longer interested in Yugoslavia's neutrality, and had little to offer in the way of material support. All it could do was to tell the Belgrade government that the United States would eventually join in and that the Western Allies would win in the end. Meanwhile, they encouraged Yugoslavia to go with Greece against Italy in Albania, which seriously preoccupied Mussolini. Joining Hitler's coalition was highly unpopular, especially in Serb opinion, which was also worried about the preservation of Yugoslavia's territorial integrity because so many Serbs were spread throughout the country. In December, Hitler issued directives for the invasion of the USSR the following May, and for helping Mussolini defeat Greece before that. Germany, Italy and Japan had signed the Tripartite Pact in September 1940. Romania, Hungary and Slovakia had joined in November 1940. In early March 1941, Bulgaria had done the same and agreed to have German troops on its soil, as a British expeditionary force arrived in Greece. Hitler now needed to know where Yugoslavia stood. In February, he had invited Cvetković and Cincar-Marković to tell them Yugoslavia also had to adhere, so as to secure its place in Europe. He offered to guarantee its territorial integrity and even not to ask for military cooperation.

Yugoslavia's position was weak. The government could no longer try and manoeuvre between Mussolini and Hitler since the Führer had effectively assumed the leadership of the war in the Mediterranean. At home, it did not even have parliamentary support of sorts, as parliament had been dissolved in August 1939 and the crown had reverted to special powers. It did not command the loyalty of a substantial portion of the population. The united opposition had been dissolved. The Serb members of the government represented at best small parties or splinters. Croat ministers wanted Yugoslavia to keep out of the war, even at the cost of concessions to the Axis Powers, at least until they became involved with the Soviet Union or the USA. There was no realistic chance of challenging Hitler's war machine. Extremists of left and right were waiting in the wings. Most Serbs (and not only them) believed that the Allies would eventually win, but because of the controlled press not much was known of life in Nazi Germany or the Soviet Union. Germany was seen, especially by Serbs, as the traditional enemy. 'Russia' was not so much a country as one of two ideologies—Orthodox Slavdom or communism.

Pressure grew, and the Yugoslav government stalled, until Hitler made a firm demand that it should join the Tripartite by 25 March, when a Japanese delegation was coming to Berlin. He was afraid of further Italian initiatives, of British action, and he generally wanted to tidy up the Balkans to protect his planned invasion of the Soviet Union. Prince Paul went to see him again, in great secrecy. Hitler gave him a five-hour lecture, during which he repeated all his arguments and concluded that Yugoslavia had no alternative. The German military attaché in Belgrade told an Italian journalist: 'There will not remain a single stone of Belgrade if the Serbs do not accept the pact'.[4] On returning, Prince Paul consulted his co-regents and principal advisers. They eventually accepted that Yugoslavia had to join the Tripartite Pact, but with some provisos to placate public opinion: respect of its sovereignty and territory, no military commitment, no transit of German troops, and support for Salonika when the war was over. However, the Germans would not publish any commitment on military matters or Salonika. The new war minister and the chief of the General Staff told Prince Paul that the army could hold out for two months at best. One of the regents had actually wanted to reject the proposals altogether, and three Serb ministers resigned. On 25 March 1941, in Vienna, Cvetković and Cincar-Marković duly signed the protocol of adherence to the Tripartite Pact, by which Yugoslavia acknowledged 'the leadership of Germany and Italy in the establishment of a new order in Europe'. The texts had been prepared in

---

4   Alfio Russo, *Rivoluzione in Jugoslavia*, Rome, 1944: 83.

advance; the additional notes were already signed by Ribbentrop and Ciano. Hitler observed that 'the Yugoslavs behaved as though they were at a funeral'. [5]

He needed to settle Greece and Yugoslavia before attacking the USSR. Force would be used on Greece. As for Yugoslavia, which he already controlled economically, it was sufficient for the time being to tie it politically. Meanwhile, the British, with the Americans, had been making last minute efforts, perceived as cynical, to get the Yugoslavs to reject German demands and to attack the Italians in Albania. The Italian minister in Belgrade described Prince Paul as being 'enigmatic to his countrymen', with the mentality of an English-educated *ancien-régime* Russian. He personally directed the policy of the government, 'which lives on from one day to the other, with no programme or aim'.[6] Yugoslavia's leaders hoped that the somewhat improved version of the Pact accepted by Hitler would also be grudgingly accepted by public opinion at home. Maček certainly considered it to be the alternative to war and the disintegration of Yugoslavia.[7] However, by accepting the leadership of Germany and Italy in the new European order, Prince Paul and his government had ended their policy of neutrality: this was the last straw for the Serb opposition. No sooner had the plenipotentiaries returned from Vienna, and the prince regent gone off for a rest in Slovenia, than on 27 March a bloodless military coup proclaimed King Peter II of age, less than six months before the regency was due to come to an end.

The regency had antagonised a substantial part of the population even before it decided to adhere to the Tripartite. Widespread demonstrations erupted on that day, first in Belgrade, then in other

---

5   Joachim von Ribbentrop, *The Ribbentrop Memoirs* (trans. Oliver Watson), London, 1954: 143.

6   Indelli to Ciano 27 September 1939, *Documenti diplomatici italiani*, IX,1, Rome, 1954: 282.

7   *Vide* the important evidence of Ferdo Bošnjaković in *Hrvatska revija*, XXVIII, 3, Munich, 1977: 321. Bošnjaković was a HSS lawyer who took part in talks between the party leadership and the ustashas in 1941 and who was later sent as Pavelić's minister in Helsinki.

Serbian towns and also outside Serbia (notably in Sarajevo, Skopje and Ljubljana). University students and secondary-school pupils appear to have been the main organisers of street demonstrations. The tension was such that the coup may well have forestalled a revolt[8] or disorders, which Tito had been expecting, but the communist leadership knew nothing in advance. Caught off guard, it could only join in the demonstrations and add its calls for an alliance with Moscow. The Comintern cautioned the KPJ: 'Do not let yourselves be carried away [...]. The time is not yet ripe for decisive engagements with the class enemy.' [9]

Whitehall had been alerted to the fact that a coup was imminent, but so had Prince Paul, by General Dušan Simović, commander of the air force, if we are to believe his memoirs. On 24 March the British minister in Belgrade had been authorised to support any subversive measure against the government, even at the risk of precipitating a German attack. British agents had encouraged a group in the (otherwise Serb) Agrarian Party (*Zemljoradnička stranka*, which was in the government, but pro-Western) and some personalities belonging to patriotic organisations, but in so doing they were merely pushing an open door. The coup was the result of a pent-up dislike of Prince Paul's régime and of its overall policy, more a spontaneous reaction than a prepared conspiracy, carried out against a weak and insecure government by officers who wanted to 'save the honour', not only of Serbia but of Yugoslavia as they perceived it. Their motives were mixed: a general dissatisfaction with the position of the Serb people in Yugoslavia; a sense of humiliation at the alliance with Germany and Italy, and the wish to stick with the West for traditional

---

8 The action of three Guards subalterns (the Croat stepson of a Serb general, the son of the permanent under-secretary of the Foreign Ministry and a Slovene) who went off to Greece to protest against the 'treason' about to be committed by the prince regent and to fight on the side of the Allies was symbolic of the rumblings in the army. Zvonimr Vučković, *Sećanja iz rata*, I, London, 1980: 45-53.

9 *The Diary of Georgi Dimitrov, 1933-1949*, Ivo Banac ed., New Haven & London, 2003: 152-153.

or ideological reasons; the feeling that siding with the Axis would encourage all those who wanted Yugoslavia to break up; and that the Allies would win in the end when Yugoslavia would be penalised for her betrayal.

General Simović, removed from his position as chief of the General Staff in 1940 by what he believed was German pressure on Nedić and Prince Paul, and now commander of the air force, hovered in the background and fancied himself as something of a national saviour. Behind the plotters stood the officer corps more generally, which supported, joined or allowed the coup, and the enthusiasm of Serb opinion. Even though Croats and Slovenes were, on the whole, appalled by what seemed to them an irresponsible slap in the face to Hitler that placed their regions in a hazardous situation, the coup showed a deep yearning for a fully representative government in an hour of need. The plotters had political contacts; they brought together party representatives, those in opposition along with those who had been in government (other than the Serb remains of the JRZ), who agreed to a broad coalition under Simović.

Prince Paul had not gone further than Zagreb. He conferred with Maček and other HSS personalities, accepted the *fait accompli*, supported Simović's request that Maček should stay on as deputy premier, returned to Belgrade, resigned with his fellow regents, and left for Greece. Maček rejected German advice not to join the new government. After some hesitation, he agreed to take on the position of deputy prime minister, along with Jovanović, the president of the SKK, and returned to Belgrade on 4 April. However, the HSS leadership had also decided that, should the government have to leave the country, Maček would stay at home and ask Krnjević to replace him. The new government confirmed the Sporazum and extended the competences of the Banovina of Croatia.

It attempted to provide continuity on the external front as well, by issuing a statement respecting Yugoslavia's international obligations, the Tripartite included, and by assuring Germany that the coup had been for purely domestic reasons. The new foreign minister was even ready to go to Berlin to offer explanations, and any concessions compatible with the national honour. All that the new leadership could otherwise do was to keep as quiet as possible, to try and win a little more time and postpone the reckoning, in the hope that British military aid and, eventually, Soviet diplomatic support would be forthcoming. Even though there had been no real British involvement in the coup, British efforts to prevent the signature of the Pact had led the plotters to expect aid should they be successful. There were top secret talks with British military representatives, who again encouraged the Yugoslavs to talk with the Greeks about an attack on the Italians in Albania. The Yugoslavs' capacity to resist had been overestimated. They were unwilling to initiate an attack, and even afraid to be overheard talking to the British. They also had secret talks with the Soviets, to try and obtain armaments, and a good word in Berlin to ward off an attack. Communist internees were released. Information obtained on German plans to attack the Soviet Union was passed on. The Soviet Union was willing to show some support to Yugoslavia, but not to risk conflict. Eventually, all that Yugoslavia got was a treaty of non-aggression and friendship, signed a few hours before the German attack, on 5 April.

When he was told of the coup, Hitler flew into a rage. Yugoslavia had reverted to being a risk factor in his Greek plan. He did not wait to see where the Simović government stood. He wanted to punish the Serbs, the main disturbers of the European order. In him the anti-Serbian Austrian streak erupted that went back to before the First World War. Germany already had a plan of attack in case the Belgrade government did not adhere to the Pact. He gave orders to invade Yugoslavia at the same time as Greece and destroy it as a state 'with merciless brutality'. A propaganda campaign was started which depicted Yugoslavia as an inorganic construct made up of mutually hostile races, with chauvinistic Serbian power seekers engaged in a belligerent course against the Reich. It set non-Serbs against Serbs and disseminated stories about Serb terror against ethnic Germans, in a replica of the campaign of vilification against Poles in the final days of August 1939. Having written to Mussolini to ask him to leave the direction of the war to Germany, Hitler issued a proclamation to the German people on 6 April, that the real enemy in Yugoslavia and Greece was England, to whose special services their disreputable leaders had sold themselves. On the same day, alleging atrocities against the German minority, Hitler attacked at dawn with no ultimatum or declaration of war.

Yugoslavia's latest plan of defence anticipated defence on all borders, except Albania where an incursion was intended to link up with Greek forces. Divisions were thinly stretched along the frontier. Troops from the north would gradually be withdrawn towards Greece, as the Bulgarian front and the north-south corridor of the Morava and Vardar valleys were firmly held. However, the Yugoslav army was caught half prepared. There were 250,000 men under arms at the beginning of March, and another 500,000 were called up for 27 March, but no more than thirty per cent of them had answered the call up within the prescribed time. The use of reservists to work on frontier fortifications was partly meant to dissimulate the call up, but it disorganised the concentration of operational units. So did the coup. When the attack occurred, troops were crisscrossing the country. Mobile forces, motor transport, tanks, anti-tank and anti-aircraft artillery were in short supply. The air force had but few modern planes. German propaganda told the Serbs they had betrayed the Pact and were thus responsible for the war; there was no point in resisting, for they would be alone and would be made to pay for it. Rumours were spread that only Serbia would be defended. Special propaganda units to subvert the Croats reinforced ustasha action. Reservists failed to report; soldiers deserted. Communist antiwar activity was just as effective, if not more so: the time to fight would be when the Soviet Union entered the war, as the fate of the Balkans would be decided by Russia and not by England.

The German 'Operation Punishment' started at dawn on 6 April with an air bombardment of Belgrade that lasted for three days and destroyed almost fifty per cent of the housing of what was supposedly an 'open city'.[10] Lightning raids put airfields out of action, destroyed most of the air force, disrupted communications and caused general chaos, thus facilitating the simultaneous land invasion. The main thrust came from Bulgaria, to link up with Italian forces coming from Albania, and to seal Yugoslavia off from Greece. The fall of Skopje on the second day of the campaign compromised the chances of a withdrawal to Greece, but Yugoslav defences in the south otherwise held for a few days. There was even an offensive into Albanian territory, with a concentric attack on Shköder (Scutari). The Yugoslavs had concentrated troops on the Albanian frontier and advanced almost to Shköder, before Italian military intelligence, which had feared and anticipated the move, and which decrypted Yugoslav communications, gave bogus reverse orders. This was realised, but not before the advance had been disrupted. By 14 April, the Yugoslavs had effectively turned to the defensive in Albania. There were other cases of efficient initiatives by lower commanders and of local resistance, notably heroic action in the defence of Belgrade by air force pilots who, incidentally, represented a good cross section of Serb, Croat and Slovene officers.

The thrust from the north was even more rapid, facilitated as it was by sabotage from ustasha sympathisers in a few key positions and by members of the German ethnic minority. By 10 April the Germans had entered Zagreb; Croatia seceded under the ustashas. A similar attempt was made in Slovenia. Regular military operations having broken down generally, the Yugoslav Supreme Command called on all units to act on their own initiative. Weak defences had been penetrated; fragments were hurled back in confusion, in panic and in defeatism; there was no reserve and no second line to fall back on. King, government and Supreme Command had left Belgrade on 6 April, and were thereafter on the move in Bosnia and Montenegro, rapidly losing control. Simović had taken on the additional wartime

---

10 The air bombardment of Belgrade killed 2,271 people as officially registered soon afterwards, but probably more in fact—anything between 5,000 and 10,000 and even more according to later Yugoslav estimates.

position of chief of staff to the Supreme Command (the sovereign being the nominal supreme commander). On the 7th Maček told the cabinet that he was going to Zagreb. Having conferred with his party leadership, he broadcast to say that he would be staying to share the fate of the people, and he appealed for order and discipline, whether in the army or at home. He had informed his cabinet colleagues and assured them that he would not disown them. At the last cabinet meeting held on Yugoslav soil, at Pale, east of Sarajevo, on 13 April, Simović resigned from his command position, to which he had General Danilo Kalafatović appointed. The Germans had that day marched into Belgrade, and Simović instructed Kalafatović to negotiate a ceasefire. It was at Nikšić airport in Montenegro, from where they were flown out to Greece on the following days,[11] to join King Peter who had already left, that the ministers learnt the armed forces were on the point of capitulating. They had not been consulted. Simović later claimed that he had intended no more than a French-type armistice.

Plenipotentiaries of the Supreme Command had gone to and returned from Belgrade to negotiate terms with the German and Italian armed forces. They were told that it had to be total capitulation, and that the German advance would continue until that had been signed. By 16 April Kalafatović was in fact a prisoner and the government had left. On 17 April the capitulation of the Yugoslav armed forces was signed by plenipotentiaries of the Supreme Command, who included Cincar-Marković in order to mollify the Germans. Poland had held out thirty-five days, France forty-three; in Yugoslavia it was all over in twelve days. The rapid victory had been achieved by air superiority and armoured power, lightning operations aiming at command centres and communications, and the advance of motorised divisions. The victory had been almost entirely German. Bulgarian territory was used as the main springboard for

---

11 Beside Maček, another HSS minister and the leader of the JMO had also stayed behind. The SLjS leader and an independent minister from Montenegro were killed in the course of the evacuation.

the attack on both Yugoslavia and Greece, but Bulgarian troops did not participate. Nor did Romanian, or initially Hungarian, troops participate, even though Romanian and Hungarian territory was also used. After Yugoslav resistance had collapsed in the north and the independence of Croatia had been announced, the Regent of Hungary proclaimed on 11 April that it was Hungary's duty to reclaim territory in Yugoslavia in the interest of the Hungarians who lived there. Italian troops then also crossed into Slovenia, after declaring war, to reach Ljubljana just before the Germans. They also proceeded down the coast, capturing the Bay of Kotor on 17 April, with the remains of Yugoslavia's small navy that had been practically inactive. Between 200,000 and 300,000 prisoners of war, 12,000 officers and over 200 generals, mostly Serbs, were taken to camps in Germany and Italy. The German armed forces had suffered 558 casualties, and the Italians 3,500. On 27 April, the German foreign ministry informed the Swiss legation in Berlin that it no longer had to protect Yugoslav interests in Germany or German interests in Yugoslavia, as it had been requested to do after diplomatic representations had been withdrawn, as there no longer was a Yugoslav state.

2
YUGOSLAVIA BROKEN UP:
HITLER'S 'NEW DISORDER'
1941

No sooner had the capitulation become effective on 18 April 1941 than the German Supreme Command announced the end of operations on the 'Serbian theatre'. Various categories of prisoners of war were allowed home (those who opted for Croatia, those who originated from the annexed territories and from Montenegro, those who belonged to ethnic minorities, and the sick) until only 181,000 were left in camps in Germany and 10,000 in Italy—ninety per cent of them Serbs. Almost all the Jews who remained in German captivity, including some 400 officers, survived the war. Many servicemen had not even seen action. Three divisions in the south had sent their men home with their weapons. Vast quantities of arms lay about.

Hitler wanted to destroy forever the 'Versailles construct' that was Yugoslavia. Serbs were to be punished; Croats brought over to the Axis; Slovenes Germanised or dispersed. Germany had already acquired a predominant economic position. It wanted to control communication lines and mineral deposits, and was ready to satisfy many territorial claimants. Italy had views about what was Italian by historic right, and what should be within its 'vital space'. When its foreign minister Ciano was called by his German opposite number Ribbentrop to Vienna on 21 April to carve up Greece and Yugoslavia, he came up against some issues that were not open to discussion, because they had already been 'irrevocably' decided by the Führer. The Reich would extend into Slovenia much further south than Rome had expected—to the very gates of Ljubljana. The territory beyond the river Mura, once Hungarian, would be returned to Hungary. Dalmatia and Montenegro were conceded to Italy, but it had to negotiate its borders and its relations with independent Croatia. Areas inhabited by Albanians could go to Italian-controlled Albania, except for the Mitrovica area with its mineral deposits which would be formally part of a residual Serbia under German control. Although Bulgaria was favoured against Albania in western Macedonia, its takeover of territory in Macedonia and south-east Serbia was to be provisional until the end of the war, to ensure its loyalty to the Axis.

The Independent State of Croatia and Italy's Three Zones

Croatia was acknowledged as being in Italy's space. Germany 'only' wanted economic advantages and a privileged status for the Volksdeutsche—the German-speaking minority. For security reasons, as the new satellite needed to organise its armed forces, it would be divided into a 'predominantly' Italian and a 'predominantly' German sphere of influence. The Germans would have preferred a government under Maček, rather than Pavelić whom they considered to be Mussolini's man. However, by 10 April when the Germans entered Zagreb, Maček had already refused their offers, although he did sign a statement asking his followers and the public to obey the new authorities. The Germans had no alternative but to accept an ustasha takeover in Pavelić's name, in advance of his return from Italy, by a prominent 'home' ustasha considered to be pro-German, the one-time Austro-Hungarian colonel Slavko Kvaternik. By arrangement with German emissaries, Kvaternik called on the commanders of the gendarmerie, the police and the Croat Peasant Party (HSS) Guard in Zagreb, to tell them to maintain order and take control of important installations. He went on to read a proclamation to passers-by in front of the Ban's residence, announcing that 'Divine providence and the will of our Ally [the German Reich...], the centuries-long struggle of the Croat people and the efforts of our Poglavnik [leader] Dr Pavelić' have determined that the Croatian state be resurrected 'on the eve of the Resurrection of the Son of God' (Easter was on 13

April), and that he was taking over on behalf of Pavelić. The Germans then entered Zagreb. Kvaternik's proclamation was repeated over the radio, followed by Maček's statement.

The collapse of Yugoslavia had provided the fascist-inspired fringe of Croat nationalism with the opportunity to spearhead the secession of an extensive state as a satellite of the Axis Powers. Its proclamation had been stage-managed by German emissaries, under the umbrella of the Wehrmacht. A significant part of the population, generally in towns and particularly in Zagreb, viewed it favourably. The ustashas had a modicum of popular support in western Herzegovina and Lika, but virtually nowhere else. However, most people accepted 'the resurrection of the Croatian state' with the feeling that the war had ended quickly and that the worst had been avoided. The HSS was split into factions, ranging from pro-ustasha right to radical left. Its leadership dreaded the use of force, but had set up a paramilitary party guard, which had been infiltrated by ustashas. The HSS Guard contributed to the takeover by helping to disarm army units and establish a measure of control. Maček was allowed to withdraw to his country home with orders not to move, thereafter reduced, in his own words, 'to the role of a helpless onlooker'.[1] Whatever Maček's intention, his statement was of great assistance to the ustashas as they settled in. It sounded like an endorsement of the new order, at a time when the King and government were still on Yugoslav soil, the Germans had not taken Belgrade, Pavelić was still in Italy, and the Yugoslav armed forces had not yet capitulated.

During the 1930s, Italy had given asylum to ustashas. Mussolini needed them to initiate the break-up of Yugoslavia, fulfil the last aspirations of *irredentismo* across the Adriatic and enhance Italy's 'space'. On 29 March, the Duce summoned the future Poglavnik from his place of residence in Tuscany and received him privately. He could put Pavelić in power, and thus believed he could strike a deal on the extent of Italian influence over the independent Croatia-to-be, and on the annexation of Dalmatia by Italy. Pavelić, who was

---

1   Vladko Maček, *In the Struggle for Freedom*, New York, 1957: 236.

anxious to take power and uncertain about German intentions, gave vague assurances. He asked for help to install himself in Zagreb in anticipation of some other German scheme. Mussolini put at his disposal the Florence radio transmitter for a couple of late evening broadcasts to Croatia, and allowed interned ustashas to join their leader. Mussolini and Pavelić had not been straightforward with each other. On 1 April, Pavelić announced to his followers the imminent fulfilment of the dream of a free Croatian fatherland within the Western, Latin and Germanic sphere of civilisation. Mussolini was then taken by surprise by the proclamation of independence on 10 April; he had not expected it before Pavelić's return. The few hundred ustashas kept under surveillance throughout Italy were brought together in Tuscany, issued with light colonial uniforms and rifles, and visited by their leader. Pavelić was received again by Mussolini, this time more officially; the one anxious to get to Zagreb as quickly as possible; the other concerned about Dalmatia; both uneasy about German intentions.

Pavelić and his ustashas were dispatched to Croatia. Reception committees along the way slowed their progress. On 13 April, they were met by Kvaternik and German representatives, and taken to Karlovac. There Pavelić had to confirm that he had made no commitments to the Italians, only to be caught up by an emissary of Mussolini's. Negotiations followed over telegrams that Pavelić would address to Hitler and Mussolini, over Dalmatia and over recognition. The Germans wanted to recognise Croatia without delay, because operations against the Yugoslav army were still going on. The Italians first wanted a formal commitment on territory. Pavelić was ready to tell his two sets of protectors, in talks that no other Croat attended, whatever was needed to consolidate his position. It was agreed that recognition would be granted by Germany and by Italy in the same terms, and that borders would be decided between the interested parties. The Karlovac hitch was the first manifestation of Italian-German tension over Croatia. Pavelić and his ustashas then entered Zagreb in the small hours of 15 April, and recognition by the Axis Powers followed. Styling himself officially Poglavnik of the Independent State of Croatia (NDH, *Nezavisna Država Hrvatska*), Pavelić appointed his first government. He explained to the newly-arrived German officials that Croats were Eastern Goths and not Southern Slavs.

Kvaternik had already issued laws to enforce the obedience of army and government personnel. Military service was imposed on all members of the Yugoslav armed forces originating from the territory of the NDH; others were forbidden on pain of death from taking any further action. An oath of allegiance to the Poglavnik was imposed on the personnel of all government, local government, public and armed services. Between 200 and 300 ustashas had returned from Italy. At the end of May they were joined by around 600 coming from Vienna, where they had been assembled from various parts of the Reich and of German-occupied Europe. Pavelić's prestige in the movement was due in part to his isolation in Italy. His contacts with the 'home' ustashas were scant. German intelligence estimated that there were 900 sworn members of the movement in Croatia at the time. The ustashas themselves put the number of their sympathisers at no more than 40,000. Although he spoke of a new order and new élite, Pavelić had to use the existing Banovina of Croatia civil service, 'ustashised' and purged. For military cadres, he relied on a number of former Austro-Hungarian officers, untainted by Yugoslavism, before he turned to those Croats who had been regular officers in the Yugoslav forces. Tension thereafter persisted between ustashas and professionals.

A revised version of Pavelić's 1933 ustasha programme served as a statute. It posited uninterrupted statehood almost from the time that the Croats arrived in their present homeland. Its ideology was drawn from extreme Croatian nationalism, from Italian Fascism and German National-Socialism, from Catholic clerical authoritarianism and from HSS peasantism. Only Croats by origin and blood could participate in the political decision-making process. The organisation of the NDH was inspired by the Italian Fascist model. Political parties and their social institutions were formally banned. Pavelić described Maček as 'an instrument of Russia and England' in an interview with an Italian newspaper,[2] and attacked those HSS leaders who had gone to London with the Yugoslav government, but the HSS founding fathers were described as forerunners of the ustasha movement.

The fifty or so communists interned by the Banovina authorities were kept in camps, but persecution of communists only went into top gear after the German attack on the Soviet Union on 22 June. Croats were called to root out the reds at home, now that they no longer came from Serbia. They were also called upon to fight the bolsheviks who had always been enemies of the Croatian people. By the end of July several hundred communists had been killed, as hostages executed for the murder of ustashas, or in the failed attempt to organise the escape of communists from Kerestinac camp near Zagreb. This was still a time when Serbs and subversive action generally were labelled 'communist'—although communists were targeted whether they were Serbs or Croats.

Once its borders had been fixed, the NDH extended over almost forty per cent of the territory of the Kingdom of Yugoslavia, to the very gates of Belgrade. Hungary had been the first to recognise it, on 11 April, so as to be freed from its pact with Yugoslavia, and to appropriate old territory. It was in January 1940 that Ciano had put to Pavelić the plan for a dynastic union between Italy and Croatia. Italy had been led to believe that the whole of Croatia would indeed be in its sphere, until Ribbentrop had told Ciano in Vienna of Germany's need to have an occupation force in a strip of territory in order 'to safeguard railway communications with Serbia'. Once the border question had been more or less settled—not without difficulty—the special relationship of Italy with the NDH was formalised with the Rome Agreements of 18 May. A prince of the Italian ruling house of Savoy, the Duke of Spoleto, was offered the crown of Croatia, but his taking possession of it was postponed, as Pavelić still hoped to get a territorial deal in exchange for the new monarch. However irrecon-

---

2　*Il resto del carlino*, Bologna, 11 May 1941.

cilable, Italian imperial irredentism and Croat extreme nationalism needed each other to achieve their separate objectives, so the coast was carved up in a compromise that left both parties disappointed. Italy's sphere of influence in the NDH was divided into two parts, one of which (Zone 2) was made up of what was left of the coast under Zagreb's sovereignty. The Croatian government was not allowed to have armed forces, fortifications, bases or arms factories there, while Italy had transit rights for its troops.

Italy annexed territories (Zone 1) around the port city of Split (Spalato) and the naval base of Kotor (Cattaro), with additions to Zara (Zadar), already an Italian enclave, which formed the three discontinuous provinces of Zara, Spalato and Cattaro that became part of the Kingdom of Italy. The demarcation line between the two spheres of influence was drawn by joint German-Italian military commissions—not without minor incidents. Ironically, German and Italian generals in Yugoslavia usually had to communicate in French. Italian troops in the annexed territories of Slovenia and Dalmatia and in the NDH, from the old border to Montenegro, and from the sea to the demarcation line, were part of the Second Army which had participated in the April campaign. They were reduced to nine divisions[3] under the overall command of General Vittorio Ambrosio, who would remain at the post until January 1942. They later became an area command—the Command of the Armed Forces of Slovenia and Dalmatia (Supersloda)—with headquarters near Fiume in Italian territory.

The relationship between Italy and the NDH was a strange one. Germany allowed Croatia to be formally in Italy's sphere, but whatever economic advantages Italy expected were reduced by Pavelić's undertakings to satisfy German needs. The Italians soon realised that they did not have the means to control anything in Croatia, yet they were saddled with an extended military presence. They made

---

3   They were two-regiment divisions of 14,200 men, stronger on paper than German occupation divisions, but increasingly below strength, with 10,000 on average, falling occasionally as low as 6,000.

27

up by sending ostensible missions to Zagreb—a legation, a military mission, a trade delegation, a Fascist Party delegation, even a secret police representation. However, the Italian minister did not present his credentials until early July, and the head of the military mission did not turn up until mid-June. There was a distinct lack of enthusiasm at Court, in the General Staff, even in the Foreign Ministry, over Dalmatia, not to mention indifference in the public at large. The territorial arrangements and the Rome Agreements turned Croat public opinion against Italy. Pavelić, who had concealed the extent of his concessions, talked of the need to make sacrifices, but could not prevent the devastating effect on the credibility of his régime.

Even though the NDH appeared to fit into Mussolini's schemes, for the Germans it was a sort of southern march for (and in economic terms, a southern extension of) the Reich. Balkan minerals and foodstuffs, and the Maribor-Zagreb-Belgrade-Salonika rail line defined Germany's sphere of control in the region. Its specific interests in the NDH were safeguarded by a confidential protocol of 16 May which, in fact, allowed the Reich unrestricted exploitation of industrial raw material, and Croatian cover for all costs connected with the presence of German troops. With the acquiescence of the ustasha government, the Germans also dismantled and took away a number of plants, paying for them into blocked accounts with German banks. They also took away workers—25,000 by the end of June 1941, rising to over 200,000 by January 1944. These workers, voluntary and not so voluntary, were paid on clearing accounts, fed and lodged in camps, while the NDH government made arbitrary and irregular support payments to their families at home.

The Germans kept only one occupation division, with headquarters in Sarajevo, but in June the 182,000 Volksdeutsche of the NDH were made into a veritable Reich-controlled state within the state under the name of 'German National Group in Croatia'. From the very first day, there were German soldiers in the streets of Zagreb, German firms received concessions to exploit resources, German former Austro-Hungarian officers came to organise Croatia's budding army, and German military and diplomatic representatives occupied an important place. A 'German Plenipotentiary General' arrived on 15 April, the same day as Pavelić, to coordinate Croatia's military efforts. A former Austro-Hungarian officer and military historian who had combined Habsburg nostalgia with Nazi sympathies, Edmund Glaise von Horstenau had held ministerial office in interwar Vienna where he had frequented Croat émigrés. The German minister to the NDH who arrived a week later was Siegfried Kasche, a Nazi Party militant since 1926 injected into the diplomatic service. Friction quickly developed between the two.

Laws, decrees and orders were issued to deal with everything possible, but with no coherent programme beyond ustashisation. Careerism, opportunism, favouritism and corruption accompanied the arbitrary and violent nature of the régime. As early as 17 April an all-embracing law 'on the Protection of the People and the State' made it legally possible to kill anybody the ustashas wanted removed, through people's courts and mobile courts-martial with retroactive powers. Loosely worded measures were taken against Jews, Serbs, Gypsies and whoever acted, or attempted to act, against the honour or the interests of the Croatian people and state. An apparatus of control and repression was put into place within weeks, under Eugen Dido (son of Slavko) Kvaternik as Director of Public Order and Security. An Ustasha Militia (*Ustaška vojnica*) was organised on the model of the German Nazi SS and Italian Fascist Blackshirts, to secure and defend the achievements of the NDH. Sworn to lifelong loyalty to the Poglavnik, it numbered some 4,500 regular militiamen, whose core were the returnees. There were also some 25,000-30,000 'wild' (irregular) ustashas who operated in the country at large.

A conscripted army was established under the name of *Hrvatsko domobranstvo*, to stress a return to Croatia's pre-1918 territorial (*domobran*) regiments. Indeed, that had been the first act of the new régime. Ex-Austro-Hungarian colonel, commander-in-chief and now Marshal Kvaternik had assigned it the task to defend the state against its foreign and domestic enemies. Officers and men were to be pure Croats. They could be dismissed, retired, appointed or promoted without regard to regulations. Officers (necessarily elderly) that had served under Austria-Hungary but had not gone into the Yugoslav army were reactivated. Before the end of the year, some 3,600 officers had applied for commissions in the Domobrans; some 2,700 ex-Yugoslav officers had been taken on. Italy was supposed to help the development of the NDH armed forces, but it did not allow the formation of Croatian units in its sphere before the Rome Agreements. The Croats turned to Germany, who obliged and thus had the main rôle in arming the NDH. The Germans decided on the size of the Croatian army, where it could set up garrisons, and provided it with discarded Yugoslav army equipment.

The Domobranstvo was made up of the land forces, the air force, the navy and the gendarmerie. The navy was purely symbolical, as the Italians had taken over the Yugoslav ships, the ports, most of the coast, and did not want a Croatian navy in the Adriatic. The air force was insignificant. The 6,000-strong gendarmerie was recruited from the old Yugoslav gendarmerie. By the summer, the land army numbered 45,000, but its officer corps was not integrated, not well trained and not dependable. It was top heavy with 100-130 generals (and admirals). Initially the highest posts were given to onetime Austro-Hungarian officers who had not served in the Yugoslav army. There were also returnee ustashas in the army. The largest group was made up of ex-Yugoslav officers, not trusted by either of the former groups and lukewarm in their loyalty to Pavelić.

General August Marić, a divisional commander in Croatia during the April campaign, captured and subsequently released by the Germans, was kept on with a succession of appointments until his resignation in September 1941 after clashes with the ustashas. He was prosecuted for helping Jews and Serbs, and for his relations with Colonel Vladimir Vauhnik, sent to Jasenovac concentration camp, released at the end of 1942 following an intervention by General Glaise von Horstenau, and interned again at the end of 1944. Vauhnik, Yugoslav military attaché in Berlin, from where he had sent valuable intelligence to Belgrade, was freed, after interrogation by the Gestapo, as a German national, born in the German-annexed part of Slovenia. Was he freed on the understanding that he would be controlled, or did he actually agree to pass information on to the German Foreign Intelligence Service? He went to Zagreb, where he was taken under the wing of General Marić, who officially used him for liaison with foreign military attachés. Conveniently stripped of his rank by the Yugoslav government in London, he operated between Italian military representatives and Croat politicians, until November 1941, when he escaped to Ljubljana just before Marić's arrest. In his memoirs, published in Argentina after the war, he describes the intelligence centre that he set up for the Allies in Ljubljana, through refugees, secret organisations, his links with Belgrade, the NDH General Staff, the Italian military and anti-Nazi Germans. He may have been thought by the Italians to have been linked to the Germans, and *vice versa*, which allowed him to work for the Allies. In June 1944, he had to leave for Switzerland.

The NDH was hardly independent; it was not a real state, but its leadership was determined it should be purely Croat. Citizenship was restricted to Aryan residents who had not worked against the 'liberation movement' and who were prepared to serve it loyally. As Catholic Croats amounted to just over half the 6.5 million population, and as the NDH stretched across Bosnia and Herzegovina, the 750,000 Muslims there were accepted as being Islamic Croats. They formed a close society that had looked to its own business, while its leaders had come to terms with the Yugoslav state. Their party, the Yugoslav Muslim Organisation (JMO), had broken up; two token Muslims were appointed to the government (one of them as token deputy prime minister).

In May 1941, the German Foreign Ministry estimated the number of Jews in the NDH at 40,000. They were targeted by racial laws on the German model, removed from public services, banned from the professions, and deprived of their property. Those who had been active ustashas before 1941 (or who were related to ustasha personalities) could be considered 'honorary Aryans'. Arrests had started the day the Germans entered Zagreb, and the first killings in May; the rounding up and confinement to camps in July. On 31 July, the ustasha paper *Novi list* boasted that Varaždin was the first town to have been 'cleansed' (*očišćen*) of Jews. On 16 December 1941, Pavelić told Ciano in Venice there were 'no more than 12,000' left in Croatia. (They had 'emigrated', added Kvaternik Jr, with a smile—Ciano noted—that left no room for doubt.) The terror against Jews culminated in summer 1942, after which there was a relative lull for the 5,000 or so survivors until the spring of 1943. Many Jews fled to Italian-occupied territory, where they were not rigorously checked, yet not welcomed either. Many refugees were turned back, and many fled again. Some of the wealthier were able to go to Italy. Eventually there were about 4,000 Jewish refugees in Zones 1 and 2 (and 500 in Montenegro). In August 1941, as the terror extended, and as the Germans pressed them to hand Jewish refugees over to NDH authorities, the Italians took measures to prevent the further inflow.

The real problem was the 1.9 million Serbs—close to a third of the population and spread over sixty to seventy per cent of the territory. Public statements described them as an alien intrusion that had arrived uninvited in Croatia centuries earlier. For them, as for Jews, there was no place in the NDH. Even before 10 April, notices had been displayed with 'No Serbs, Gypsies, Jews and dogs'. Immediate measures were taken to remove what indicated their presence, such as place names, the Cyrillic script, or the name 'Serb' Orthodox (replaced by 'Greek-Oriental'). They were, like the Jews, dismissed and expropriated, arrested and rounded up. There is no written record of a statement allegedly made by Mile Budak, the minister of education and religious affairs, that Serbs would be expelled, converted or killed, although people talked about it and remembered it. Other statements in that style by the same minister and by the minister of justice were recorded in the press.[4] The Italian journalist Alfio Russo

---

4   Such as: 'We do not want to commit any crimes, but as they came with the Turks they [the Serbs] shall now have to go'; 'This land can only be Croat,

relates a conversation with Pavelić in late April, when the Poglavnik said Serb rebels would be killed.—And what if all Serbs rebel? —We shall kill them all.[5]

The Germans initially wanted to send 250,000 Slovenes from northern Slovenia to Serbia, and replace them with ethnic Germans, but the German military in Serbia had objections. The various German and NDH authorities eventually agreed in June on a programme of 'orderly transfers': 170,000 Slovenes to Croatia, a corresponding number of NDH Serbs to Serbia, another 5,000 'politically tainted Slovenes' to Serbia. Less than 9,400 Slovenes were in fact 'transferred' to Croatia, where they were made unwelcome, while another 17,000 simply fled, before Himmler decided to end the programme. The transfer of Slovenes was relatively 'orderly' compared to that of Serbs, who were moved out at night, at thirty minutes notice, with 50 kg of belongings and a minimum of cash. Prominent people were the first to go, including about half the Orthodox clergy, then the population of selected villages in order to destroy continuity of settlement. Mass expulsions had started well before the agreement, until in October the Germans put an end to the transfer of Serbs as well. They estimated that 14,000-18,000 Serbs had by then been 'transferred' to Serbia, besides 90,000-120,000 simply expelled, and 180,000-200,000 who had fled. A decree had formalised concentration camps in November 1941 under Kvaternik Jr, after most of them had been set up (there would eventually be as many as twenty). The largest was the Jasenovac complex reclaimed from marshland at the confluence of the rivers Sava and Una. In April 1942 the Ustasha Surveillance Service said that it 'can now accept an unlimited number of inmates', by which time the camps there had become killing cen-

---

and there is no method we would hesitate to use to make it truly Croat and to cleanse it of all Serbs'; 'They are enemies who settled by force, and so they must go, willingly or forcefully'; and variations thereof.

5   'Li uccideremo tutti'. Russo, Rivoluzione: 108.

tres. The number of deaths at Jasenovac—of Serbs, Jews, Gypsies and undesirable Croats—remains a subject of controversy.[6]

In the first shock of defeat and collapse, the Serb population of the NDH was passive. 'Flying' ustasha bands roamed the countryside, spreading terror. More often than not they came from the outside, mobilised local marginalised individuals, and gave them power over life and death. There were instances of murders even before 10 April. Mass killings and expulsions started in late April in areas within easy reach of Zagreb. The notorious massacre at Glina, 50 kms from Zagreb, occurred on 12 May, when two to three hundred were burned to death in the Orthodox church. There was a turn for the worse after Pavelić's visit to Hitler on 6 June, when the Führer advised: 'If the Croatian state is to be really stable, a nationally intolerant policy should be pursued for 50 years'. In Bosnia and Herzegovina, the ustashas made use of the discontent felt by many Muslims against the inter-war agrarian reform. They revived First World War memories of Austrian-encouraged pogroms of Serbs by Muslims, and of the troubled transition period at the end of the war when Serb peasants took land and sought revenge. The ustashas again enlisted what Muslim notables would later describe as 'the dregs of society', who happily paid off old scores. They involved as many Croat or Muslim individuals as they could through the distribution of looted property.

---

6   The demographer Bogoljub Kočović, author of the most serious study of the number of victims of the Second World War in Yugoslavia, estimates the total number of Serbs who died in the NDH at between 370,000 and 410,000 (latest edition, *Sahrana jednog mita. Žrtve Drugog svetskog rata u Jugoslaviji*, Belgrade, 2005). Tomislav Dulić writes of the Jasenovac complex: 'Regardless of the fact that there did not die seven hundred thousand [a figure often quoted] prisoners at Jasenovac, an estimated one hundred thousand still make it one of the largest camps in Europe during World War II' (*Utopias of Nation. Local Mass Killing in Bosnia and Herzegovina, 1941-1942*, Uppsala, 2005: 281). Kočović too offers a tentative estimate of around 100,000 (correspondence with author, January 2007). Researchers at the Belgrade Museum of Victims of Genocide have so far recorded between 80,000 and 90,000 who died at Jasenovac, over half of whom were Serbs (*Politika*, Belgrade, 29 January 2007).

The terror sought to encourage flight, and make it impossible ever to revive intercommunal life. It sought initially to depopulate border regions with Serbia and Montenegro that were difficult to control, and perceived as being a symbolic border between 'East' and 'West'. It was increasingly accompanied by a state-sponsored and fear-induced programme of conversion that disregarded canonical procedures and told Catholic bishops who was acceptable for conversion, and who was not. The programme was a tragic farce. It was most successful in regions more or less under ustasha control, and gradually came to an end when it was obvious that conversion was no guarantee of security. By the winter, three Orthodox bishops and 150 other clergy had been murdered (219 clerics by the end of the war).

The Roman Catholic Church generally greeted the setting up of the NDH. Archbishop Alojzije Stepinac of Zagreb had been considered 'Yugoslav' enough to be appointed to that top post at the age of thirty-nine in 1937. However, his allegiance was to the Catholic Church and the Croat nation, and he had become more and more of a Croat nationalist. His stand against Freemasons and Marxists, and also against other Christians, was not uncommon among conservative Catholic prelates of the time. Although no ustasha, he initially welcomed the new Croatian state, if not its ideology. He called on Kvaternik and on Pavelić, ordered a Te Deum to be celebrated in all churches, and instructed the clergy to do its duty towards the NDH, which he expected to be run according to strict Catholic teaching. Many priests viewed the new régime with favour. Individual clerics were ustasha adherents, active as theoreticians, propagandists, officials, and even killers. Many more simply watched with satisfaction the destruction of the Orthodox Church in Croatia. This was especially true in Bosnia, under Archbishop Ivan Šarić of Vrhbosna (Sarajevo), an enthusiastic ustasha supporter.

Generally, however, the bishops were more circumspect, some even hostile, as they came to fear that ustasha brutality would harm the cause of Catholicism. Misgivings started very soon, with the Rome Agreements and the reserved attitude of the Holy See, leading to what Stepinac's biographer Stella Alexander called the 'complexities, the contradictions, the paradoxes and dilemmas'[7] that were to paralyse the Catholic Church of Croatia. The Archbishop of Zagreb received letters from bishops, priests, politicians and ordinary people, asking him to intervene against the treatment of Serbs and Jews, and he did. From May, he wrote to the interior minister and to the Poglavnik, protesting discreetly, as though he could not bring himself to believe the worse about the behaviour of people who were Croats and Catholics, and as though Pavelić himself were not responsible.

The Catholic hierarchy could not accept the authority the régime assumed in matters of faith and doctrine. The ustashas were determined to keep the matter of conversion in their own hands. Stepinac protested against the violence and the disregard of canonical procedures—to no avail. The bishops had met in conference in June, when he had led them to a visit to the Poglavnik. When they met again in November, not all were able to attend, but they sent a collective remonstrance to Pavelić, repeating that conversion should be without constraints, and exclusively within the province of the Church. They referred to the damning reports they had received and which tinged the Catholic Church with infamy. As Orthodox individuals and entire communities asked for conversion to avoid persecution, and as Catholic laymen and priests also argued that it was indeed a way to save lives, the Archbishop issued confidential instructions to put no obstacles to such conversions. Although he realised that they would in most cases be for the duration of 'these sad times' only, he nevertheless wrote to the Pope on 3 December that the prospects for conversion appeared to be good, provided the rules were safeguarded. Meanwhile Pavelić, who referred to Stepinac as 'that ass',[8] paid no attention to the protests beyond issuing a decree in November giving converts the same formal protection as other citizens.

---

7   Stella Alexander, *The Triple Myth. A Life of Archbishop Alojzije Stepinac*, New York, 1987: 5.

8   Quoted from Jozo Tomasevich, *War and Revolution ... Occupation and Collaboration*, 538.

Those Serbs fortunate enough fled to German-occupied Serbia or to Italian-occupied coastal areas. Others sought refuge in forests and uplands. What began as a panicked flight turned into a disjointed rebellion. It began in early June in eastern Herzegovina. As Italian forces had transferred power to the NDH, the ustashas had arrived, armed their sympathisers, found support among the Muslim villagers and brought in army units. They had ordered the surrender of arms under pain of death, begun to arrest and kill prominent Serbs, and massacre entire villages. Villagers rose, obtained aid from Montenegro and disarmed the gendarmerie. The revolt was essentially apolitical, organised by local personalities (priests, teachers, officers, local politicians, cattle merchants). It quickly took on an ethnic bias. In a poor region that had rebelled in the past against Turks and Austrians, Muslims were always 'Turks', and Croats were now 'ustashas'. The ustashas were hard put to defend Catholic and Muslim settlements.

Serb nationalist propaganda had intensified in Bosnia after the setting up of the Banovina of Croatia in 1939. Many of the rebel leaders had been members of nationalist and patriotic organisations, such as the veterans of irregular chetnik formations that had fought behind enemy lines in the Balkan Wars and in the First World War. Although they called themselves chetniks in 1941, they were no more than armed bands that had progressed from self-defence against ustashas to attacking Muslim villages. New factors intervened in eastern Bosnia in July that provided some structure. Spurred on by the invasion of the USSR, the communists, from their cells in Sarajevo and around the Tuzla mines to the north, began to organise partisan units, but their ambition to move from imperialist war to revolution surpassed their capacity. Officers of the Yugoslav army also came from Serbia to help the insurgents, with armed bands mostly made up of refugees from Bosnia. The officers were accepted as competent professionals and holders of royal commissions. By the end of August, the area within, and west of, the Bosnian bend of the river Drina was in their hands, and they controlled communications with Serbia across the river. In the Romanija massif east of Sarajevo, the communists had been able to organise a larger force, whose advantage lay in the fact that it was able to recruit some Muslims and rein in more extreme anti-'Turkish' behaviour.

Their disadvantage lay in their avowed purpose to aid the Soviet Union by diverting German resources from the Eastern Front. German forces had rarely been attacked, and the officers with the insurgents hoped that the Germans would not intervene, but communist-led partisans started interfering with railway centres and army stores. The Germans eventually did intervene in support of NDH forces, and by late September, considerable changes had occurred in eastern Bosnia. The northern part had been pacified. The insurgents were not up to fighting regular forces. Officers, who themselves often operated independently of each other, complained of indiscipline. The partisans managed a somewhat better fighting spirit and discipline, because of the political control and indoctrination by party activists, but there were too few of them. Officers feared losing the initiative to the communists; the latter feared desertions to the chetniks. In late September and October they managed joint operations, but dissensions appeared over liberated territories. Some officers then approached the German military as the enemy occupying power according to international law, assuring them that they were only fighting Croat rebels against the legal Yugoslav government. Their approach failed to stop the Germans while it provided the communists with a useful propaganda weapon, but partisans were not yet ready to turn against chetniks.

By the end of July, the uprising had flared up on both sides of what had been in the past the border region between Habsburg and Ottoman dominions—in western Bosnia and on the borders of Croatia proper where there was a concentration of Serbs. The KPJ's influence on Croat peasant masses was nil. The Serb peasantry of Croatia had been represented by the Independent Democratic Party who had supported the HSS for the sake of Serbo-Croat peace within Yugoslavia. With the advent of the NDH, the Serbs of Croatia were left in a political vacuum that the KPJ would eventually fill, but not before it had overcome the confusion it had been in until the attack on the USSR. In Croatia between April and July 1941, it had, on the one hand, tended to accept the new borders while, on the other, preparing for a pan-Yugoslav revolution.

The uprising in the western parts of the NDH started on the Dalmatian border. It liberated the area between Drvar and Knin. There too, communists appeared in their own name after the invasion of the USSR, causing differences among the rebels over booty and the administration of insurgent territory. The revolt spread northwards into the western Croatian border areas and into central Bosnia. It was popular, massive, anarchic and rural; the cities remained quiet. Once the enemy within immediate reach had been destroyed or driven out, developments depended on agreements and jealousies between such local leaders as had survived the initial massacres. The communists succeeded in taking over in the plain regions of Srem and Slavonia and in Croatia's western frontier districts, but their cadres were outsiders—indoctrinated urban Croat party activists who had to work with illiterate or semi-literate Serbs, limit their vindictiveness and find a way of appealing to Croats and Muslims.

By the end of August, the NDH authorities realised they had lost control of most of Lika and Kordun, and of vast tracts of Bosnia and Herzegovina. Ustasha terror had been so blatant that it had shocked the Axis. The Germans had rapidly withdrawn most of their forces from their zone, and what they left did not interfere beyond protecting their communication lines. The Italians, who had been slower to withdraw because of the boundary dispute, had come to regard the ustashas with aversion. The latter nevertheless had to turn to their protectors for help. As the Germans were busy in Russia, and the NDH was meant to be the Italians' protégé, the task was handed over to them. Italian troops went back into their Zone 2 in September. They sought to pacify with as little loss of life as possible. They launched a propaganda campaign to convince the population they had come as protectors, appealed for an end to the insurgency, and did not always ask for weapons to be handed in. The insurgents had no interest in taking the Italians on; most of them went home. Many local leaders were willing to remain quiescent, and to settle for peace and safety in the countryside. Even the communists realised their partisans were neither keen to fight the Italians nor up to real military action. They had, after all, started in the belief that the Red Army would easily beat the Wehrmacht, which was not yet the case.

Pavelić had not expected the Orthodox peasants to rise in self-defence. What happened was not a movement against the foreign occupants or even against the ustasha régime. It was the reflex of isolated villagers in danger of extermination. The Serbs of Bosnia generally lived in a pastoral economy, on the slopes of a series of massifs divided by basins and canyons. Every summer, they moved their flocks up to mountain pastures. For centuries, whenever there was danger, entire villages retreated up. This is what had happened again in the summer of 1941, as bands were formed, taking arms from isolated gendarmerie stations and smaller NDH garrisons, occasionally with the complicity of Domobran officers, who looked with dismay and even with fear on the atrocities.

German arrangements for the NDH had been hasty. Hitler cared only for economic interests, with enough order to safeguard them, but without tying up German troops that were needed elsewhere. No sooner had unrest started than most Reich representatives on the spot blamed ustasha policy, which had fuelled the insurgency and destabilised the NDH. The German General in Zagreb reported in June: 'The ustashas have gone raving mad'. Glaise had imagined Hitler as the avenger of the old Habsburg Monarchy against Yugoslavia, bringing order and security for all. Instead, the destruction of Yugoslavia had brought chaos. Glaise took an instant dislike to Pavelić and the ustashas, but he also disliked the Italians. Well informed of the massacres, he missed no opportunity to raise the issue with Pavelić, with ustasha officials, and in his reports to Berlin. Horrified German reactions (none of which were made public) poured in. They were inspired by revulsion, by the desire to preserve Germany's reputation, and by the fear of total chaos in the area. Over the summer, Pavelić was moved to order harsh punishments for those who enforced the law in an illegal manner, with arrests and some executions, and, eventually, the prohibition of the activity of 'wild' ustashas. However, these measures were little more than cosmetic, as Hitler's encouragement to pursue a 'nationally intolerant policy' over fifty years was worth more than Glaise's admonishments.

Italy's three new Adriatic provinces formed the *Governatorato* of Dalmatia under Giuseppe Bastianini, a diplomat and onetime ambassador to London, who was placed directly under Mussolini. In principle, all the institutions and laws of Italy were extended to the new territories; in fact, race and corporation laws were not. Out of a population of 380,000, 14,000 claimed to be Italian, of whom only 4,000 had opted for Italian citizenship after 1918. The old Yugoslav civil service, public services, and even the professions, were to be gradually purged, replaced or incorporated. Names were italianised. Steps were taken to introduce the Italian language in the administration, in schools and in sermons. However, all these measures had to be scaled down or postponed because of the lack of qualified personnel. Reactions to the occupation were mixed and changing. The movement of people was controlled by official passes, but they were freely issued. The shock of the arrival of Italian troops was followed by a feeling of relief when comparisons were made with ustasha rule. The effect of the restoration of food supplies, services and utilities, was spoilt by the thuggish behaviour of local and imported fascists. All such reactions were intensified in Split, the biggest port of the Yugoslav coast, and an industrial and commercial centre, where the Rome Agreements had provided a special administration to appease Pavelić. Most of the 'super-Italians' lived there, alongside the many ustasha sympathisers who had come in the hope of taking over. The city had a generally pro-Yugoslav bourgeoisie opposed both to the NDH and to Italian rule, and it had communist cells. Serb and Jewish refugees, as well as Yugoslav army officers, had found their way there, and so had Ilija Trifunović Birčanin, a veteran chetnik commander of earlier wars who had been close to the British.

The massacres and rebellions in the NDH, the German invasion of the USSR, and the risings in Serbia and in Montenegro, had shattered what remained of the illusion that life could be more or less normal for the duration of the war under Italian occupation. There were incidents in towns, acts of sabotage undertaken by communists, and officers talked of forming small resistance groups. Over the summer, communists began to leave the towns for the mountains. Split was also the centre of a movement of civic resistance to italianisation. The Italians were not prepared for armed resistance; they reacted with arbitrary arrests, internments and the institution of special tribunals under the law for the Defence of the State that imposed 276 (including twenty-three capital) sentences in 1941. They too lost their illusions. The military had been told to disinterest themselves from Croatia's internal affairs. Yet they had to contain a situation created by the ustashas' extremism. Italian soldiers had witnessed scenes of massacres. Military intelligence knew that an insurgency was under way, with vindictive action by Serbs against Croats and Muslims. The occupation forces were caught in the crossfire. When they were within easy reach, soldiers and subalterns reacted with spontaneous gestures, crossing lines to save children and old people. They took photographs. They occasionally disarmed ustashas.[9] The officers' oath included the 'protection of the unarmed', which they used to justify themselves when they were reminded that 'the Croats are our allies'. Garrison commanders intervened, and the Italian press carried vivid reports from August.[10]

---

9   When Vjekoslav Simić, a Franciscan attached to the ustasha command at Knin, was beaten up by Italian soldiers on 19 June, the commander of the army corps simply noted '*Bene!*' on the report of the incident.

10   Corrado Zoli, of the Bologna daily *Il resto del carlino*, used the method of conversations, letting people whom he met on his way—Germans and Croats—tell him and his readers how the horrors were usually carried out by young ustashas sent in from the outside, how the Germans did not have enough troops, and how the only hope was for the Italians to take over. Curzio Malaparte's reports for *Il corriere della Sera*, Milan, provided material for his novel *Kaputt* (1944).

When in late July Serb rebels in the mountains turned on NDH garrisons, and interrupted communications, the first contacts occurred between them and Italian garrisons in the Tromedja region where Dalmatia, Bosnia and Croatia meet. They asked for food, ammunition and protection. They made it clear they had no quarrel with the Italians. They would stop fighting, if Italy helped them or annexed the area. The latter idea was taken up. Serb notables from the hinterland to the Italian enclave of Zadar had had links with the city. A number of ex-Yugoslav Radical Union (JRZ) parliamentarians were persuaded to initiate a request for an extension of annexation or occupation; their plea was published in the press. The Italian top brass convinced Mussolini that to extend the occupation to the entire coastal area was the only hope to limit the insurgency. It feared that, with the ustashas, the situation would get worse. The communists, well organised in Drvar in western Bosnia, outside the de-militarized zone, were trying to influence the rebellion in Lika. The Germans, who were tied up on the Eastern Front and busy with the insurgency in Serbia, were ready to hand over control of much of the NDH, starting with the coastal zone. In order to facilitate an Italian takeover, talks with the Lika rebels moved on to a higher level, between the chief of staff of Supersloda and the rebels' negotiators. Eventually the Serb delegates agreed to stop operations in Italian-controlled territory and to help Italian commands prevent communist infiltration.

The aim of the decision to reoccupy the demilitarised zone of the NDH was to end the insurgency in the hinterland to Italy's new coastline. Orders were given to Supersloda to disarm and dissolve ustasha units, evacuate Domobrans, purge Croatian personnel, and cooperate with local authorities accepted by the population. By way of concessions to NDH sensibility, token Domobran units were allowed to remain under Italian command, and a Croatian administrative commissioner was assigned to Supersloda. On 7 September Ambrosio issued a bilingual proclamation announcing that, in agreement with the NDH government, he was assuming military and civil authority in the area. Severe sanctions would be taken against those who might want to hinder it. The population was invited to return to its villages; Italian armed forces would guarantee 'their safety, their freedom and their goods'.

Italian troops encountered little or no opposition, as insurgents returned to their homes or withdrew outside the territory. In Drvar, the communists had established a base whose influence was a threat to Italian control. Drvar was a small industrial centre where NDH rule was so loose that the area had been mainly spared massacres; there was little interference with communist activity. The Drvar communists had expressed their solidarity with other rebels, while trying to take them over, issuing propaganda that the Red Army was about to reach Yugoslavia. The ustashas were spreading rumours that the Duke of Aosta, onetime viceroy of Ethiopia and a prisoner-of-war of the British, had negotiated a deal on behalf of the royal house of Italy, and that the reoccupation of Zone 2 was a prelude to Italy's change of camp. They also managed more anti-Serb action as they moved out. Meanwhile, the dominant feeling for many Serbs was to exact revenge, so that local Croats and Muslims also sought protection. The Italian command issued orders to check its officers' 'Serbophile tendencies' and to protect all in need.

As the situation calmed down in the coastal zone, it flared up in the Bosnian hinterland. By the end of September, the Army General Staff in Rome felt that it had to fill the vacuum between the demilitarised zone and the demarcation line, where ustashas and communists still exerted their influence and threatened Italian positions, but where NDH authority was minimal. After a joint operation with Croatian and German forces from the north, and with the help of intelligence and propaganda from local chetniks with whom they had negotiated, Italian troops entered Drvar. The move into Zone 3, which then started officially on 9 October, was more difficult. Nevertheless, the first results were judged favourable, as by the end of October, most bands appeared to have ceased their activity. The designations of Zone 1 (annexed territory), Zone 2 (the demilitarised coastal area of the NDH where the Italian army had taken over civil as well as military powers) and Zone 3 (which the Italians merely occupied) were adopted formally. For a while, Italy occupied about half of the territory of the NDH, all the way up to the demarcation line with the German area. In practice and in the longer run, the effort had to be limited to keeping fortified towns and open lines of communication. There were no fresh troops to allocate, and by the onset of winter the Second Army's hold was precarious.

In Zone 2, the greater autonomy of action of Italian commanders allowed a sophisticated approach which caused differences within the ranks of Serb insurgents. The influence of communists fell as the us- tasha danger passed. Non-communist groups were generally known as chetniks, but Italians could not always tell the difference between chetniks and partisans. All those who declared they were from the annexed territories were taken under Italian protection. Jews were no longer required to wear distinctive signs. In the coastal cities, there was much vacillation in local opinion, and divisions were not clear cut. There were attempts at setting up links between communists and traditional parties, whose feelings were with the Allies but who did not think the time had come to fight the Italians. The HSS was even more confused than the others. 'Whatever we do, the final outcome of the war will be as the English want. So any action by us is futile, as the English will decide everything', a former HSS member of parlia- ment in Dubrovnik told a KPJ emissary, as communists continued to believe that the Soviet Union was unbeatable.[11] The rival influences of hinterland chetniks and communists were felt, and the business community was ready to help both sets. It kept Trifunović in hiding in a Split suburb. It managed bogus deals with Italian contacts (with whom they listened to the BBC) that could be claimed as a form of resistance in so far as they provided funds for civic resistance, for pamphlets and for intelligence gathering.

It was also in the autumn of 1941 that three personalities emerged in the Serb anti-communist camp of the Italian-controlled part of the NDH. Radmilo Grdjić, before the war a journalist with the inde-

---

11 Mato Jakšić, *Dubrovnik. Sjećanja*, Belgrade, 1966: 146.

pendent Belgrade daily *Politika* and secretary-general of the official Sokol gymnastic organisation, had been due for evacuation by the British, but had ended up in Split before returning home to Mostar after the Italian reoccupation. He approached the Italians for support in organising help for Serb widows and orphans; he contacted HSS city council members. All in all, he appeared as a competitor to the local, mostly Muslim, KPJ organisation, which was already active helping the families of communist victims. Grdjić too, like the communists, began to acquire arms from NDH and Italian stores to send to armed groups. Dobroslav Jevdjević, once a member of the right-wing Organisation of Yugoslav Nationalists (Orjuna, *Organizacija jugoslovenskih nacionalista*) and lately a parliamentary candidate of the opposition Yugoslav National Party (JNS), was also in Herzegovina. He had approved of the setting up of the Banovina of Croatia, and the fact that he had also advocated a large Serb counterpart to include most of Bosnia-Herzegovina had brought him close to the chetniks associations. Both men established links with Birčanin in Split. The Orthodox priest Momčilo Djujić turned up as a relative newcomer among the chetnik commanders of the Tromedja area. By double-dealing between Italians and communists, he managed to raise a local fighting force which secured his area from ustasha incursions and kept the communists at bay, without too obvious contacts with the Italian military, who described him as a *filibustiere*.

In mid-December, the German Supreme Command realised that more had to be done in the NDH than merely protect mines and railways. It wondered whether the Italians were disposed to occupy it all, as German troops were needed for the Eastern Front. Mussolini was ready to accept on the spot; his generals wanted to think it over. There was panic in Zagreb, and opposition, from both Glaise and Kasche. By the end of the month, it was Hitler who had thought better of the idea to let the Italian army into the German zone of the NDH.

If in April the Independent State of Croatia had met with the acquiescence of a majority of Croats, by the end of the year much had changed. Pavelić had originally been able to widen his base by taking over the extreme right of a split HSS. He initiated a campaign to attract more of the Peasant Party's militants through manifestations of public support. The press was able to boast that, during August and September, some 7,000 HSS members (including twenty-two former MPs) had signed up to join the Ustasha Movement. However, the hard-core following in lowland Croatia, the farmers and small-town artisans, remained passive, indifferent and even hostile. Dissatisfied with Maček's attitude, Pavelić kept him isolated. In October, he had him arrested with a number of other personalities, and interned at Jasenovac until May 1942, when he was placed under house arrest. His arrest increased the feeling of disappointment and discontent felt below the surface. Of the rest of the HSS leadership, some were with the Yugoslav government in exile in London; others in the Italian-occupied coastal zone; half a dozen remained in Zagreb under the party's vice-president, August Košutić.

The Muslims' JMO leader Džafer Kulenović, who had been a minister under both Cvetković and Simović, had not gone into exile.[12] Although the party had spent almost as many years in government as in opposition, the formerly landowning Muslim class had its grudges against the pre-war régime. The loss of their share of crops from tenants had much reduced their standing, at times to poverty, and with them affected others linked to their way of life. The ustashas recruited a sizeable number of Muslims who willingly helped with the persecution of Serbs. Although Pavelić talked of how purely 'Croat' Bosnia's Muslims were, and even about returning to them the land that had been redistributed to Serb peasants, his chief representative in Bosnia and Herzegovina was a leading Catholic Croat ustasha returnee, Jure Francetić, and much of the ustasha apparatus there was in the hands of Catholic clerics. Kulenović was nominally kept

---

12 Kulenović had succeeded as JMO leader on the death in 1939 of Mehmed Spaho, who had considered himself an 'undefined' Yugoslav, whereas of his two brothers, one defined himself as a Croat, and the other as a Serb. The Spaho brothers symbolised the way in which the Muslims of Bosnia and Herzegovina were divided into 'undefined Yugoslavs', Croats and Serbs.

on in the NDH government, but did not effectively see Pavelić until August, when a JMO delegation was received by the Poglavnik as a counterpart to what the HSS had done. The JMO leader and other Muslim personalities from various walks of life who had previously identified themselves as Croats did initially side with the new régime. However, most Muslims were lukewarm, neutral, even opposed, as they sought to protect their group interests.

Many turned against the ustashas' policy of using Muslims against Serbs; they became worried about their own situation in the general lawlessness of Bosnia. In the summer, under the initiative of Muslim clergy, notables from Sarajevo, Mostar, Banjaluka and other towns met and signed resolutions calling for an end to the killings, and condemning the participation of Muslim 'scum' that invited retribution from Serbs. They appealed to the authorities to restore order and to ensure the safety of life and property for all citizens. The protests were phrased in a way that avoided direct criticism of the régime. The signatories came from the upper ranks of Muslim society; they lacked a coherent political vision; and did not achieve a wider mobilisation. The resolutions came as an unwelcome surprise to the ustashas, but did not stop the persecutions. Some Muslims turned to expressing their dissatisfaction by deserting from the Domobrans, by joining Orthodox rebels, by forming self-defence bands, by appealing for German protection. Little was left of the early Muslim support for Croatian independence. Meanwhile Sarajevo remained the main centre of power for the ustashas in Bosnia, because it was the German command centre. It was also a place of safety for many Muslim refugees from eastern Bosnia and Sandžak who had fled from chetnik attacks, and who numbered more than 50,000 by the end of the war.

Things had gone badly wrong for the NDH by the end of 1941. Its economy was in decline, as the ustashas' aryanisation and croatisation policy was merely a camouflage for individuals and groups to lay their hands on Serb and Jewish property. Declining revenues had to satisfy the rising demands of German and Italian occupiers, themselves in disagreement about the exploitation of their ally. Even though only a small number of Croats and even fewer Muslims had taken a direct part in the massacre of Serbs, they had started a fratricidal struggle in the mixed regions. Extreme Croat nationalism had set up a pan-Croat state in the ruins of Yugoslavia, and attempted to croatise it by terror. In return, Serb insurgents had started to repay atrocity for atrocity. Catholics, Orthodox and Muslims in the mixed regions became locked in a vicious struggle, each willing to eradicate others from its territory, and forced to turn to foreign conquerors for protection. Yet the German General in Zagreb could report in June that, in reaction to the atrocities of the ustasha régime, some pro-Yugoslav feelings were beginning to reappear; Italian military intelligence in July, that feelings against the régime were such that communist propaganda was likely to turn the most unlikely people into partisans; and by the end of the year, Italian soldiers picked up HSS leaflets in the countryside that urged peasants 'Patience! The day of liberation is near'.

The German-Controlled 'Serbian Residual State'

What remained of Yugoslavia after the various annexations, redemptions, resurrections and restorations, was called by the Germans the 'Serbian residual state' and kept under their control because of its strategic resources (non-ferrous metals) and routes (the Danube, rail links between Central Europe and the Mediterranean). It had no status other than that of an occupied territory. Of the foreign diplomats in Belgrade, only the Italian minister remained as an observer. The territory was that of Serbia before the Balkan Wars, give or take to fit Germany's interests. Thus south-eastern districts acquired by Serbia at the Treaty of Berlin in 1878 were handed over to Bulgarian occupation and administration, while northern districts of what is now Kosovo were kept as part of Serbia because of mines and valley communications. Romania did not want to claim the Yugoslav part of Banat (present-day eastern Vojvodina); even less did it want Hungary to have it. It was thus left attached to Serbia, but run by the local ethnic German minority, given the privileged status of 'German National Group in Serbia and Banat' (120,000, with another 8,000 in Belgrade).

Because of Hitler's timetable for the conquest of the USSR, the Wehrmacht's 'battle-worthy' units were withdrawn from the Balkan theatre in a matter of weeks. They were initially replaced in Serbia by two occupation divisions (of three regiments at first, eventually down to two). In June Serbia became an area command subordinate to the newly-designated Armed Forces Command Southeast of Field-Marshal Wilhelm List in Salonika. However, the occupation divisions of Serbia and the NDH were kept under a separate Command for Special Purposes LXV. The Nazi 'new order' multiplied overlapping and clashing administrations. Not only was the command of occupation troops at first separate from the German General in Serbia, but the latter had an administrative staff, whose head, Harald Turner (brought over from Paris), was effectively the civil administrator, and a foreign policy adviser from the foreign ministry in Berlin. Economic affairs were under the Plenipotentiary for Economic Affairs. There were various intelligence and security services, such as the military intelligence Abwehr, the Nazi Party intelligence SD (*Sicherheitsdienst*), the Gestapo secret police, with its prisons and camps, and the criminal police.

Germany took immediate steps to gain control of all usable raw materials. The occupation authority assumed control of war production and basic transport facilities. What important mining, industrial, banking and insurance enterprises Germany did not already control, it sequestered or acquired in one way or another. The British-owned Trepča Mines, being enemy property, was placed under German administration. A majority of shares in the Compagnie française des mines de Bor had been bought out of money owed by the Vichy government for occupation costs. The former consul general in Belgrade, Franz Neuhausen, was the Plenipotentiary for Economic Affairs, with complete control over Serbia's economy. Germany wanted to maximise the territory's resources with a minimum of troops. It hoped to be able to do so with the help of Bulgarian soldiers, ethnic German SS volunteers, native auxiliaries, a Serbian puppet administration, strict controls over a wide range of matters, and draconian rules harshly enforced. On 1 May the German military commander appointed a low-grade Serbian Administration of ten commissioners who were put in charge of the ministries, under the control of Turner and Neuhausen, as a simple instrument of the occupation régime.[13] It was headed by the commissioner in charge of the Interior Ministry, Milan Aćimović—a former Belgrade police chief who had had a six-month stint as home minister under Stojadinović, with good pre-war anti-subversive credentials. The main task of his administration was to get the population to accept obedience to the Germans, to help restore basic services, to identify and remove undesirables from public services.

The Yugoslav débâcle was felt most acutely in Serbia. There was bewilderment, humiliation, disillusion and despair, a feeling that the Allies, the state, the army and the Croats had all failed. The political structures had been destroyed. The mainstream politicians who remained withdrew into passivity. German propaganda blamed communism, plutocracy and Jewry for having tricked the Serbs, and the pro-German advocates of a return to Serbian roots and traditional values duly attributed the collapse to foreign influences. The unification of Yugoslavia in 1918 was seen by them as an error; the coup of 27 March as an act of lunacy paid for by the 'English'. The news of the massacres in the NDH (brought by refugees and, more vividly at times, by dead bodies floating down rivers) produced a wave of resentment against Croats and Muslims. As the Germans restored order in Serbia, and then railways, telephone, water and power, there was an audience for those who argued that the occupying power

---

13 Cvetković, who had retired to his home town Niš, had, at the time of the armistice, suggested saving something of the régime such as it had been when Yugoslavia had joined the Pact, with the two regents who had remained in the country and himself as prime minister. Cincar-Marković had been consulted, but did not want to take part in any collaborationist administration.

merely wanted peace and order, and that the prime duty of patriots was to stop anything that could cause further suffering to Serbs.

There were also many, particularly among the officers, who did not share the belief that Hitler had definitely won. Britain was battling on, the United States were expected to go to war, and the Nazi-Soviet Pact could not last long. Many would not come to terms with a rapid capitulation signed without government approval. With overflowing prisoner-of-war camps in the Reich, the Germans had not rounded up all Yugoslav military personnel. Serbia too had plenty of servicemen that had not been captured. There were 1,200 officers in Belgrade alone who refused to work with the collaborationist administration, and there were those who had not laid down their arms or returned home, who had hoped to make their way to Greece or gone into hiding, in order to continue the war.

Much confusion has been caused by the use of the word 'chetnik'. The army had begun to set up 'chetnik' detachments for operations behind enemy lines in case of war, but they had never been operational. The most common usage of the word between the wars was for members of the original chetniks' veterans associations from the Balkan and First World wars who had since been joined by relatives and sympathisers. They had been expected to act as a volunteer territorial reserve in case of war, but in outlying Serb areas they had increasingly become nationalistic and were disliked by non-Serbs. After 1932, Trifunović Birčanin had given way as their overall leader to a more right-wing rival, Kosta Milovanović Pećanac. They were the most famous of the old chetnik 'voivodes' still alive in 1941. The former had been in touch with the British, who had thought of him for possible guerrilla action after the collapse of regular operations. The latter, who had been close to the JRZ government, appears to have received official funds to organise guerrilla actions in southern Serbia, where he had a following among fellow veterans, in the event of an invasion. He had operated there in 1916-1917, and in April 1941 he did indeed organise armed bands, almost immediately involved against Albanian bands that attacked Serb settlers and villagers. Groups of disbanded military personnel also called themselves chetniks.

Colonel Dragoljub (Draža for short) Milhailović was one of those regular army officers who did not accept the legality of the capitulation.[14] In April 1941 he had been chief of staff of the Yugoslav Second Army in northern Bosnia. On learning of the capitulation, he made for Serbia with a small following. There is no evidence that the move was part of a pre-arranged plan to organise resistance. He had served from Slovenia to Macedonia, in Belgrade in the Guards and in the Military Intelligence section of the General Staff, and as military attaché in Sofia and in Prague. He had spent some time in France after attending a course, and was a great francophile, known also later for his pro-British views. He had been critical of Yugoslavia's defence dispositions, and there was no love lost between him and his onetime superior General Nedić. There is no reliable evidence that he was linked with the conspiracy of 27 March 1941 or with any British intelligence or special service. One cannot be certain of what he had in mind when he arrived at Ravna Gora, a plateau in north-western Serbia, on 13 May. Access to it was difficult, yet it overlooked the Western Morava valley. He knew it well from the First World War, and had friends there. He found out that German troops were few and far between in Serbia, that the local administration and *gendarmerie* remained intact, and that many officers like him had escaped capture.

---

14 The lack of personal sources (diary, private correspondence) makes it difficult to write about Mihailović's intentions and views. The surviving documents are his almost obsessive instructions (relating mainly to matters of military administration), his radio messages to the government in exile (saying what he wanted them, or the British, to know), and Axis intercepts of his radio exchanges with real or nominal subordinates. On several occasions, he had to destroy or bury his archives, or leave them for safekeeping to trusted individuals, who in their turn had to destroy or bury records. What was retrieved by the communists could have been selected or otherwise rearranged. The only reliable memoir by someone that was close to him is by a fellow officer, Zvonimir Vučković, *Sećanja iz rata*, 2 vols, originally published in London 1980 and 1984.

He appears to have decided to restore some sort of underground order, starting in Serbia which he knew well. This meant establishing links with fellow officers who were in hiding or had formed their own detachments; obtaining the confidence of the local population; determining the feelings of the local authorities; gathering intelligence and securing contact with the Allies and the Yugoslav government abroad. He understood that the war against Germany would be a long one. Although he does not seem to have thought of starting immediate active resistance, he envisaged his movement as one to be coordinated with outside plans and support. However critical of Simović he and other officers were in the days following the collapse, Mihailović was a legitimist. He had no political agenda beyond maintaining, if only symbolically, the persistence of the Yugoslav state, and opposing the mood of defeatism. For the time being, he kept with him only a small nucleus of officers with an armed guard, which he called the Command of Chetnik Detachments of the Yugoslav Army, so as to establish continuity with the planned pre-war special operations detachments. The Germans immediately noted that a Colonel Mihailović, who had not recognised the capitulation, had arrived on Ravna Gora and was continuing to resist.

For the first few months, Mihailović groped towards a network of officers and non-commissioned officers who had not been captured, and of reliable people within the administration and gendarmerie. He set up links with those armed groups that had already been formed in Serbia, and in neighbouring areas of Herzegovina and Bosnia. With the help of local government offices, he began to draw up lists of conscripts and reservists for possible use. The only civilians to go out to Ravna Gora were a handful of intellectuals from the Serb Cultural Club (SKK), who took charge of propaganda. They did not belong to the political mainstream, tended to blame the Croats generally and the Yugoslav state establishment for the defeat.

The most influential were Dragiša Vasić and Stevan Moljević. Vasić, a writer and a republican, otherwise a reserve colonel, set himself up as Mihailović's right-hand man. In August, he proposed an advisory Central National Committee to be made up of available representatives of Serb parties, of patriotic societies and of prominent individuals. Their reluctance to come out in the open further embittered Vasić towards politicians. He was a man of contradictions, a republican who had been to Moscow and turned strongly anti-communist, but whom the right accused of being a left-winger, if not a Soviet agent. Moljević, a lawyer, was an obsessive nationalist who, having at first been Vasić's protégé, turned into his rival. In June he produced a plan for a post-war Yugoslavia, rounded off to take in whatever *irredenta* could be claimed. It would rid itself of its minorities, and would gather all Serbs in a Serbian unit through population exchanges. Such a Serbia would dominate Yugoslavia, and thus the Balkans, but it would have to do it through 'the breadth of its views and the extent of its vision'. Six months later, in December, after he had come to know of the massacres in the NDH, he wrote of the need to act quickly at the time of liberation, to set up borders with Croatia, to punish culprits, and to carry out the necessary population exchanges. One does not know what Mihailović made of it; he was not politically minded, stuck to the Yugoslavia that he knew and served, and welcomed those non-Serbs that rallied to him. Although he was aware of the limitations of his enterprise, in Serbia let alone outside it, Mihailović saw himself as the embodiment of the Yugoslav armed forces that had not capitulated. By June, he was planning guerrilla warfare, for which he was expecting help from the outside. Meanwhile he would act through propaganda, intelligence and sabotage. However, there could be but one resistance movement, that of the Yugoslav army bound by oath to King and country. His aim, for the time being, was to minimise reprisals and avoid clashes, with occupiers and competitors alike, while he set up his organisation.

The main competitor was the KPJ, whose leadership was summoned by Tito to a consultative meeting in Zagreb in early May. They noted that the old state was dead, that a break-up of the Nazi-Soviet Pact was imminent, and that the Communist Party should prepare itself to seize power in alliance with the USSR. Tito and the Central Committee then moved to Belgrade, where conditions were better under German occupation than in Zagreb under usta-sha surveillance. When Germany attacked the Soviet Union on 22 June, the Comintern instructed all communist parties to alleviate the struggle of the Soviet people by starting guerrilla action. The KPJ manifesto that Tito wrote was, cautiously, a summons to prepare for such action. The Belgrade police immediately initiated arrests. As Comintern calls became more pressing, the Central Committee met to decide how to respond. The Party hierarchy was turned into a military chain of command; its network put on a war footing. Central Committee members were despatched to various parts of the country, to take charge of autonomous centres, adapted to the realities of partition, occupation and local mood. On 12 July, the call to arms went to 'the workers, peasants and citizens of Yugoslavia', to the Serbian, Croatian, Slovenian, Montenegrin and Macedonian peoples, and to 'Muslim brothers'. KPJ statements were published through underground communist papers.

For the KPJ, the break-up of Yugoslavia had meant the end of a régime that had persecuted it, but its leadership, like Mihailović, asserted its right to jurisdiction throughout the territory. During the ambiguous period of April to June, when the Soviet Union accepted the liquidation of Yugoslavia, communists ceased to mention its name, yet Tito worked hard to maintain the cohesion of the party that he led. Contradictions lay below the surface, factions reappeared and central control was not as strong as it seemed. The interval was used to reconstruct the KPJ clandestine network, acquire arms, and find recruits among those embittered against the pre-war régime. With the attack on the USSR, Tito was free to join in, and exploit, a popular cause by reviving patriotic slogans. In Serbia particularly, they stuck a responsive chord, at a time when Mihailović's cautious action had restored some optimism. Like the officers, the KPJ appealed to all those who wanted to continue the war against the Axis. In doing so, the communists were also helping the Soviet Union, 'our dear socialist fatherland'.

They believed in the invincibility of the USSR. Tito remained in Belgrade, where the victorious Red Army was awaited following the expected German defeat in Russia. He was tempted to emulate Lenin and carry out an accelerated revolution in wartime—to destroy the remaining institutions of the old régime and the class enemies, to gain the leadership of national forces through a people's front that the KPJ would infiltrate and eventually dominate. This was not according to the wishes of the Soviet leadership, which was keen to keep its alliance with the West and hence avoid revolutions, but it had more pressing tasks than to control all communist parties all the time. What Stalin wanted first and foremost was action to impede Germany. Events in Serbia, particularly in western Serbia, unfolded rapidly during July. The KPJ began to organise its own bands, soon to be known as 'partisans' (a term borrowed from the Russian), made up of party members and generally urban sympathisers that had left the towns. People took to the woods and hills after the crops had been brought in, to join the first guerrillas to be found, in order to attack military convoys and smaller garrisons. The KPJ was a small clandestine party, but it had an all-Yugoslav if as yet imperfect underground network, leadership, discipline, indoctrination, determination and faith, while Mihailović, whatever his intentions, had begun as one man on one mountain in Serbia. In the cycle of uprisings of the Serb population of Yugoslavia in the summer of 1941, Serbia comes last chronologically, but whereas elsewhere they were amorphous, local and leaderless outbursts, the one in German-occupied Serbia crystallised into a two-headed resistance which showed that Yugoslavia had not been destroyed as thoroughly as Hitler had intended.

Having been told that he could have no reinforcements, the German military commander tried to marshal native forces. The commissioners sponsored an 'appeal to the Serbian people' to restore order and ensure a successful 'national revival'. It obtained 307 signatures—notorious collaborators and pre-war Axis-leaning politicians, but also intellectuals, scientists and churchmen, many of whom signed under pressure. Meanwhile the German occupation authority, with help from the Foreign Ministry in Berlin, was looking for ways to strengthen the collaborationist administration. The outcome was the appointment, on 29 August, of General Nedić as president of a 'Serbian Government'. He had commanded the Southern Group of Armies in the April campaign, and had not been taken into custody. Since the defeat, he had turned against the mistaken experiment of Yugoslavia and its alliance system. Believing that the future belonged to Germany, he was anxious that the Serbian people should be able to survive under the Nazi New Order. Even so, strong pressure had to be put on him to accept, threateningly from the Germans, indirectly through several Serbian personalities worried by the possibility of Serbia being partitioned among Germany's allies, and by the communist influence over the uprising.

His twelve ministers were commissioners who had been retained (including Aćimović at the home ministry), followers of Ljotić, the leader of the Zbor movement, and three fellow generals. He was allowed to use the media to press his appeals not to provoke more severe policies, and to put forward his ideology of a return to simple rural life with the stereotyped qualities of 'Mother Serbia'. He made much of the fact that he was allowed to use Serbia's old flag and coat of arms, and even King Peter's portrait. He denounced the communists and those who had brought on the war; he castigated English plutocracy, bolshevism and political parties. His slogan of saving Serbian lives was popular. His government had no status under international law, and no power beyond that delegated by the Germans.

The Nedić government was authorised to set up a Serbian State Guard (SDS, *Srpska državna straža*) to keep internal order. Planned initially to number 17,000, it absorbed the old gendarmerie, and gradually rose to 24,000. Those who joined generally considered themselves to be the continuation of the pre-war gendarmerie on the basis of international law. The SDS did not have enough officers, and was unreliable. The only reliable collaborators the Germans could find were the adherents of Zbor. Ljotić, who had been consulted before Nedić's appointment, and who preferred to exercise his influence offstage, was allowed to set up a parallel force of Serbian Volunteer Detachments of 3–4,000 (rising eventually to 12,000), made up of his followers with added refugees, who also invoked the absentee King along with St George. Having completely turned to Serbia with a clear-cut totalitarian solution and an Orthodox emphasis, Ljotić offered the Germans a force of indoctrinated auxiliaries, committed to opposing Judaism, freemasonry, communism, democracy and Mihailović. Pećanac, with his ragbag 'black' chetniks, made his peace with the occupation authority. He was licensed to keep some sort of peace, under remote supervision, in his patch of southern Serbia. With a varying force of 3–6,000, he remained very much a law unto himself, forfeiting what little reputation he still had, until he was killed by Mihailovic's men in 1944. Yet another source of recruits was the 'White' Russian émigré community. Some 2,500 of them (later to expand to 11,000), stimulated by their anti-communism and by talk of being led back to Russia, volunteered to join the Russian Security Corps, whose prosaic duty was to protect industrial installations working for Germany.

Mihailović's men had been the first to 'go underground' or 'take to the woods', in so far as they were military personnel that had not surrendered. Although they had had defensive encounters with the Germans, reprisals and the tales from the NDH made them reluctant to go into armed struggle except against the ustashas across the border. Mihailović provided some arms and officers to go to eastern Bosnia. This was particularly the case with Major Jezdimir Dangić, who had commanded the gendarmerie unit that had escorted King Peter to Nikšić airport, and whom Mihailović sent across the Drina in August. By that time, the withdrawal of German troops, the belief that Russia was too big a morsel for Hitler to swallow, added to the feeling that something had to be done to help the Serbs in Bosnia, had raised the fever in Serbia. Mihailović was pushed into premature action. By appealing to legitimacy, he achieved preponderance in sympathy, if not in militancy. Meanwhile communists were also rousing peasants against the local government machinery and hampering Mihailović's organisation. Some officers were eager to attack the Germans, as a release from their own frustrations, and to retain support in the face of communist competition. Others were diffident towards the partisans, and sensed danger to the population confronting reprisals. The KPJ had sent emissaries to Mihailović and came to some agreement with him. At the end of August both sides went into action, sometimes jointly, capturing prisoners.

From Belgrade, Tito was finding it difficult to keep up with developments. He realised that the arrival of the victorious Red Army was no longer imminent; he was concerned about the way communist action was developing from region to region, and troubled about the need to make a deal with Mihailović. He left the capital and made straight for a meeting with Mihailović, some 15 kms north of Ravna Gora on 19 September. Tito argued in favour of uniting their forces in full-scale operations; Mihailović, for an end to a premature general uprising that exposed the population to reprisals. Tito suggested a plan for a share of the booty and of the administration of territory; Mihailović objected to disrupting the old administration. An uncertain *modus vivendi* was reached. Tito went on to a gathering of KPJ leaders on 26-27 September, where it was decided to stimulate risings all over Yugoslavia, so as to create areas under communist rule, but to avoid fighting occupation troops; the Supreme Staff of the Peoples' Liberation Partisan Detachments was set up under him.

While the rival insurgent leaders debated, the German military reacted with vigour. They considered armed resistance by civilians as terrorism, and reprisals against the population of occupied territories as a legitimate deterrent. As the armistice protocol had brought legal resistance to an end, the death penalty was immediately introduced for 'Serb soldiers' found with arms, strengthened on 28 April by the announcement that one hundred Serbs would be executed for every German killed. As the number of diversionary acts increased, Serbia was declared a war zone, village houses were torched, and the first concentration camp was set up outside Belgrade for hostages, internees and captives. Executions started at the end of July. The 'Serbian solution' to the rising had failed, but as the Germans could not afford to bring in reinforcements for more than a short time, they would terrorise the population into submission. Troops were now brought in from Greece, Romania and Croatia, followed by a division from France and, ultimately, another division from Russia. General Franz Böhme was sent from Greece to take charge with the new position of Plenipotentiary Commanding General in Serbia. General Walter Kuntze replaced List at Command Southeast in Salonika.

A general ruling had just been issued by the Wehrmacht High Command, on the basis of Hitler's order of 16 September 1941, which became the formal basis for measures to be taken in all occupied areas: one hundred executions for every German officer or soldier killed, fifty for every wounded. Every such act had to be 'regarded as being of communist origin'. Böhme was instructed to apply the order in Serbia for German nationals, ethnic Germans, Bulgarian military personnel, individuals in the service of the occupation authority, and, eventually, for members of the Serbian government, its local representatives, and officers of collaborationist formations, with insistence on the harshest literal interpretation. The anti-Serb prejudices of Wehrmacht commanders—especially if they had served the Habsburgs—lived happily with Nazi anti-Slav racism, and coincided with the wish to punish those who had rejected the German alliance. Orders were given for lists of hostages to be drawn up by every local command, and to arrest as many as could be kept in internment—communists, Jews, 'nationally' and 'democratically' inclined individuals. For Mihailović and his officers, their worst fears were coming true: the situation in Serbia threatened to become as dire as in the NDH, and all for very little gain. Mutual suspicions between hardliners on both sides of the resistance developed into incidents.

By the beginning of October, traffic over most of Serbia was at a standstill, several smaller towns were in insurgent hands as the result of the action of mutually suspicious 'chetniks' and 'partisans', and joint sieges had begun of larger towns. Their respective commands were in Požega and Užice, 15 kms apart. The latter, with a small-arms factory and a branch of the National Bank, was the capital of what came to be called the partisans' 'Užice Republic', where they destroyed land records, introduced communist symbols, held a parade for the anniversary of the October Revolution, and organised Communist Party courts and executions for militants guilty of pre-war factionalism.

The Germans went into counter-action. Ten soldiers having been killed and fourteen wounded in a joint partisan-chetnik attack on Kraljevo, 1,700 hostages were shot there on 20 October, in spite of attempts by the local Serbian administration and the local Zbor branch to mitigate the punishment. Ten Germans having been killed and twenty-six wounded in the attempt to free a platoon captured by partisans as the German platoon was returning to Kragujevac, men and boys were rounded up in and around the town, in streets, shops, homes and schoolrooms between 18 and 21 October, this time with assistance from the Serbian Volunteers; 2,778 were shot, the executions continuing beyond the required quota.[15] The reprisals against the civilian population exacerbated the tension between chetniks and partisans. The communists' ranks were thinning again, as Mihailović's influence grew; the officers feared for the social fabric and for their own authority. Tito and Mihailović resisted advice to attack the other side quickly; another meeting was arranged, but could not take place before 26 October because of German operations. Once again, some consensus was achieved on secondary issues. German intelligence noted that the talks had taken place and failed. For Tito, Mihailović was 'a pleasant-mannered but not an outstanding' officer.[16] For Mihailović, Tito was a mystery. The communist

---

15 These figures are now agreed by German and Serbian scholars. Until recently, the inflated figures of 6,000 and 7,000 were advanced and widely believed.

16 Fitzroy Maclean, *The Heretic. The Life and Times of Josip Broz Tito*, New York, 1957: 109. In the English edition Maclean has Tito say: 'A nice, pleasant-mannered sort of man—a typical regular officer' (*Disputed Barricade. The Life and Times of Josip Broz-Tito, Marshal of Jugoslavia*, London, 1957: 145).

leader was believed to be Russian, and did nothing to dispel the mystery. It helped his aura with the rank-and-file of the partisans; it hid the fact that he was a Croat, and that he had already been to the area in 1914 with the invading Austro-Hungarian forces.

Mihailović's popularity surpassed that of the partisans in Serbia, and it was spreading further afield. Yet he was depressed by the realisation that the insurgents were not able to protect the population from the Germans' punitive expeditions. The number of victims in Serbia, particularly as exaggerated at the time, coming on top of those in the NDH, led him to fear that the very survival of the Serb nation was at stake. The strains in relations between chetniks and partisans had become such that the German offensive tore the uprising apart. Mihailović and Tito may have realised that they could not afford to fall out, but they could not, even had they wanted to, overcome the accumulated distrust. As broken agreements followed provocations, zealots on both sides (some chetnik commanders in particular) were eager to break off. From 31 October they attacked and captured towns from each other. Even so, both leaders still sought to bring hostilities to a halt, as ceasefires alternated with ultimatums. The fratricidal war affected fighters on both sides; ordinary people were horrified by their bloody discord and frightened by the reprisals.

Böhme shortened the front against the rebels, for more concentrated striking power in selected areas. The final assault started on 25 November, as winter was setting in, with mobile troops, armour, air power, and a contribution from Nedić's SDS. Tito and Mihailović had one last conversation over the telephone to check each other's intentions: Tito would defend his positions, and Mihailović disperse. More wisely, the partisans withdrew from Užice on 29 November. Tito headed for the rugged Sandžak region separating Serbia from Montenegro, hardly daring to hope that the Germans would stop their pursuit at the boundary line with the Italian zone—which they did. The inhabitants saw them off in silence.

The development of Mihailović's authority owed much to the legitimacy he had acquired by linking up with the Yugoslav government in exile and with the British. In July, King Peter and the government had reassembled in London, arriving by way of Greece and the Near East; they had declared that Yugoslavia was still at war, and would continue to fight until victory. A radio link had been established in September. Even though Mihailović asked for discreet support rather than propaganda, and London urged restraint, stirring stories soon appeared about the Yugoslav resistance. To play up Mihailović's heroic image was a response of sorts to Soviet demands for a second front, and a morale booster for occupied Europe, at a time when nothing more could be done. The initial success of the rising in Serbia was due to a false sense of security and popular enthusiasm, spurred on politically by determined communists and organisationally by reluctant officers. Allied London had lionised the Yugoslav government in exile and the young monarch. The Soviet government had restored diplomatic relations with them. General Simović deluded himself with false comparisons between the Serbian government in exile during the First World War and his own government; he had no armed force, beyond a couple of small ships, a dozen planes and a few hundred officers and men that had been able to join the British in Egypt, until contact was established with Mihailović. On 15 November, the BBC announced that Mihailović was the commander of the Yugoslav armed forces in the homeland. At a time when the Allied world had little good news, the accomplishments of 'the first resistance in occupied Europe' were inflated to legendary proportions.

The first Allied mission to occupied Yugoslavia was a joint British-Yugoslav team, hurriedly organised by the British Special Operations Executive (SOE), to report on what was happening. Landed by submarine on the Montenegrin coast in late September, it arrived at Mihailović's headquarters by way of Užice and partisan headquarters a month later, just as the rising in Serbia was beginning to fail. All that the British could do was to try and patch things up locally between chetniks and partisans, while advising Mihailović to husband his resources in the hope of better times ahead. The link gave him a psychological boost, and confirmed him in the view that his original strategy had been correct, but the communists were convinced he had received directives to attack them.

The partisans had suffered a heavy defeat. Tito had believed that Germany was about to be defeated in Russia; he had not expected such a massive revolt, and had had to make do with peasant fighters, who did not want to fight away from their homes, who were reluctant to accept much discipline, let alone indoctrination, and who did not understand the communists' revolutionary rhetoric. When repression burst the bubble of optimism, popular mood turned against the insurgency, and the communists' difficult relations with the officers broke down. Mihailović too was in a desperate situation. He had been unable to impose command discipline on his officers. The British could not supply arms. Faced with loss of morale, desertion and shortage of ammunition, he clutched at straws. Nedić was opposed to both resistance movements, but whereas the communist-led partisans were, for him, nothing more than agents of Moscow bent on destroying the traditional order, he considered Mihailović's chetniks as being merely misled by London: they could perhaps be induced to change their ways. Although General Böhme had told him that Mihailović was a German problem in which he was not to meddle, Nedić may have tried to neutralise him in early September, by suggesting, through intermediary officers, to no avail, that he move to Bosnia. In late October, the idea of a 'legalisation' on the model of Pećanac's chetniks, which would secure an end to the reprisals and a source of arms to fight the communists, was put to Mihailović.

It is impossible to ascertain how much of it came from an officer of Mihailović's organisation in Belgrade, how much from within the Abwehr, how much from Mihailović himself, and exactly what each of the three had in mind. Did the Germans want to sound out Mihailović, or talk him into capitulating, or entrap him? In spite of opposition, the Abwehr did go ahead, and Mihailović did, however reluctantly, come to a meeting with the Belgrade head of German military intelligence, on 11 November, at Divci, on the frontline between German-controlled and chetnik-controlled territory. To the surprise of all who had been involved in the preliminaries, it turned out that the German command, who were about to quell the rising, merely wanted to see if it could not get Mihailović to conform to the capitulation that had put an end to military operations seven months earlier. There was talk of arresting him, before he was allowed to leave. Three weeks later, orders were issued for an operation to destroy his headquarters and detachments in the Ravna Gora area. Although he had ordered his detachments to disperse, on 6-7 December Mihailović barely escaped capture as some 500 of his combatants were taken. On 10 December, a German bounty of 200,000 dinars was offered for him through the radio, the press, leaflets and posters, followed on 13 December by a similar NDH bounty should he cross the border. It was a coincidence that on 7 December, the BBC announced that Mihailović had been promoted to brigade general (corresponding to the British rank of major general) when he had gone to earth and off the air waves. In the words of Simon Trew, 'he was a general without troops'.[17]

If he had not personally come to a Pećanac-type arrangement, 2–3,000 of his men did enlist in a new category of auxiliary 'legal' chetniks created by Nedić to help maintain order. There is no reliable evidence that the order came from Mihailović, even though it seems that he approved. He might have wanted to avoid committing himself, or to leave his commanders a free hand. Some crossed to Bosnia to fight the ustashas. Most of his men were sent, or simply went, home. 'Legalisation' had its advantages. It provided Nedić with more men to act against the remaining partisans. It offered Mihailović a way for part of his chetniks to survive the winter with a minimum salary and an alibi provided by Nedić's administration. The disadvantages were numerous. There was more confusion than ever over who and what the chetniks were. Although Mihailović increasingly avoided the term, his men were popularly called chetniks. Individuals

---

17 Simon Trew, *Britain, Mihailović and the Chetniks, 1941-1942*, Basingstoke & London, 1998: 95.

and entire formations would move from one category to another. The Germans, had no control over the 'legalisation'; they did not go out of their way to prevent it, but they proceeded to make their first arrests of Nedić's officers.

Mihailović's men had often clashed with Ljotić's volunteers. At times, they had clashed with the SDS, in spite of some contacts between officers who had been colleagues before the war. With his legalised chetniks, Nedić had acquired auxiliaries, but also worms within his administration, as Mihailović increasingly sought to infiltrate it. As 1941 drew to a close, General Mihailović led an itinerant existence, with the barest of staff and bodyguard. Of his 'Yugoslav army in the homeland', there remained a few scattered platoons in the hills, and fragments of a support network in the towns. The communists had been defeated, but his own organisation had been severely damaged, and his men forced to make accommodations with, or at least camouflage as, collaborators in order to survive. The very failure of the premature rising appeared to prove him right, and he was determined to go back to his original plan. However, he saw that in order to put himself beyond the reach of the Germans, he too had to leave Serbia. Böhme, his mission accomplished, was replaced by General Paul Bader, who consolidated all military functions in Serbia as Plenipotentiary General. During the summer of 1941, remnants of the Yugoslav army, more or less co-ordinated by Mihailović, joined by Tito's communists, had caused serious trouble for the Wehrmacht and cleared, if not actually liberated, whole areas of Serbia. Mihailović's influence and strength had been greatly exaggerated. Yet it was he whom the Allies, the Germans and the natives generally seemed to consider the leader of a rising that appeared to be more important than anything that had happened hitherto in occupied Europe.[18]

---

18 According to German documents, from 1 August to 5 December 1941 German casualties in Serbia amounted to 203 dead and 378 wounded; 11,522 insurgents died in combat, 21,809 hostages were executed.

As large-scale action came to an end, the German military presence in Serbia was again reduced to two occupation divisions, but a more important rôle was thereafter assumed by the German police apparatus, the ethnic German SS and the Bulgarian army. In December, Bulgaria was requested to extend its occupation zone almost to the river Ibar to the west and the Bor copper mines to the north. A Bulgarian Occupation Corps of three divisions had its command at Niš, subordinated to the German command in Serbia which also retained exclusive political and operational control. Bulgarian occupation covered forty per cent of the territory, Banat excluded. This was precisely what Nedić had feared at the time of his appointment. His protests and his threat of resignation (even of suicide) were to no avail.

Germany had originally intended to operate all war-production facilities, but with the rising, it was decided to dismantle armaments and explosives factories, and to remove machinery, tools and equipment to Germany. By March 1943, this had been carried out. The mining of copper ore at the Bor installations, seriously damaged by Yugoslav forces in April, was started again in November. By September 1942, it supplied sixteen per cent of German consumption, despite labour and other problems, just as the Trepća lead mines provided thirteen per cent of the Reich's needs. Antimony mines, much destroyed during the insurgency, were in operation again by June 1942, and meeting sixty-two per cent of Germany's needs. All in all, industry in Serbia was not so much taken over as destroyed, by military action, by the manner of production for the war effort, by turning out labour to work on repairing and operating railways and mines, and to go and work in the Reich. Insurgency, reprisals, removal of plants, and action to incite workers to work in Germany, all contributed to the departure of over 40,000 workers to the Reich by 1943. The cost of repairing industrial installations was borne by the Serbian government, along with compensation claimed for war damage to German property, and ever-increasing occupation costs.

No sooner had Belgrade been occupied than anti-Jewish measures began to be applied in a haphazard manner. Jews had to register, under pain of execution, with the security Einsatzgruppe; they were made to work on clearing ruins and retrieving bodies, loading and unloading rail wagons and river barges. On 30 May, an order of the military commander introduced the full panoply of German racial laws regarding Jews and Gypsies. Large-scale arrests of Jews as hostages started with the uprising, while confiscated Jewish property was sold at a fraction of its pre-war value, usually to Volksdeutsche. The latter and Serbian Volunteer Detachments were 'drilled' into assisting arrest and deportation operations. Internment camps under the jurisdiction of the Gestapo were set up in former military and industrial installations on the outskirts of Belgrade, for Jews and other hostages. There were also smaller camps at Šabac and other places for Jewish refugees from other countries. Jews (assumed to be communists) were hostage fodder, always selected for reprisal executions. In October, the Plenipotentiary General ordered the immediate arrest of all male Jews and Gypsies, and, as ever more space was needed in camps for other internees as well, they were quickly executed. Orders were subsequently issued for the internment of women and children.

As part of their counter-insurgency plans, the Germans had set up a large concentration camp on the grounds of the Belgrade Fair (*Sajmište*) intended for the population of rebel areas. Across the Sava (now in Novi Beograd), hence technically in the NDH, it was nevertheless the preserve of the German police apparatus in Serbia. As the rising was put down without resorting to such large-scale internment, the camp was used for other purposes. From December 1941, it took in surviving Jews and Gypsies, mainly women and children, reaching a maximum population of 6,900 by the end of the year. They would all be killed by May 1942, to make way for other inmates; after March their liquidation was accelerated by the use of mobile gas chambers brought specially from Berlin.[19] The German military could boast that Serbia was 'free of Jews' ('*Serbien ist judenfrei*').[20]

The German command had set up a Jewish committee in Belgrade to help it carry out its initial measures. It had a Jewish and Gypsy affairs section organised as part of the Special Police at the Prefecture of Belgrade, under Gestapo control (other sections dealt with foreigners, the 'DM [Mihailović] movement' and communist action), with even a Serb Jewish police officer. The Nedić administration, and even more so Zbor, went along with the German measures; the Serbian police and even more so Serbian Volunteer Detachments provided passive or active assistance. Yet the responsibility for initiating and implementing the liquidation of some eighty per cent of Serbia's 15,000 Jews, along with other Jews who happened to be in the territory, rests firmly on the Germany military authority. The Jews from Serbia who survived were the prisoners of war in Germany and Italy, those who initially were able to obtain travel permits for Italian-held areas, pass off as Serbian refugees, hide away from towns with baptismal certificates obtained from willing clergy, or join the resistance, always at the mercy of those who risked their lives by protecting them.

The Nedić government contributed to the maintenance of order, with ordinances to impose registered residence, limit and control

---

19 Sajmište was then turned into the main transit camps for resisters and internees, partisans, chetniks and others, on their way to labour locations and concentrations camps, in the Reich and elsewhere, for the whole of Yugoslavia, and from October 1943 for the whole Balkan area, until its evacuation in July 1944. In the spring of 1944 it had 4,000 Italian prisoners of war. The Association of the Old Sajmište Memorial estimates the number of victims in the camp at over 10,000 Jews and over 13,000 others.

20 '*Keine Judenfrage mehr*', was how the head of the Gestapo put it. On the expeditious way the Germans dealt with the 'problem' in Serbia, and on the role of the Wehrmacht in particular, see Raul Hilberg, *The Destruction of the European Jews*, 3rd ed., New Haven CT & London, 2005, section on the Balkans. Hilberg has since further revised his work, adding more details, for translated editions. The latest and fullest is the French, *La Destruction des Juifs d'Europe*, Paris, 2006 (Les Balkans: 1259-1593).

travel, enforce the denunciation of unregistered individuals, and prevent any form of public protest. The collaborationist press campaigned against the corruption of the pre-war régime, with its political parties, banks, concessions, 'and other dirty instruments of its so-called democracy'.[21] In a climate of unemployment, corruption and general impoverishment, it railed against the bourgeoisie that was still living off its ill-acquired riches, and against the pro-Western intelligentsia that had done nothing to help the people. It denounced the whispered propaganda coming from these circles. Its loudest condemnation was for Mihailović and the communists, who were but paid agents of London and Moscow calling for more sacrifices from the Serbian people.

The idealisation of patriarchal village collectivism as opposed to the decadent West was inspired by the writings of Russian Slavophile writers via certain Orthodox Church personalities such as Bishop Nikolaj (Velimirović), who, after having been influenced by Western religious and philosophical thinkers, had in the 1930s preached a sort of Orthodox nationalist revival. Although he had provided one strand of inspiration for Ljotić's movement, he had opposed both Zbor and the Tripartite Pact, and had refused any support to the German occupation. He was interrogated by the Germans on account of his British links, subsequently apprehended on suspicion of contacts with the chetniks, and kept under house arrest in various monasteries. The head of the Serbian Orthodox Church, Patriarch Gavrilo, a staunch opponent of the Tripartite who had blessed King Peter when the monarch was about to leave the country, was also interrogated and subsequently interned in monasteries. Divided and disrupted, deprived of its head, the Serbian Orthodox Church limped on under a locum tenens, Metropolitan Josif of Skoplje (Skopje), expelled from his see to Belgrade by the Bulgarian occupation authorities. While some of the clergy in Serbia did collaborate with, and even militate in, Zbor, some clerics sided with the partisans, and most of them sympathised with Mihailović.

---

21 *Srpsko selo*, Belgrade, 18 September 1941.

One area in which the Nedić government showed helpful initiative was that of the refugees, who flooded in from the NDH, from Bulgarian, Hungarian and Albanian-controlled territories, and from the German-annexed part of Slovenia. In May 1941, at a time when their number was nearing 180,000, it set up a Commissariat for Refugees, which started by registering them. Many did not register, so that estimates of their number vary; it could have been as high as 400,000 (including 86,000 orphaned children). That represented ten-eleven per cent of the territory's population which, nevertheless, and in spite of its own difficulties, manifested a high degree of solidarity. In order to feed them, the Commissariat managed to buy surplus wheat and obtain donations from producers. Placed initially in camps, they were gradually dispersed and well received throughout Serbia. To a point, they made up for a deficit in labour; they also joined the SDS, the Serbian Volunteers, chetniks and partisans. The Germans, who were worried by their impact on the economy and on security, tried to stop their influx, and even obtain their repatriation.

Italian-held Montenegro; Albania's, Bulgaria's and Hungary's annexations; Slovenia

Italian troops coming up the coast from Albania had moved into Montenegro on 16 April 1941 before going on to Dubrovnik to meet those coming down from Italy. The plan was to restore Montenegro as a small satellite state, but the Italians were not quite clear about its borders, head of state or local opinion. Their intelligence was based on a group of émigré loyalists of the Petrović-Njegoš dynasty, deposed in 1918, and on the mistaken belief that all Montenegrin 'Greens'—the so-called 'green' party that had opposed the unconditional unification with Serbia into Yugoslavia in 1918—pined for outright independence, whereas most of them were 'federalists' who would have been satisfied with a Montenegrin unit within Yugoslavia. Federalists had maintained some influence in the Cetinje area, and the King and Queen of Italy had a sentimental attachment to Montenegro (Queen Helen was a daughter of King Nicholas), but the presumed claimant would not hear of a restoration. Prince Michael, Nicholas's grandson, who lived in France and had been interned by the Germans in Germany, was a staunch Yugoslav with Allied sympathies. His refusal confounded Italian planners and their circle of separatist followers. The borders were an even more serious issue. Italy had bagged Kotor; Albania wanted fringe areas with an Albanian population that had been part of Montenegro in 1914; the NDH wanted to extend into Sandžak. King Victor Emmanuel was opposed to such 'mutilations' which made Montenegro less viable and wounded its pride. He was successful in obtaining that Mount Lovćen, the mythic symbol of Montenegro, should be excluded from annexation by Italy.

The Italians behaved with goodwill. Prisoners of war were freed. Food supplies and other goods started arriving from Italy at low prices. One division was retained for garrison duties, thinly spread throughout the territory. The pre-war administrative apparatus generally remained in place. Mussolini planned an ambitious programme of public works. A diplomat was sent to Cetinje as High Commissioner to prepare for the restoration of the Kingdom of Montenegro. What the Italians failed to realise was that their handful of nostalgic separatists had almost no support, and that no sooner were preparations started than a region-wide conspiracy was astir to counter it. The purposefully easy-going character of the occupation made it easy. The region had been Yugoslavia's last bastion, where King and government had gone to before flying out, and yet there had been no real military operations in Montenegro itself. Most men had been called up in one locally-based division. After some initial success in Albania, they had gone home with weapons and equipment. Some 400 regular Yugoslav army officers, many non-commissioned officers and civil servants, as well as KPJ militants who were natives of Montenegro, had returned home. Even after the attack on the Soviet Union, no measures were taken against communists outside cities, while their rating as pro-Russians rose. Even more than elsewhere, they believed that the Germans would soon be defeated in Russia, and that the KPJ should make the best of it. Milovan Djilas of the KPJ leadership, sent to his native Montenegro to make preparation for guerrilla action, had travelled from Belgrade with false papers and a regular visa from the Italian Legation.

The occupiers' goodwill elicited nothing but contempt from a population that nursed its wounded pride. Djilas writes: 'Only in armed conflict could we affirm ourselves and force the enemy to understand us and grant us recognition'.[22] The Italians planned to have a Montenegrin Assembly meet on 12 July—St Peter's day, according to the Julian calendar, Montenegro's patron saint—to adopt a 'Declaration on the Restoration of Montenegro', but found it almost impossible to gather seventy-five hand-picked and paid delegates, because of the latent tension under the apparent calm. The arrival of thousands of refugees from border regions, and rumours from Albania made it impossible to keep the new territorial settlement under wraps until after the event. The main rôle at the Assembly was assumed by Sekula Drljević, a Montenegrin independentist who had come from Zagreb, and who hurried the proceedings.[23] The declaration read to, and acclaimed by, those delegates who were still in town, restored Montenegro's sovereignty in the form of a constitutional monarchy whose destiny was united to Italy, and asked the King of Italy to name a regent.

Italy's Montenegro restored was stillborn. Its proclamation triggered a general uprising. After a week, the Italians were left with only the three major towns of Cetinje, Podgorica and Kolašin, and the coast. Apparent calm and reliance on their clients had led them to live for a while with the illusion of popular support. The uprising took them by surprise. The communists immediately went into action. Able-bodied men gathered in villages; the local gendarmerie

---

22 Milovan Djilas, *Wartime*, London, 1977: 22.

23 He had been successively a minister and leader of the parliamentary opposition under King Nicholas, partisan of the union with Serbia, republican and federalist, before becoming a separatist linked to right-wing circles in Croatia.

joined them. Officers assumed command while communists did their best to inject some organisation and to take over. It was coincidence that the Central Committee's call to the peoples of Yugoslavia went out on 12 July. The Italian military presence was dispersed in many very small units. Tiny garrisons surrendered when confronted by several hundred well-armed and well-officered peasants, and forty-three Italian soldiers were killed on the first day. The snowballing revolts went on to attack, and obtain the surrender of, battalion-sized garrisons. Surprised, disillusioned, and shocked by the mutilated corpses of some of their own men, the Italians reacted haphazardly by arresting and by executing some of those denounced by separatists. They then mounted a counter-offensive. On 15 July, General Alessandro Pirzio Biroli, commander of Italian forces in Albania, was given full powers to put down the revolt in Montenegro.

The insurgents had gone back to the traditional pre-1914 levy pattern according to districts and clans. The main commanders to emerge were Colonel Bajo Stanišić who had returned from Herzegovina, Major Djordje Lašić who had escaped capture in Slovenia, and Captain Pavle Djurišić. Tito suspected that Djilas was acting too independently, as he steered a course amid a succession of differing instructions, from the initial preparation of small-scale action to full-scale uprising, between creating a KPJ-dominated political organisation and a military structure, between the fighters' urge to attack the Italians and the local militants' wish to destroy the establishment, and differences within the local party organisation itself.

General Luigi Mentasti's XIVth Army Corps based at Shkodra (Scutari) in Albania, with elements of five divisions added to the one already in Montenegro, repressed the revolt within a month. About 67,000 Italian soldiers were used. Albanian and Muslim irregulars from border areas, who remembered the Montenegrin occupation of 1913, moved ahead and secured their flanks. Mussolini, who was anxious to restore order quickly without having to ask for German help, wanted to resort to the execution of hostages, but left it to the military. Pirzio Biroli issued directives to repress vigorously, but to avoid 'acts of revenge and useless cruelty'. In the process, dozens of villages were burned down, hundreds of inhabitants were executed, 10,000-20,000 were interned, and the irregulars were allowed to loot and burn freely for a while. Enthusiasm subsided. Local notables wanted resistance to be continued only against those Muslims who were acting against their Christian neighbours. Embittered communists turned against the peasant mentality, as only the ideologically committed continued to fight. Having heard of ustasha and German terror, most people felt that it was safer to tolerate the Italians, such as they were. Armed groups made contact with the occupying troops to end the revolt. The main aim of the rebellion had been achieved once the setting up of a separate client state of Montenegro had been stopped. Having peaked at over 30,000, the rebels disintegrated.

The Italian response had immediately exposed the insurgents' lack of unity and their military weakness. Peasant fighters abandoned their positions and went home. Differences between officers (still mostly uniformed, and in command) and communists (who were organising the movement, and placing their 'politkoms'—political commissars) had appeared almost immediately—over surrender terms to Italian garrisons, and over the administration of 'liberated' territory. Carried on a surge that was difficult to control, the officers did not have the ability to challenge the communists' organisation, and the communists were not able to find enough officers whom they could control. Djilas tried and failed to get Stanišić to accept overall military command. When on 18 July he managed to set up the Command of People's Liberation Troops of Montenegro, Boka (Bocche di Cattaro) and Sandžak, it was in fact his own command with the advice of such officers as were willing to accept communist control. By that time, the Italian offensive had broken through. In less than a month, important centres were reoccupied, Italian prisoners freed, and the command of the XIVth Army Corps transferred to Podgorica, but the revolt grumbled on until December.

Pirzio Biroli reported on the situation on 12 August. He judged that it would be dangerous to persist with the idea of setting up an independent Montenegro under Italian protection. The mass of the population was against it. The territory envisaged was too small to be viable. He suggested either an enlarged *governatorato* to take in the now Italian *Provincia di Cattaro*, Metohija, Sandžak and eastern Herzegovina, or a straightforward annexation. In order to win back the confidence of the population, he advocated a more pro-Serb policy.[24] In October, Mussolini decided on direct military rule over Montenegro such as it had already been delimited. Pirzio Biroli was appointed Military Governor; he announced a policy of maintaining peace and order, and of leniency towards the rebels. The old civil administration was retained whenever possible, under Italian military supervision. Most internees were released. New strict directives were issued for the taking of hostages—only if necessary, from localities and families known to be linked to rebels, for no longer than ten days, and in decent conditions of detention. No real attempt was made to disarm the population.

The Italians wanted peace. They realised that the best they could have was control of the towns, the coast and communications. Garrisons were strengthened in fortified towns, but links with the countryside were virtually severed. The remaining rebels were tolerated as long as they desisted from active hostility. Communists in Montenegro had used their pre-war anti-government links with separatists, who organised talks between partisan and Italian military representatives. Nothing came of them, except prisoner exchanges. Increasingly, the lead among Montenegrins was taken by those who realised that it was necessary to adapt to the reality of occupation while waiting to see what turn the war would take. In towns and in the more exposed regions, local committees were formed to negotiate practical compromises. The communist-controlled insurgents who had retired to the hills came out openly as partisans. The 'nationalist'

---

24 '[The peoples of the Balkans] are all more or less untrustworthy, but the least untrustworthy are the Serbs', he wrote to the Supreme Command in Rome. During the First World War, he had served in Salonika and on the Macedonian Front, where he had been in touch with the Serbian army and decorated with a high Serbian military award.

(non-communist) rebels who had also retired to the hills were concerned to protect their patch from Muslim raiders and communist committees.

There were differences within communist ranks. The passage of the SOE mission with its Yugoslav officers through partisan territory on its way to Serbia had rekindled the distrust of the British, as rumours spread of Mihailović's action. Whereas Djilas pleaded for tactical elasticity, in order to win over or neutralise other insurgents, others were intent on executing Italian officers, peasants who deserted, traitors of all sorts, and even fractious party members. The regional KPJ unleashed a reign of terror wherever it could, to wipe out potential competition. As the partisans' 'Užice Republic' in Serbia was about to collapse, Tito asked for help from Montenegro in men, food and loot through Sandžak. He also recalled Djilas, who left in early November, thinking that he might be shot for something that he had done (or not done). The failed attempts to capture isolated northern garrisons to establish a passage to Serbia was a further blow to communist morale. Tito added confusion with his subsequent letter of 21 December (Stalin's birthday) to the communist leadership of Montenegro. He announced that Red Army victories in front of Moscow inaugurated a new stage in the struggle against the invaders, in the sense of sharper class differences, yet also criticised the Montenegrins for committing 'ultra-left and worse errors'.

The differences in outlook between communists and nationalists were particularly pronounced in northern Montenegro, with its traditionally close ties with Serbia and its 'frontier' mentality towards Muslims. It was there that ustasha manipulation of the Sandžak Muslims and the flight of the Orthodox from the area annexed to Albania was mostly felt. Djurišić was popular in his own Vasojević clan. Whereas communists wanted to carry on with the revolution, by turning against 'traitors', 'kulaks' and 'spies' (particularly if they were Muslims), Djurišić and his fighters were impatient to go on with the uprising by marching into those districts and turning on the Muslims and Albanians. As their forefathers had done at the time of the Eastern Crisis of the 1870s, they would kill 'Turks' so that 'Turks' would not kill 'us'. There were differences also among the officers themselves, as some (particularly those who had come from other regions) opposed the trend. One of these, who had known Mihailović since 1928, decided to go and see him. Captain Rudolf Perhinek, a Slovene who had participated in the uprising, felt that resentment in Montenegro against the communists had become greater than against the Italians, but that nationalists were fragmented and isolated. He arrived at Mihailović's headquarters after Major Zaharije Ostojić, a Montenegrin who had come with the SOE mission and reported that 'all Montenegro is red'. Mihailović eventually sent Perhinek back as his delegate, with written authority to organise Yugoslav army units there, and oral approval for Lašić (whom he knew) to command in Montenegro, and Djurišić in Sandžak. Mihailović had also talked in vague and contradictory terms of the need to put off civil strife, to 'remove enemies' and to bring them to justice. However, because of the outbreak of civil war in Serbia and of German operations, Perhinek was not able to return to Montenegro before late December.

Meanwhile, the situation there had deteriorated. Civil strife had indeed started, and Italian repressive measures stepped up again, with the death penalty for armed insurrection and sabotage according to the Wartime Military Code. An impatient Djurišić had set out himself in early December to meet Mihailović. Winter conditions prevented him from getting through an area saturated with German troops. He returned without having seen Mihailović, but after having encountered Perhinek, who transmitted the gist of Mihailović's instructions. He was also told that the rising in Serbia had been put down and that Mihailović was possibly dead. Not satisfied with Perhinek signing on behalf of Mihailović, Djurišić had the latter's signature transferred to a formal order of appointment so as to make it more legitimate. He thereafter claimed to have visited Mihailović at his headquarters, to have been appointed and given instructions by Mihailović personally. He also appears to have forged the lengthy order of 20 December, allegedly signed by Mihailović, directing him to eliminate both communists and Muslims.[25] The situation in Montenegro at the very end of 1941 was then more or less under control, but a control limited to essentials. Where the Italian writ did not run, what remained of the insurgency was getting ready for bloody civil strife. Italian repression, in spite of the fascist rhetoric of official pronouncements, could not be compared to German repression in Serbia. Hard-line fascists such as Governor Bastianini of Dalmatia considered Pirzio Biroli's military government of Montenegro to be too lenient.

In their operations from Albania in April, the Italians had used irregular bands. Giuseppe Bottai, the Italian Minister of Education whom Mussolini had sent on a 'visiting' appointment to Albania as Inspector General of Irregular Forces, described them as a combination of patriots and brigands who vented their 'anti-Serbianism'.[26] Yugoslavia's ethnic Albanians saw Italian troops as liberators; a great demonstration was organised in Tirana to celebrate the liberation of Albanian lands and to call for the creation of a Great Albania, but the government there did not immediately know what territories it could 'redeem'. The Germans wanted to keep the northern tip of present-day Kosovo, to control the Trepča mines and the Belgrade-Skopje railway. They came to an arrangement with local Albanian collaborators to whom they handed over the local administration. This was subsequently formalised with the Nedić government when the area became an autonomous Albanian region within Serbia. Still, the Germans backed anti-Italian Albanian propaganda from their bit of Kosovo, and supported similar Bulgarian moves in Macedonia.

25 The authenticity of the order, of which there is no original, has generally been accepted by most authors, Yugoslavs of all persuasions and others. The reconstruction of Djurišić's moves and the convincing case for the forgeries is made by the Canadian historian Lucien Karchmar, *Draža Mihailović and the Rise of the Chetnik Movement, 1941-1942*, New York, 1987: 396-8 and 427-30. Perhinek's rôle and testimony according to author's correspondence and interviews with him December 1978–July 1980.

26 Giuseppe Bottai, *Diario 1935-1944*, I; Milan, 1994: 261.

In the bulk of Kosovo and Metohija and in the Debar (Dibra) area of western Macedonia destined for Albania, there was a period of transition that lasted until the end of 1941. The Italian diplomat sent as civil commissioner bravely tried to steer through an ordered change, to work out compromises and to dampen the nationalist ardour of Albanians, who were backed by the government in Tirana and by the Italian *luogotenente del Re* (regent) himself—Francesco Jacomoni di Sansovino. Eventually three new provinces were added to Albania and entrusted to a special Ministry for Liberated Territories. The move was a popular one, both in the annexed areas and in 'old Albania'. Non-Albanian public employees were expelled. Serbs were persecuted, looted and murdered. The Albanian population welcomed the opportunity to pay off old scores, particularly against the settlers who had come after 1919 under the terms of the agrarian reform. Emigrés who had gone to Albania returned to recover their property and to organise the persecution of Serbs and other Slavs. Serbs left in tens of thousands—5,000-10,000 to Italian-occupied Montenegro, 23,000 to German-occupied Serbia. Many ended up in camps, to be used as labour on fortification works and in mines. It was several months before Italian and German authorities intervened, to offer some protection to those who had remained, in cities and plains at least.[27] No resistance, chetnik, communist or otherwise, made any headway in the area in 1941: Serbs were terrorised into impotence.

---

27 The estimates of Serbs who had left Kosovo by 1944 vary between 70,000 and 200,000; of Albanian newcomers to Kosovo, between 15,000 and 300,000. The upper limits are incompatible with Yugoslav census figures for what is now Kosovo: 149,000 Orthodox Serbo-Croatian speakers and 331,000 Albanian speakers in 1931; 200,000 Serbs and Montenegrins and 498,000 Albanians in 1948.

There were some 400 established Jews, mostly in Priština, and 100 refugees from outside Yugoslavia. In November 1941 they were joined by 300-400 Jewish refugees from Serbia, who had come with papers provided by the Italian legation in Belgrade and some of whom went on to Dalmatia. In March 1942 those who originated from German-controlled areas were handed over and sent to their death.

Bulgaria had broken off diplomatic relations with Yugoslavia on 15 April, but it was not until after the capitulation that Hitler allowed its troops to enter Yugoslav territory, under strict control, as competing Albanian and Bulgarian claims were being sorted out. By the end of the month, the Bulgarians had been allocated and duly occupied most of Yugoslav Macedonia, a chunk of south-east Serbia with the districts of Pirot and Vranje, and a small part of Kosovo. With two divisions in Macedonia and two in Serbia (55,000 men), they set up the headquarters of their Fifth Army in Skopje. By enabling its territorial aspirations to be generally satisfied, Hitler was later able to get Bulgaria to supply more troops for extended occupation duties in Serbia. Bulgaria did not follow Germany in attacking, or even breaking off with, the Soviet Union. The Bulgarian army would not have fought against the Russians. It could, however, extend its occupation duties in the Balkans, thus earning, and preparing for, formal annexation of the occupied lands.

The Sofia government treated Yugoslav Macedonia (though not the Serbian districts it occupied for the Germans) as a liberated extension of Bulgaria—legislatively, administratively, militarily, educationally, linguistically and ecclesiastically.[28] It was taken for granted that the inhabitants were Bulgars, unless they were obviously Serbs, in which case they were pressed to leave. Inter-war settlers of the agrarian reform were first deported, and then all who had registered as other than Bulgarians were told to depart within two days. In spite

---

28 During the Balkan Wars, in the zone of Serbian occupation of Macedonia, the Serbian Orthodox Church had been quick to take over from the Ecumenical Patriarchate (already mostly serbianised locally) and from the Bulgarian Exarchate. In June 1913, Bulgarian clerics and teachers were all made to sign that they were resigning and departing voluntarily. At the end of 1915, when Serbia had been run over, it was the turn of the Bulgarian occupation authorities to re-bulgarianise through their church by deporting and interning in Bulgaria all Serb ecclesiastics who had not left. At the end of the First World War, when the region became part of Yugoslavia, the Serbian church once again eliminated all traces of a Bulgarian ecclesiastical presence. In 1941, the three dioceses of the region were 'annexed' to the Bulgarian Exarchate, the Serb bishops and all priests considered to be Serbs were expelled and replaced by clergy from Bulgaria.

of resistance by the German authorities in Serbia, 62,000 people had left by the end of 1941, according to Bulgarian official figures. Otherwise, the Bulgarian occupation was broadly welcomed since it brought to an end two decades of imposed serbianisation.

The favourable disposition turned sour after a few months, when people realised they had exchanged serbianisation for bulgariani-sation. As they were increasingly incorporated into Bulgaria's war machine, through conscription and requisitions, dissatisfaction set in. By the autumn, restrictive measures were being taken against Jews, and Jewish refugees from Serbia made to register. The few who did were consigned to the German authorities, but it was not before March 1943 that a general roundup was undertaken, preliminary to the handover and transportation to extermination in Treblinka (Po-land) of 7,250 Jews.

The expulsion and the departure of so many Serbs reduced the potential for resistance. Bulgarian-feeling Macedonians accepted the new régime and so did other Macedonians for the time being. The appointment of Šatorov at the head of the regional commit-tee of the KPJ had been a calculated risk. He defected with his re-gional organisation to the Bulgarian Communist Party which the Comintern in Moscow at first seemed to accept. After the German attack on the USSR, Moscow gave satisfaction to Tito by accepting that pre-war boundaries marked the limits of jurisdiction between communist parties. However, Bulgarian and Yugoslav communists continued to jockey for control of the Macedonian party organisa-tion. Lazar Koliševski, sent by Tito to replace Šatorov, was arrested by the Bulgarian police in November 1941. There were but few com-munist militants in Macedonia, and their sympathies were mostly for a Balkan federation, if not for Bulgaria. For the next two years, the KPJ lost control of the situation in Macedonia.

Whereas the Bulgarian quasi-annexation wanted to treat the in-habitants of Yugoslav Macedonia as liberated compatriots, so long as they accepted it, such an approach was not possible for Hungary's historical nationalism in the territories that it wanted to reclaim. After it had recognised the NDH, Hungarian troops occupied Bačka, Baranja and, further north, the smaller area of the river Mura, which led to a cold war with the NDH. The deportation of all who had come after 1918 started within weeks. Although plans to deport 150,000 to Serbia were opposed by the German command in Belgrade, the Hungarian military managed (by immediate action, and then by internment and gradual discreet expulsions) to get rid of 50,000–60,000 inter-war settlers, mostly to Serbia. Various economic measures were taken against Serbs and Jews, with the subsequent redistribution or sale of property to over 13,000 families—mostly ethnic Magyars from Bukovina and elsewhere. The 'southern territories of the Crown of St Stephen' were fully reincorporated by law in December 1941. A systematic policy of magyarisation was enforced, except on the German minority (189,000), which enjoyed its own status. The peak of terror against Serbs and Jews was reached in January 1942. Yet pre-1918 Serbs and Croats thereafter had citizenship rights, lower-ranking and Hungarian-speaking public employees were retained, landowners and businessmen looked to protect their interests, and one Serb (a former senator) and one Croat (a former parliamentary deputy) sat in the Hungarian parliament. Resistance was almost impossible in open plains.

The situation in Slovenia was different yet again. There had been demonstrations in Ljubljana in favour of the change of government in Belgrade on 27 March 1941, the Slovene People's Party (SLjS) had joined Simović's all-party cabinet, and a new SLjS Ban, Marko Natlačen, had been appointed. However, the party leader Father Fran Kulovec, sensing Hitler's wrath about to descend on Yugoslavia, made a desperate last-hour attempt on 5 April to see whether Slovenia could not be spared. He received no answer, and was one of the victims of the German bombardment of Belgrade the next day. In Ljubljana, representatives of Slovenia's parties immediately set up a National Council under Natlačen. They tried to negotiate some sort of special status, but to no avail as Slovenia was destined to be partitioned between Germany and Italy.

Under the agreement finalised in Berlin on 8 July 1941, Germany took two thirds of the territory (10,260 m^2) and three quarters of the population (800,000) with all important economic assets. Northern Slovenia, already occupied by German troops and formally annexed on 1 November, was to be germanised, or rather made German again as it had allegedly once been, as a march at the southern end of the Reich. Himmler was put in charge of an elaborate programme of ethnic engineering. Plans were drawn up for the deportation of 250,000—the politically undesirable, the 'intelligentsia', those 'inimical to the German state and people', those who had settled after 1914 (essentially Slovene immigrants from the regions that had been assigned to Italy), all the 'ungermanisable' (*nichteindeutschungsfähig*) Slovenes, as well as the inhabitants of a 10-20 km border zone with Italy. They were to be sent to Serbia, to the NDH, and even to Bulgaria's new territories. Their place would be taken by ethnic Germans brought in from Italy and Romania. Those deemed acceptable for 'regermanisation' (*Wiedereindeutschung*) were to be sent to indoctrination camps in the old Reich. Hitler told his officials: 'Make this land German again' (*'Machen Sie mir das Land wieder deutsch'*).

Mass internment of people liable to deportation began immediately, and forced resettlements took place from June to November, although quotas were several times revised downwards. Large-scale movement was hindered by the popular unrest that it caused, and by resistance from the receiving authorities (in particular the German military command in Serbia). There is considerable confusion concerning numbers, since many also fled on their own. Perhaps as many as 80,000 may have left in one way or another—50,000-60,000 of them deported. 35,000-36,000 were taken to the old Reich (16,000 eventually retained for regermanisation). No more than 2,000-3,000 ethnic Germans were imported. Ruthless germanization entailed the closure of all Slovene schools and cultural institutions, the enrolment of the population in German mass organisations, mobilisation in the German army, and the expulsion of the intelligentsia (including ninety per cent of clergy,[29] eighty-four per cent of engineers, 60 per cent of teachers and forty-five per cent of doctors). There were brutal reprisals for even minor offences (306 executions in 1941), with only the most desultory resistance before the middle of 1943. The Italians complained of brutal SS raids across the border.

Hitler had decided that what the Reich did not need could go to Italy. He certainly did not want Ljubljana, which was the centre of Slovenia's political and intellectual life. What he left to the Italians was of no real benefit to them; it attracted no irredentist passion or dynastic sentimentality. They annexed it, probably because the Germans had annexed their part, and as a safeguard against possible further German advances. Their *Provincia di Lubiana* (340,000 inhabitants, 100,000 in Ljubljana, with 20,000 refugees from the German zone) had a special status. The Italians brought in the upper levels of the provincial administration, but otherwise kept on most of the existing employees. The population was exempted from military service. Slovenian and Italian were joint official languages. The province was placed under a High Commissioner, assisted by a Consultative Council meant to represent political trends, education, industry, commerce, banks, agriculture, employers and employees. They included Natlačen and Ivan Pucelj, a liberal who had been a minister throughout King Alexander's reign.

To begin with, the Italian occupation changed little outwardly. Humiliating though it was, it compared favourably not only with the Reich annexation but also with what the ethnic Slovenes in pre-war Italy had to go through. All the cultural institutions were kept, with the Academy and the University of Ljubljana. Normal cultural life continued, except that existing teachers' and students' organisations were replaced with official Italian ones. No measures were taken against the Catholic Church (or any other church) and its organisations. The Catholic Church, Bishop Gregorij Rožman of Ljubljana

---

29 Some thirty Slovene Catholic priests ended up at Jasenovac camp in the NDH, and twenty at Dachau. Bishop Ivan Jožef Tomažič of Lavant (Maribor) was kept under house arrest.

in particular, was seen as an important channel of communication. It generally accepted the Italian régime as the new *de facto* political authority; it kept its regular contact with the Holy See (and through that channel with the wider world, including the Yugoslav governments in exile).

However, Italian rule had its contradictions. The High Commissioner was Emilio Grazioli, a leading fascist of the border region who had been active in italianising the Slovene minority there, and who introduced all the fascist trappings. The Consultative Council was not consulted and soon withered away. The majority trend in Slovene politics had been the SLjS, shaped by Christian personalist thought and Catholic social doctrines, Yugoslav-inclined and generally autonomist. With the aid of the clergy, it had garnered its strength in the countryside. It had usually been in government, to the point of joining Stojadinović's JRZ. The liberal trend was well represented in the upper urban strata, and among university and secondary-school teachers. Once Yugoslav to the point of centralism, it had fragmented over King Alexander's dictatorship. The Marxist trend was also urban, divided between the social-democrats, those who had joined the Socialist Party of Yugoslavia, and the communists in the Slovenian section of the KPJ, who were more petit-bourgeois intellectuals than industrial workers. The contradictions manifested by Italian rule, the failure of an approach that had little substance, the truncated territory of the province, and the comparative mildness of the occupation, all prompted a resistance that was almost impossible on the German side.

The KPJ's Slovenian section went into action differently than in other parts of partitioned Yugoslavia. At the forefront were its refugees from the German and Hungarian zones; it sought to give a moral boost to a people divided up between Germany, Italy and Hungary. It set up a Liberation Front (OF, *Osvobodilna fronta*) with Christian socialists and left-wing liberals; it talked of 'former Yugoslavia' as having fettered Slovenia. As disillusionment with the Italian régime set in, as Natlačen and Pucelj resigned from the Consultative Council, as liberal students organised 'negative demonstrations' in Ljubljana (such as not going out at certain times on King Peter's birthday and other pre-war Yugoslav national holidays), they moved to sabotage, armed attacks, and total domination of the OF. The traditional parties thought that immediate armed resistance was pointless. Instead they began to form cadres for an underground organisation that would emerge against occupation forces when the time seemed ripe. By November, they had established links with Mihailović and with the exiled government, who similarly cautioned against premature action. Officers, delegated by Mihailović, contacted the non-communist partners of OF and the SLjS's 'Slovenian Legion' cadres. OF stigmatised them all as reactionary 'White Guards'.

As early snows set, armed bands of partisans from across the old Italo-Yugoslav border pressed peasants for support and attacked Italians who no longer felt safe outside towns. Grazioli realised that his intended nominal advisers were caught between OF pressure and advice from London. Natlačen called on Bishop Rožman to denounce the OF as a communist organisation with a dangerous policy. By the end of 1941, communists had started liquidating 'traitors' who denounced the partisans and who recruited officers for groups that were outside OF. Those who wanted to temporise were frightened and slithered towards collaboration.

⚘

The events in the Balkans before the German conquest of Yugoslavia and Greece had given the Allies the brief illusion that the conquering might of the Axis could be arrested. The about-turn in Belgrade on 27 March 1941 had contributed much to the illusion. When King Peter and his government arrived in Britain, they were received as heroes, in spite of the rapid collapse of their country's defences. The news of the risings that followed in the summer boosted British public morale. For a while, the eighteen-year old monarch became the symbol of Yugoslavia's struggle to keep its freedom in alliance with Britain. The Soviet government, which earlier on had come close to accepting the fact of the country's partition, was heartened, in the summer, to hear of uprisings that diverted German forces. The exiled ministers in London regarded the news with mixed feelings. It enhanced their standing. At the same time, the Serbs among them were alarmed by the bloodshed, and the Croats by the emphasis on the Serb nature of the resistance. The government had been formed as a broad representation of disparate parties; it had had no time to agree on a programme; it was not a working team, let alone a war cabinet. Croat ministers were reluctant to condemn the ustasha massacres loudly and clearly; their Serb colleagues were reticent to bind themselves publicly again to the 1939 Sporazum. The former's reluctance interlocked with the latter's reticence. For long out of office, now all together in office but in exile and under the shock of events at home, they were already politicians of another age who did not realise that their achievements, ideals and followings were being destroyed by the war.

The news of the developing civil war between insurgents was greeted in dismay in London. The British wanted to believe that Mihailović stood a better chance of re-establishing unity than the communist-led partisans, especially since he had told his government that he was on his way to stopping the fratricidal struggle that the others had started. The risings had generally been Serb, but they were joined only by the fact that Serbs were treated collectively as vanquished foe. An Italian special correspondent in Zagreb had noted: 'All those who, within the old [Yugoslav] borders, consider themselves to be different from Serbs have run to some better protection'.[30] If the risings had been Serb, in some way or another, they had also been local, fragmented and diverse. They were not even really against Hitler's 'New Order', for the Germans in Yugoslavia held on to what they controlled in different ways, with different interests, in what was more like a 'new disorder'.

---

30 *Il popolo d'Italia*, Milan, 3 May 1941.

3
INSURGENTS LEFT TO THEIR
OWN DEVICES—1942

Mihailović's Sabotage Action in Serbia; the 'Ravna Gora Movement'

In London in the dark days of 1941, the Belgrade coup of 27 March had contributed to a passing feeling of optimism. The risings were seen as a sequel—the beginning of a sustained resistance looking to Great Britain. Mihailović was the kind of leader the British had hoped might emerge, and they played him up. In January 1942, Slobodan Jovanović took over a reshuffled Yugoslav government in London from General Simović. The exiled Yugoslavs were themselves keen to be associated with an officer who had expressed loyalty to his government and to the Allies. He was appointed Minister of War *in absentia* and promoted again. In June he was also made army (full) general and appointed chief of staff of the Supreme Command, which was transferred back to Yugoslavia. Jovanović wanted to improve the position of the government by contributing Mihailović's resistance to the Allied cause, while helping him obtain unity among, and loyalty from, the insurgent forces. Mihailović now officially called his followers the Yugoslav Army in the Homeland (JVO—*Jugoslovenska vojska u otadžbini*), to distinguish them from the few Yugoslav forces in the Middle East.

For most of 1942, the war went badly for the Allies. By July the British were pushed back to the borders of Egypt. The United States suffered reverses in the Pacific until midsummer. The Soviet Union was still in dire straits. The possibility of the Western Allies opening a second front on the European continent forced Hitler to keep troops there that could otherwise be sent to the Russian front. Because he did not trust his allies and feared they could make a deal with Germany, Stalin was careful not to antagonise them. The Soviets maintained they had no links with the Communist Party of Yugoslavia (KPJ); they told Tito to camouflage its rôle, and seemed to attribute importance to Mihailović. Nevertheless, Allied interest in the Balkans actually lessened in 1942, and the insurgents were left to their own devices. They survived by mimicry and mobility, as they extended their constituencies and fought each other.

When London built up Mihailović as leader of an all-Yugoslav resistance that did not exist, German-occupied Serbia was actually the only area where he had set up an organisation, and yet he had gone underground again. The uprising had been crushed; civil war between the insurgents had started. Having realised there would be no second front in Europe for at least another year, Mihailović would go back to preparing a future rebellion to be coordinated with the Allies. He would aim to bring together all who could contribute to strengthening the JVO, and avoid further useless loss of life. He remembered the bloodletting of the First World War, and was gripped by fear that Serbs, caught between ustasha massacres, German repression, and mistreatment under Hungarian, Bulgarian and Albanian rule, would be wiped out of existence. The Serbian Orthodox Church had similar fears, as its Bishops' Council appealed for peace in its Christmas pastoral letter, which Ljotić harshly criticised in his newspaper for not condemning the insurgents. Mihailović resolved there would be no new rising until the enemy was weaker and the Allies nearer at hand.[1] He and his staff spent several months hiding around south-west Serbia. Meanwhile Nedić had returned to the idea that Mihailović should leave Serbia, and organise the Serbs outside Serbia. In late March, discussions were held with the collaborationist Home Minister Aćimović which came to nothing.

---

1   So he told a British officer who had escaped German capture, before leaving Serbia in May 1942 (Christie Lawrence, *Irregular Adventure*, London, 1947: 232).

The Serbian government then publicly summoned Mihailović and other officers to surrender within five days, before they arrested and interned their relatives, including Mihailović's wife. As the Germans also increased their action to liquidate Mihailović, he decided to put himself altogether beyond their reach and to follow the example of the partisans. Early in May, he left for Sandžak, and thence for northern Montenegro, followed by his staff, but without any troops. He appointed General Miroslav Trifunović to be commander of Serbia. From northern Montenegro, he pursued the setting up of the JVO and extended his contacts, keeping Serbia as his centre of gravity. He built up a good intelligence network, which allowed him to tell the British of German movements through Serbia. From the summer he also undertook sabotage in the Morava and Ibar valleys. In the autumn this was stepped up at the request of the British to hinder the transport of supplies to the Aegean ports, with the cooperation of Serbian local authorities and railway personnel.

Mihailović's command was in close contact with Montenegro and eastern Bosnia. He had connections with independent chetnik leaders of the Italian zone. In the Independent State of Croatia (NDH), he approached HSS politicians, onetime officer colleagues serving in the Domobrans, and Muslim notables. His links extended right up into Slovenia through officers and politicians. One should not underestimate the potential authority that the King and exiled government could still convey in many quarters. The presence in occupied Yugoslavia of an important member of the government in exile was a strong symbol. Having left Serbia, where he had been forced to adapt his organisation to prevailing conditions as the only way of preserving it, Mihailović found even more complex situations. He did not have sufficient authority to change them, but could not admit it for fear of reducing his authority even further. Yet he hoped that he would in time be able to make changes, with the help of his government and of the Allies. He designated regional commanders, and appointed delegates, but they had little grip over local actors. He tried, at least where he had more control, to set up the framework of future territorial operational units, but it was difficult to maintain an 'army', even a secret one, in a state of war under the vigilant eye of occupation forces. To maintain the cohesion and the fighting spirit of his men without successful major encounters was an illusion. From his base, he issued orders, directives, exhortations and threats, generating again much paperwork, some of which—including pre-signed blanks—found its way to enemy hands. From May 1942, his radio communications were intercepted and decoded, essentially by the Germans. If his organisation infiltrated the security of his native opponents, it was in turn penetrated by agents of all sorts.

'His' commanders, even the regular army officers nearer at hand, generally had a proprietary attitude to their respective districts. They were loath to operate outside their patch, difficult to remove, insubordinate and at loggerheads. Mihailović did not have much choice, for there was a shortage of available officers. Most were in prisoner camps. Many officers, even in Serbia, were fence-sitters; the more senior were unwilling to fight a guerrilla war.[2] The further they were from Mihailović's headquarters, the more local commanders became warlords who paid lip service to the King's representative, but took orders only when it suited them. As for the fighters, they remained essentially traditional guerrillas, local and seasonal, even when officers tried to mould them into an organised force. Mihailović provided a symbolic authority that seemed to hold them all together, but he followed events more than he could initiate them. The mass adherence of Serb chetnik bands to Mihailović made it difficult for him and his nominally Yugoslav army to find an audience among non-Serbs. His non-Serb officers complained that the atmosphere around them was 'too Serb'.

Particularly since he had left Serbia, Mihailović came to see in the communists the main obstacle, with the Ljotićites, to his unification of 'national' forces. From December 1941 and over the winter, the partisans went through a period of crisis. Most were sent or simply

---

2   Only one general served under Mihailović, whereas there were four generals in the collaborationist government, and some thirty sat it out in Belgrade.

returned home; and many went over to the chetniks, as communists also settled accounts among themselves. They were hunted down in areas where they had antagonised the population. With inadequate intelligence and poor morale, 1,000-1,500 fighters from Serbia had gone into Sandžak, to join 500 local partisans. The region was nominally Italian, but the partisans met Muslim militiamen, whom they had underestimated and who were defending their own territory and coreligionists, while Nedić's Serbian State Guard (SDS) and legalised chetniks were in hot pursuit across the demarcation line. Generally speaking throughout Yugoslavia there was no class-conscious proletariat to provide recruits for the KPJ, and there were not many workers among the partisans. By mid 1942, 42,000 workers from Serbia (rising eventually to 100,000) had been recruited for work in the Reich. Most of the others stayed on at their jobs. The poor would join the resistance in periods of high tide, and otherwise gravitate towards collaborationist formations which offered better conditions. KPJ cadres were still weak in military terms, as they did not trust officers willing to fight alongside them. The communists' rhetoric and action against class enemies, bourgeois, kulaks, traitors and anglophiles did not endear them to the middle and upper peasantry whose support was essential to any resistance organisation. The KPJ was criticised even by the Comintern, who feared that its radicalism would limit its appeal and endanger the war coalition with the Western Allies.

Occupied Serbia was relatively quiet for a while after the rebellion had been quashed. German forces were reduced again to three weak occupation divisions. A top-level meeting at the German SE Command on 28 September 1942 concluded that the 'D[raža] M[ihailović] Organisation' (as the Germans called the JVO) was the biggest rebel organisation in Yugoslavia. It had already for some time been rebuilt in Serbia, collecting funds and supplies, and enlisting for future mobilisation. It was careful to avoid overt action that could provoke the Germans. Whereas the administrative staff of the Commanding General favoured concessions to Nedić, to build his government into a force capable of competing with Mihailović for the loyalty of the population, the SS and police apparatus under August Meyszner argued that Nedić was but the public face of the DM organisation.

The JVO devoted particular attention to penetrating the SDS and the legalised chetniks. Mihailović's new status, British propaganda, the gradual turn of the war and the fact that no anti-German action was required for the time, other than protecting known cadres and providing intelligence, made it relatively easy to obtain their secret allegiance. Pressure was also placed on outright collaborators by public condemnations of Nedić, Ljotić and Pećanac, by royal decrees stripping of their rank Nedić's generals and a number of other officers, and the denunciation of traitors 'placed under the letter Z'[3]—all announced over the BBC. Within a short time, the Nedić administration was riddled with Mihailović sympathisers, and many SDS officers considered themselves part of the JVO. They could thus go about the destruction of the remaining partisan units in Serbia with the approval of Nedić, of the German General and of Mihailović. Only Ljotić's Volunteers were as relentless in their action against Mihailović's men as against Tito's—if not more so.

There was a delicate interplay in 1942 between Nedić's and Mihailović's forces in Serbia. Most of the population saw Nedić as the one who kept some order and lessened the effects of the German occupation—particularly in towns. Civil servants and government pensioners, SDS and inactive officers, were dependent on Nedić for their livelihood; many shared his anti-communism, if not the propaganda that blamed Mihailović for most of Serbia's misfortunes. Nedić's personnel and officers were also beginning to think of their future if and when Germany was defeated, and were thus willing to render services to the representative of the Yugoslav government.

---

3 There were about one hundred of these, all servants of the Nedić administration. The meaning of 'Z' (whether it stood for *zaplašiti*—frighten—or *zaklati*—slay) was left deliberately ambiguous. Of the personalities listed, only two were killed—a notorious Ljotićite and a deputy home minister.

SDS units were 'disarmed' by the JVO; ammunition, intelligence and funds leaked away. Mihailović even asked that officers infiltrated into the SDS be publicly condemned by the exiled government, for better protection of their subversive work. Outside towns, the Nedić administration did not impede the work of Mihailović's movement, even though the latter had very few men actually under arms, as opposed to those available for call up. In late spring to early summer that year, parts of Serbia were so calm that everyone seemed to gather at the Vrnjačka Banja watering resort—the writer Ivo Andrić, future Nobel Laureate for Literature, who sent Mihailović a message of sympathy;[4] another writer, the communist Marko Ristić; Mihailović's commander of Serbia, General Trifunović; and various members of the German General's administrative staff.

Himmler had written to Turner on 23 August: 'Anything that can in any way contribute to the strengthening of the Serbian government, and thus of the Serbian people, must be avoided.' The farming out of a good third of Serbia to the Bulgarian occupation corps had been a terrible blow to Nedić, and the Germans planned to entrust more territory to it. By the middle of 1943, only the immediate vicinity of Belgrade, the Bor mines and a 150 km strip along the Danube were under direct German occupation. The Serbian government had no control over the occupation authorities' increasingly harsh economic measures. They were ruthless in squeezing as much food as possible—through compulsory deliveries, imposed penalties for insufficient deliveries, sequestration of hidden stocks, as well as purchases on the market—to the point of endangering the population's minimum needs. Unsatisfied by the way in which the Serbian government handled the collection of the assigned amounts of wheat, they put their own military and police to the task. They imposed huge occupation costs that fluctuated according to their needs, and which

---

4   A writer-diplomat who had been minister to Berlin at the time of the German attack, he had been brought back to Belgrade and told that, as a Croat, he could go to Zagreb. He chose to spend the war years in Belgrade, writing his major novels.

the Serbian government could only meet by increasing taxes, its debt to the National Bank and the banknotes in circulation. On 25 March 1942, the government as a whole addressed a memorandum to the German General, complaining that its authority was so reduced that it appeared to be no more than the tool of the Germans. It suggested that it be given a legislature and a regent, who would be head of state, leader of a national party and commander of the SDS. The memorandum irritated the Germans, who shelved it. In September, Nedić tried again to complain about Bulgarian forces, occupation costs and food requisitions. He actually submitted his resignation, but thought better of it. Ljotić withdrew his ministers from the government, so as not to have to share responsibility for economic measures.

By midsummer the Germans were worried by the revival and the subversive potential of Mihailović's organisation, which they estimated at 100,000 adherents. Most of the officers with the legalised chetniks had gone underground again. German intelligence knew that younger officers were pressing for action, and that Mihailović had specified that generalised action would coincide with the opening of the second front. There were several waves of arrests of army officers still living at large and of SDS officers suspected of links with the DM organisation. Most were sent to prisoner-of-war camps. Many, from officers to postal and railway employees, were executed by the Gestapo for being 'DM agents'. While refraining from armed confrontation with occupation troops, the JVO was helping in the obstruction of requisitions, increasing the collection of intelligence on German rail traffic, and passing to the sabotage of rolling stock. In the autumn, Mihailović was requested by the British Middle East Command to interrupt lines of communication going through Serbia to the Aegean ports. On 8 November, following an appeal by Jovanović to redouble efforts, he announced a campaign of total civil disobedience in Serbia. The Germans knew that his reports to London were exaggerated. Nevertheless, his sabotage action was serious enough to warrant a serious response. The Germans threatened to punish each act of sabotage by the execution of one hundred hostages. They disarmed, interned and dissolved most of the legalised chetniks. They purged the SDS yet again. They reorganised Ljotić's Volunteer Detachments into the Serbian Volunteer Corps (SDK—*Srpski dobrovoljački korpus*), whose members were sworn to fight to the death communists and chetniks, and placed them under the German General. They incorporated the Russian Security Corps into the German army and expanded it by taking in Russian émigrés from outside Serbia.

Motivated by a belief that he was making a valuable contribution to the war effort, Mihailović had taken his task seriously, prepared to accept enemy counter-measures. The requests were presented to him as essential to help the Allies in the Western Desert, but Simon Trew questions whether the Serbian railway system was in fact all that important to supply the German war effort in Africa, particularly in November after the second battle of El Alamein. Did the British believe that the Belgrade-Salonika line was of greater importance than it actually was, that it was too difficult a target for unescorted bombers, and that results could be achieved by Yugoslav guerrillas in return for insignificant material support? Or was it that the JVO's usefulness in Serbia at that stage fitted into Allied deception plans?[5] At any rate, Mihailović's action in September-December 1942 damaged the Serbian railway system seriously enough for Allied leaders to pay tribute to him for contributing to their African success, and for the Germans to interpret it as a preparation for future action. They returned to mass terror. SS General Meyszner took over the Serbian special police. The new Seventh SS Volunteer Mountain Division 'Prinz Eugen', made up of ethnic Germans, and trained for anti-guerrilla warfare, went out on punitive expeditions. It was commanded by General Arthur Phleps, an ethnic German from Transylvania who had successively been an Austro-Hungarian and a Romanian army officer before joining the Waffen SS in 1940. Thousands of hostages and sympathisers of 'saboteurs', 'DM supporters' and 'communists'—all of whom were denounced, mostly by the Vol-

---

5 Trew, *Britain, Mihailović and the Chetniks*, 148-59.

unteers—filled concentration camps. The Gestapo smashed through a series of DM centres in Belgrade. The Nedić government ordered the arrest of all who obeyed Mihailović's disobedience order. It is estimated that during December 1,600 JVO combatants were killed in clashes with occupation and collaborationist troops, or executed. At the end of the year, Patriarch Gavrilo and Bishop Nikolaj, whom the Germans suspected of having been in touch with Mihailović, were moved away from the Belgrade area to a monastery in Banat until September 1944, when they were taken to Dachau. All these measures brought to an abrupt conclusion much of the anti-German action that Mihailović had started up again since the summer.

The Serbian countryside in 1942 was crisscrossed by armed formations. There were German and Bulgarian occupation troops, collaborationist SDS and Volunteers, and chetniks—Mihailović's, legalised varieties, and 'wild' chetniks whom it was difficult to categorise. They changed colours according to time, location and whom they met. It was often difficult to distinguish patriotically or politically motivated action from banditry. The rural population was fearful of reprisals and not particularly keen on resistance, except when it protected them from attacks on their livelihood. Villages were left to their own devices, with many of their menfolk in captivity or 'in the forest'. They had to put up with requisitions by the authorities, and with requests by guerrillas for food, cash, help and manpower. The state administration at that level had mostly disappeared or was under the control of some 'free administration'—generally that of the JVO and of its military commanders. Peasants inclined to Mihailović, but they were anxious not to provoke the Germans. Small partisan bands just about survived in southern Serbia. Pro-communist and pro-German extremes concentrated in towns, particularly in Belgrade, where the majority was by then mildly in sympathy with Mihailović. City dwellers resented the fact that peasants had got rid of their debts through inflation, and that they had more food. Inflationary pressure, however strong, was less than in Croatia, because of ever stricter policies adopted by the German Plenipotentiary for

Economic Affairs. However, German requirements, refugees and a markedly reduced production affected food supplies, the struggle for which among claimants became more determined. Lack of food and the black market characterised urban life. The collaborationist régime chastised the indifference of the capital's 'affluent high society', while real war profiteers were often protected by the German authorities.

It was not before the summer that intensive bulgarianisation, conscription, rationing, and the influx of civil servants and teachers from Bulgaria resulted in sufficient resentment in Macedonia for any groups to try and make use of it. The old anti-Yugoslav Macedonian activists who had returned from exile were the first to feel frustrated, and found allies among the divided communists. In the absence of inter-communal violence and of widespread suffering, the only way for the KPJ to make a comeback was to adopt anti-Serb 'Macedonianism', but Tito selected a loyal Serb communist to do it. Svetozar Vukmanović Tempo was the new emissary sent to Skopje in September. Tempo, who did not arrive until the end of February 1943, was told to clarify the KPJ's approach to Macedonia, and to try and set up an autonomous communist organisation, on the lines of what had been done in Croatia and Slovenia, which could also have ties with Sofia. For the JVO, all the Bulgarian-occupied area was part of Major Radoslav Djurić's command from April 1942. He worked closely with the SDS and with legalised chetniks to counter Bulgarian and communist action, so as to have as many men who could readily move around, but he was hampered by both local legalised chetniks and by the Bulgarian police who made a series of crippling arrests before the end of the year.

We know that Mihailović was in favour of the legal continuity of the Kingdom of Yugoslavia. As a loyal officer for whom the war had not come to an end, he would not let himself be enlisted for any reform, but he does not appear to have understood that he could not create an underground army on the basis of regular call-up, and motivate guerrilla fighters for a simple return to the 'constitutional' status quo of 6 April 1941. The intellectuals of the Serb Cultural

Club (SKK) who had joined him in 1941 continued to discuss the setting up of a political advisory committee to elaborate post-war reforms, and by the end of 1942 they were again with Mihailović in Montenegro. Moljević and Vasić competed for the position of *éminence grise*. Between them they fathered the idea of a 'Ravna Gora movement' to come out of the resistance, which would reorganise Yugoslavia into a state with social justice and without political differences, and one where Serbs would never again be trapped under non-Serb rule. Moljević mulled over the old SKK idea of a territorial unit within Yugoslavia called 'the Serb lands', but one that he saw through the prism of the NDH experience, that would extend to all the territory inhabited by Serbs and be purged of all who were guilty of treason and massacre. He made his way to Montenegro to try and convince Mihailović to become a political leader, to call a halt to the 'London farce' that was the Yugoslav government in the British capital, to take decisions rather than instructions, and tell the exiled politicians there what they should do.

There were more discussions, at JVO headquarters in Serbia, about the constitution and the territorial claims of the new post-war federal Yugoslavia; the structure of Serbia within it; the punishment of traitors and the removal of disloyal minorities; the nationalisation of important economic institutions, wealth redistribution, and even giving the vote to women. There was talk of an interregnum after the liberation during which a provisional government stemming from the resistance would carry through essential changes and hold elections. Much of it was unrealistic and contradictory. Vasić edited a newspaper for a time, and a small group of similarly-minded intellectuals busied themselves with more transitory publications, but their content hardly amounted to a coherent programme. They expressed their faith in the Serbian fatherland within a new Yugoslavia that extended into Austria and Italy; they made patriotic calls to resistance and generally agreed that there would be no return to the *status quo ante*. They attacked ustashas, communists and Ljotićites. General Trifunović, whose views were sympathetic to the Democratic Party, did not like the tendency to denigrate political parties. However, many officers, faithful to the pre-war rule that they should ignore politics, continued to be suspicious of them in general, those expressed by 'chetnik ideologues' as well as those expressed by communists. Mihailović continued to issue instructions to that effect. He had no political stature; he had reservations towards politicians; he wanted to avoid political discussions in time of war; he had no political alternative to offer. In his instructions, he laid stress on the fact that all under his command were the regular army of Yugoslavia, which was at war, and he repeated his conviction that Germany would be defeated. His personal ethos appears in some non-military directives, such as the one on how to educate the young in a 'feeling of honour, dignity, honesty, humility, social justice, Yugoslav brotherhood, and Slav solidarity', with a sense of civic duty towards King and fatherland. For girls, the stress was on family and home.[6] Around him, in the JVO Supreme Command, two conflicting tendencies began to take shape in the course of 1942—one for a 'movement' coming out of the resistance, and the other for an advisory body of political parties. Mihailović himself, as far as can be judged from the extremely limited evidence available, gradually began to move towards the latter.

All that while, the fountainhead of his legitimacy, the exiled government itself, was based on weak legitimacy. The Simović cabinet had been brought together as a representation of parties to compensate for the absence of an elected parliament, but it had little other unity of purpose. It carried with it into exile the burden of military defeat added to that of unresolved ethnic and constitutional issues, hideously magnified by recent events. The exiled party leaders, who believed that they would, with an Allied victory, return to their pre-war positions, were reduced most of the time to saving these positions, while mutual distrust made them act as if they could survive

---

6 From the Headquarters of the Yugoslav Army, 6 September 1942 [Peter II's birthday], in Milan Vesović, Kosta Nikolić and Bojan B. Dimitrijević, ed., *Rat i mir Djenerala*, Belgrade, 1998, I: 131.

only at the price of deliberately avoiding real issues. The whole of 1942 turned out to be one long cabinet crisis. By the end of the year, the divided and confused Yugoslav government in exile was losing the sympathy of its British hosts. On taking over, Jovanović had understood that the link with Mihailović could be a useful one, but the government failed to provide guidance for those at home who were still expecting it. Collectively, it did not know enough about what was happening in Yugoslavia, as each group of ministers listened only to what it could interpret optimistically from its own intelligence. Not before the summer of 1942 was direct but tenuous communication, which did not go through British transmission, established with Mihailović.

Even the British had limited intelligence, interpreted variously according to strategic needs, and varying conceptions of how resistance in occupied countries should be managed. Having initially viewed revolt in Yugoslavia as premature, they warmed to it as a useful diversion of Axis troops from the Eastern front. Inability to influence it by providing any real material help made radio propaganda all the more important. The Mihailović myth thus produced was worse than useless to his movement. In the course of 1942, the various individuals and bodies responsible for British policy came to the view—not without contradictions and divisions—that the original rapport to Mihailović had to be changed. By the end of the year, the Yugoslav government in exile had received conflicting signals of these discussions, but it was told that there was no change in policy.

The 'Italian-Chetnik Condominium' of Montenegro

The winter of 1941/42 had been a hard one in Montenegro. The rising had been suppressed, but fighting had flared up between the insurgents. Many rebels had come from neighbouring regions. There were even more refugees, causing an estimated sixty per cent rise in the population and who were a source of manpower for all armed bands. The KPJ turned against all opponents real or potential before they could be formed into a rival movement on the model of Mihailović's in Serbia. Action against the occupying forces was stopped in order to concentrate on removing all adherents of the former state before the victory of the Red Army over fascism. Tito, the communist leadership and the main partisan force from Serbia tried to set up winter quarters in Sandžak so as to link up with the partisans in Montenegro. The area had generally been given up to bitter winter cold and roving native bands that fought over small towns. The partisans' disastrous attempt to capture Plevlja from its Italian garrison on 1 December 1941 was followed by widespread desertion, terror, plunder of villages, the execution of captured Italian officers, of party 'fractionalists' and even of 'perverts'. Tito went through a spell of depression; he had a lucky escape on 12/13 December when the Italians almost captured him. On 21 December—Stalin's birthday—he formed the First Proletarian Brigade out of the 1,200 best partisans that had come out of Serbia and Montenegro, as the armed force of the KPJ, with hammer-and-sickle banner. The Comintern did not think that the name was helpful. During their 47-day control of Kolašin in January-February 1942, the partisans killed some 300 of the town's 6,000 inhabitants, throwing the mutilated bodies into mass graves which they called the 'dogs' cemetery'. The popular mood in Montenegro turned completely against them. Their Supreme Staff moved on to east Bosnia, as their hold over the 'free territory' in northern Montenegro disintegrated.

Their last fling may have been at a meeting on 8 February where they appear to have declared the liberated territory of Montenegro an integral part of the Soviet Union.[7] Three days later, Colonel Stanišić proclaimed a revolt against them on the territory of his Bjelopavlići clan north of the Podgorica-Nikšić road, and fighters flocked to his banner. The Italian 'Taro' Division seized the opportunity to go out and relieve Nikšić. In danger of being caught between them

---

7   Stephen Clissold (*Whirlwind. An Account of Marshal Tito's Rise to Power*, London, 1949: 84) and German military intelligence (*Kriegstagebuch des Oberkommnandos der Wehrmacht, 1940-1945*, II, 1, Frankfurt am Main, 1965: 138) note the declaration, but there is no trace of it in partisan sources.

and the partisans, Stanišić concluded a non-aggression agreement with the divisional command. Captain Djurišić's chetniks then took back Kolašin, which would remain their stronghold until May 1943. Having turned the tables on the communists, Stanišić and Djurišić between them had by the end of May driven the communists out of the greater part of Montenegro. The Italians had been benevolent neutrals, or even providers of ammunition and other supplies. The partisans still held on to the north-western fringes that connected them to eastern Bosnia. They also retained a precarious footing in the mixed Orthodox-Muslim eastern border. In Sandžak, the Italians had let local chetniks and legalised chetniks from Serbia do most of the work.[8] When Djilas returned to Montenegro in March 1942, he found an alienated land which he no longer recognised. 'Death was nothing unusual. Life had lost all meaning apart from survival'.[9] Communist terror and popular reaction to it played into the hands of the Italians. Montenegro was garrisoned by the XIVth Army Corps under General Luigi Mentasti at Podgorica, while the Military Governor, General Alessandro Pirzio Biroli, resided in the old capital, Cetinje. Entrusted with full civil and military powers, he faced a new situation, linked to events in Serbia, the civil war between insurgents, and the bitterness of separatists who felt that Italy had let them down. The Italians had been caught unprepared. Essentially concerned with the maintenance of order in what had reverted to being enemy territory under Italian military authority for the duration, Pirzio Biroli wanted peace. An old-fashioned officer and gentleman who was liked by his troops, and who had also been a colonial governor, he had tried both amnesty and reprisals; he had even been ready to discuss with the communists.

In February and March, a series of events paved the way to indirect rule, as the anti-communist reaction led people almost to forget they were under foreign occupation. A group of civilian notables in

---

8   Nedić had tried to suggest to the Italian military attaché in Belgrade a joint Serbian-Italian occupation of Sandžak.

9   Djilas, *Wartime*, 147-8.

Podgorica formed a committee, ostensibly for charitable purposes, that opened talks with the Army Corps Command, while officers organised volunteers for Stanišić's force. It was through these that Stanišić was approached for a more extensive agreement. The Italians would supply him with arms, ammunition, clothing and food while he pursued his struggle with the communists. In return, he would not fight the Italians for the duration of the war. A similar agreement appears to have been reached with Djurišić.[10] Reserve and active officers meeting at Podgorica elected General Blažo Djukanović commander of all 'nationalist' forces in Montenegro. A popular figure appointed Ban on 27 March 1941, he was living in Cetinje under house arrest. Stanišić and Djurišić having formally acknowledged him, Djukanović became the official spokesman for the nationalists in Montenegro. It had been Pirzio Biroli's idea to have the anti-communists deal with the communists. He had at first wanted to unite them for the purpose under Krsto Popović, a onetime brigadier in the Montenegrin army before 1918 who had gone to Italy with supporters of the deposed King Nicholas, and returned to Yugoslavia in the 1930s. Popović was the most reliable from the Italian point of view. He had organised a militia of italophile 'Greens', but it was not possible to link him to the other commanders, who had fought as insurgents with the communists, and some of whom were already connected to Mihailović.

Stanišić had been the most popular and the most authoritative of the commanders in the rising. He controlled the heart of Montenegro, right up to Herzegovina and across the border, and stood for total union with Serbia. He was considered soft towards the communists, so that his revolt against them had been a turning point. Djurišić in the north and across into Sandžak, had turned Kolašin into a chetnik fortress after warding off a partisan attempt to capture

---

10 These agreements, from captured chetnik sources in the Yugoslav archives, do not survive in Italian military records. Italian copies may have disappeared after the collapse of September 1943. It may also be that they were not considered formal enough to be filed back in Rome.

it again. He claimed to be acting in the name of Mihailović, even though their relations were problematic. Pirzio Biroli now went to General Djukanović, in the hope that he could deliver a more formal top-level arrangement that tied the rival local commanders to the maintenance of public order and the prevention of action against the Italian authorities. Between them they negotiated the agreement of 24 July 1942. Djukanović was recognised as overall commander of all native armed formations, whose operations needed Italian approval. He would be assisted by an advisory National Committee of delegates from the districts. Three area commanders were designated—Djurišić, Stanišić, and Popović—with responsibilities corresponding to Italian divisional arrangements, each with a mobile 'legalised' force of 1,500 men. The Italians would provide them with heavy weapons, ammunition, food and a fifteen-lira daily allowance; Djukanović would be responsible for their enlistment and control. The nationalists had to accept that Popović be given formal responsibility over the Cetinje and Bar districts. In counterpart, they obtained an assurance of basic food supplies, the accelerated liberation of internees, and the immediate withdrawal of the Albanian bands that had participated in counter-insurgency. The officers who had acknowledged Djukanović accepted a compromise that left them in control of their territories, on condition they left the Italians alone in the towns. Djukanović was elected chairman of the National Committee, effectively selected by the commanders, and whose functions remained ambiguous. An official communiqué announced that the Governor had responded to the nationalists' offer to collaborate in the restoration of order. On returning from a 1,000 km tour of Montenegro by car, Pirzio Biroli wrote to his brother on 8 August: 'Ho fatto un bel giro [I've been on a good trip...] Montenegro has become the most pacified region in the whole of Balcania'.[11]

The Italians controlled the coast, the larger towns, and the roads linking Cetinje, Podgorica and the coast. Popović's Greens controlled the poorer and less mountainous southern districts where they

11 *Balcania* was the term used officially by the Italians for Yugoslavia.

were concentrated. His area was out of bounds for the other commanders, who accused him of offering refuge and protection to the communists. Certain links remained between the two 'pariah' parties of pre-war Montenegro, Popović's sons were themselves with the partisans, and communists found it easier to survive in his territory or in Italian-controlled towns. Had it not been for Italian protection, the Greens would have been wiped out by the centralist nationalists. The division of Montenegro between federalists and pro-Serbian centralists helped Pirzio Biroli's indirect rule. Stanišić, who controlled the central districts, turned out to be closest to Djukanović, who left him free in military matters. He set up his headquarters in the monastery at Ostrog. Djurišić lorded over the northern districts. For most of the time, he was quite independent and a law unto himself. Clissold has described the whole set-up as an 'Italian-Chetnik condominium';[12] more accurately, it was a power-sharing arrangement between the Italian military, Montenegrin Greens, and two sets of unionist chetniks. Djukanović was in Cetinje with no force under his direct control, and with a National Committee that does not appear to have had any political significance. The Italians brought food to Montenegro, and generally remained in their garrisons. Their payments to the legalised units were irregular and in arrears. They did not seem to mind that the commanders also maintained varying numbers of territorials. The Italians themselves maintained the gendarmerie and armed smaller irregular bands, all of which were infiltrated by chetniks, and through which more ammunition reached the commanders. Popović's and Stanišić's formations participated in mopping up operations alongside Italian forces in their areas.

The émigré chetnik writer Mihailo Minić describes Kolašin as 'the capital city of the chetniks for the whole of Yugoslavia'.[13] Once a Turkish and Muslim settlement, it had been taken over by Christian Montenegrins in successive phases between the 1850s and the 1920s, by killing, pillaging and buying up land on the cheap. It was the capi-

12 Clissold, *Whirlwind*, 83.
13 Mihailo P. Minić, *Rasute kosti, 1941-1945*, Detroit, 1965: 139.

tal of Djurišić's territory, and it was in that territory that Mihailović arrived with his staff and British liaison officer, at the time of the terminal battles between chetniks and partisans, when local chetnik commanders had already made their peace with Italian forces. He changed his location a couple of times before settling down near Kolašin, in the village of Gornje Lipovo, which became the nominal headquarters of Mihailović's JVO from which he continued to re-mote-control the movement in Serbia. By mid-July, Italian military intelligence had located his presence, with radio transmitter and British mission in attendance, but they had also understood that it would not affect whatever they wanted to do at the time. Mihailović discovered something of the complexity of the situation when he arrived in Montenegro. Local chetnik commanders considered their arrangements with the Italians as an expedient. The majority of the population was conscious of a tradition that had led to union with Serbia in Yugoslavia. At his trial, Mihailović claimed that he had not known what had happened in Montenegro before he actually arrived there in June, and that he had to accept the situation as he found it. Djurišić and Stanišić had made it clear to him they would acknowl-edge him as a moral leader, even formally as commander, but that in practice he would be obeyed only in so far as his orders coincided with their interest. He had no troops; they had theirs. He had to be satisfied with their acknowledgement, and let them conduct their own policies, if he hoped to retain, and eventually increase, his in-fluence over them. He complained that Italian military intelligence knew much better what they were up to than he could ever know. He could only try and exploit the differences between them. He accepted Djukanović, but delegated officers to act as chief of staff to his com-mand in order to check him. The first of them was Lašić, who did not get along well with Djukanović. The Italians tried to keep up with those links, and feared losing control over them.

Not being able to change the situation, Mihailović wanted to make the best of it. He certainly approved of the destruction of com-munist forces, but was more ambivalent (at least initially) about the

Italian connection. He had brought with him to Montenegro his status as representative of royal Yugoslavia and of its British allies, which he believed would give him some clout to deal with the rival chetnik commanders. Realising its limits, he would only use it to try and get them to prepare to take over from Italian forces at the time of the Allied landing. Meantime he would exploit their links to receive arms, supplies and food. In September, he set about reminding all who were under his command that they were no 'national army' but the regular Yugoslav army. He asked them to make good use of, rather than be used by, the Italians, and to avoid personal contact with their commanders. Regular officers who had come with him and who were not from Montenegro found it difficult to adjust to an atmosphere where family and clan were all-important, with barely a nod to a notional Yugoslavia and its JVO. There was great dislike between officers on Mihailović's staff and the Montenegrins. The relationship with Djurišić was particularly odd. Mihailović pretended not to know of Djurišić's forgeries, and Djurišić pretended not to know that Mihailović knew. Mihailović lived a few miles away from his nominal subordinate and under his protection, with the Italians pretending not to know that he was there. He needed Djurišić's loyalty, and helped him in return by providing him with legitimacy, and with Yugoslav government and British cash. Their superficial show of mutual loyalty has left a legend of presumed close relations, whereas Djurišić was loyal to himself only.[14] He was a dominant personality, who inspired popular loyalty, who managed to instil some military discipline into guerrilla tactics, and whom the communists respected as an opponent.

Mihailović had also come to a totally different political milieu, whose primary preoccupation was not so much the world war as the local struggle against communists. Anticommunism in Montenegro was as extreme as its communist counterpart. Northern Montenegro

---

14 In the summer of 1942 he told Hudson that he was available to act independently and in defiance of Mihailović (F.W.D. Deakin, *The Embattled Mountain*, London, 1971: 151-2).

was not only virulently Serb, but its contacts with Serb forces set up in Herzegovina and Dalmatia had led some people to want to cut loose from the Croats even at the price of sinking Yugoslavia. Anti-Muslim prejudices ran deep. In such an atmosphere there emerged among local chetniks the idea to hold a conference of young chetnik 'intellectuals' to discuss the reorganisation of the Yugoslav state and society after the war, and appropriately to commemorate 1 December—Yugoslavia's Unification Day. A 'youth conference of chetnik units of the Yugoslav Army on the territory of Montenegro, Boka [Boka Kotorska or Bocche di Cattaro, the province annexed to Italy] and Sandžak' met at the village of Šahovići near Bijelo Polje, well attended by teachers, journalists, lawyers and other small-town 'intellectuals', mainly from Djurišić's and Stanišić's units. Representatives from Djukanović's and from Mihailović's staff were in attendance, but the show was entirely dominated by Djurišić. The debates and resolutions expressed extremism and intolerance. The resolutions posited the restoration of a monarchical Yugoslavia, to begin with a temporary chetnik dictatorship after the war. Claims were put forward to Albanian, Bulgarian, Romanian, Hungarian, Austrian and Italian territory. Serbs, Croats and Slovenes would live within their respective territories, without minorities. The state would take over industry, larger trading institutions, banking, publishing, education and health. Many such ideas, which had featured in East-European authoritarian regimes from the Baltic to the Aegean, were being discussed, though not in so extreme a version, in SKK circles under the influence of Moljević, who, with Vasić, had come to join Mihailović again in late 1942. The Šahovići resolutions have since gone down as some sort of a chetnik credo. However, Mihailović had had no hand in the congress, even though he had done nothing to counter it.

By the end of 1942, the situation in Montenegro within its Italian borders appeared stable. The Italians had given up any idea of a satellite state. The military had opted for indirect rule. Prince Michael was back in France (after his aunt, the Queen of Italy, had intervened in his favour), soon to be involved with the French resistance, through whose channels he had written to his cousin King Peter II to assure him of his unfailing loyalty to Yugoslavia. Mihailović was ensconced in the village of Gornje Lipovo, nominally in command of all Montenegrin commanders except the Green Popović. The stability was deceptive. Even with no real operations, the Italian army during 1942 counted 1,426 dead, injured and missing. The chetnik commanders barely accepted and rarely obeyed Mihailović. Lucien Karchmar has noted that what united the Montenegrin chetnik commanders was their short-term community of interests with the Italian military, which lulled them into complacency.[15] The Italians continued to pay salaries to civil servants, allowances to 'prisoners of war on conditional leave', and to distribute wheat, flour and salt, yet Montenegro continued to suffer hunger.

Border regions also suffered from the continued settlement of old scores between Orthodox and Muslims. The latter had been organised and then abandoned by the Italians. Sandžak in 1942 was even more of a no-man's-land. Both Mihailović and Tito needed a corridor through it to link Serbia, Montenegro, Herzegovina and Bosnia. It was the turn of the Serb-speaking Muslims there to be left to the mercies of armed Serbs. In Metohija, the Italians tempered the excesses of albanianisation which threatened to destroy the fragile peace of Montenegro. The Governatorato of Montenegro, backed by the Foreign Ministry in Rome, attempted a compromise formula for the regions with mixed population, but came up against the intransigence of the Albanian government, backed by the Italian Luogotenente in Tirana, who had accepted a more nationalist government in order to broaden support for the régime. Yet there was almost no sign of Serb rebellion in Kosovo in 1942. A Kosovo chetnik corps had been set up composed essentially of Serb refugees gathered on the border with Montenegro. They attempted occasional forays, to be hounded mercilessly by a Tirana-backed local Albanian militia, or assassinated by what little communist organisation there

---

15 Karchmar, *Draža Mihailović*, I, 416.

was. Rivalry between the Cetinje Italians and the Tirana Italians was almost as bad as between chetniks and communists.

Tito's 'March' Across Bosnia; Battle without Mercy

The move of Tito's Supreme Staff and of his main force from Užice to Foča, in the highlands of south-east Bosnia, occurred in the middle of confused events. Defeated in Serbia, the partisans knew of successful risings elsewhere, and wanted to link up Montenegro and Herzegovina. Their leadership needed winter quarters to reorganise, but in eastern Bosnia they discovered that there were hardly any communists among the insurgents. The commanders were responding to Mihailović's influence; most combatants were fighting for 'King and country'. Tension between the three inward-looking communities was another obstacle to communist influence. After the crimes committed by ustashas against the majority Serb Orthodox population, too often with the help of Muslims recruited to beef their numbers, Serbian bands had gained the upper hand, and were eager for help and leadership to defend their villages and avenge their dead. The local Serb peasantry welcomed the partisans, but in order to involve them in action against Muslims and Croats, while the KPJ was looking for industrial workers and urban youths and trying to earn the confidence of non-Serbs as well. Tito had already turned his best combatants into a 'Proletarian Brigade' to avoid their contamination by local recruits. The latter were formed into 'volunteer detachments', but no amount of indoctrination by political commissars could as yet make them reliable anti-chetnik fighters. The situation was even worse in Herzegovina, where the communists were totally unable to counter anti-Muslim prejudices. KPJ activists shared them; partisans settled accounts in Muslim villages with a clear 'class' conscience; and Italian military commands could not as yet clearly differentiate between chetniks and partisans.

Tito managed to gather sufficient forces to acquire control over a strip of territory in the region of the upper Drina. It was not far from Montenegro, where he still hoped to redress the situation. Foča, where he settled at the end of January, had changed hands several times; its population was reduced to a handful of old people, women and children, but the town had not been destroyed. (It would change hands ten times in the course of the war.) The ustashas had arrived from the outside, picked up what recruits they could, including many Muslims, and methodically slaughtered Serbs, working their way down from the top of the social pyramid. Serb bands had then come, the ustashas had left, and the 'Turks' had been targeted. The region was pillaged and burned. Foča was turned into a slaughterhouse. The chetniks killed indiscriminately. In so far as they had any aim other than revenge, it was to frighten Croats and Muslims into leaving the area. Reluctant to fight other Serbs, they did not put up much of a fight against Tito's men. In Foča the communist leaders mulled over the crisis the movement was going through. They thought about the future, and decided that the near future lay in eliminating the 'fifth column' through class terror. The victims were chetnik commanders, organisers and sympathisers, richer peasants, gendarmes, lukewarm communists, Muslims and Croats whose villages continued to be pillaged, people who no longer wanted to fight or who thought differently.

The communists' rivals had concentrated in Herzegovina. With the help of Montenegrin partisans, attacks were launched on their strongholds to prevent the development of a southern zone of nationalists linking Herzegovina and Montenegro, and to acquire much needed supplies. Mihailović's influence had been on the rise with the arrival of Major Boško Todorović from eastern Bosnia. Todorović had gone some way towards getting the disunited chetnik groups, many of whom had already made accommodations with Italian units, to concentrate on fighting the ustashas, to let the Italians deal with the communists, and to be chary of links with the occupation power. The communists managed to kill him. They failed in their attempt to kill Grdjić in Mostar after he had made contact with Mihailović. They went on to kill more than five hundred leading chetniks—as estimated by the KPJ Regional Committee for Bosnia-Herzegovina on 28 April 1942. As a result, the struggle against the occupiers had taken second place in Herzegovina, the peasants had been alienated, and the surviving nationalists driven into the arms of the occupying forces. The arrangements entered into by Italian corps commanders involved no longer-term political plans. They were based on common opposition to communist bands. Their aim was to keep the armed chetniks under control, install trusted local authorities, and generally counter ustasha intrigues. The generals also thought that local chetnik commanders might influence Mihailović not to heed any advice from London to initiate action against Italians as well as against Germans.

Once in Foča, Tito was able to resume direct radio contact with the Comintern. He admitted that his situation was critical and begged for aid. At the same time, he claimed a force of 200,000 combatants, which he could raise to 500,000 if a second front (preferably Soviet) were started in the Balkans. He also amply provided Moscow with details of his rivals' misdeeds and of British intrigues. The Soviets helped by forwarding intelligence about German moves, and by no longer mentioning Mihailović in their media. They told Tito that his movement had set a heroic example, but that technical difficulties prevented them from sending aid. (That was also what the British told Mihailović.) They had to break it to him that the Red Army was not about to arrive in the Balkans. Precisely because they too were obsessively distrustful of the British, they were anxious to avoid anything which could endanger the Allied coalition. While they encouraged Tito to continue striking at the Anglo-Saxons' 'hangers-on and agents as lackeys of the occupiers and enemies of the people', and providing hard facts against Mihailović, they also advised him to disguise the obvious communist character of his movement.

Tito was at times driven to despair by the Comintern's instructions, but he accepted that the interests of the USSR, as guarantor of the Yugoslav revolution, were paramount. Stalin's priorities in time of war anyhow allowed Tito some freedom in domestic affairs. The KPJ leaders took stock of Moscow's advice and of the situation they faced. A new broader line was devised to enlist, control and lead all patriotic forces within the Peoples' Liberation Movement (NOP, *Narodnooslobodilački pokret*) and Peoples' Liberation Struggle (NOB, *Narodnooslobodilačka borba)* against the occupiers and their auxiliaries, and to condemn all who refused to rally. The narrow line of class struggle and communist hegemony remained within the broader patriotic line. Moša Pijade, the veteran Belgrade communist journalist, translator of Marx and chief KPJ organiser in Montenegro in 1941, wrote out the rules for the new order of people's committees in liberated areas, while Tito formed a Second Proletarian Brigade, as well as a 'shock battalion' to liquidate those who refused to rally.

The partisans had moved into a region where the chetniks were already strengthening their position. The Germans were worried. After the suppression of the rising in Serbia, they viewed eastern Bosnia as a new focus of resistance that affected the safety of the mines. The idea was mooted in the German Supreme Command of asking Italy to occupy the whole of the NDH. Glaise von Horstenau, who did not like the idea, leaked it to Zagreb as an 'Italian plan'; Hitler vetoed it. SE Command then ordered General Bader to carry out an operation with German troops from Serbia and from Sarajevo, with the help of NDH troops, to get rid of the accumulation of guerrillas in eastern Bosnia. The insurgents had got wind of it and generally avoided contact. The Germans concentrated on towns and communications, with little desire to comb mountains in violent winter weather. Major Dangić proposed an informal non-aggression agreement. Sympathetic Abwehr officials in Belgrade favoured a deal with the chetniks of the region while they cleared the partisans, but all that they could obtain was a directive from Bader to treat as prisoners of war chetniks captured without resistance. The partisans agreed locally with ustashas not to fight each other in instances when they both concentrated against chetniks. Through a series of evasive measures, melting away, crossing the line and re-forming, they were able to complete their regrouping in the Foča area. Chetnik leaders believed the ustashas had actually helped the partisans take the town.

117

North and west of the partisan area was another no man's land on the Serbian border. Mihailović's officers had come to organise the local chetniks, to steer them away from revenge against Muslims, to help the passage of refugees and prevent the return of communists into Serbia. Local chetniks did not really want them, particularly when they realised that they brought no material support. As Bader also came round to the idea of using chetniks across the Serbian border to keep ustashas and communists at bay, Dangić turned up in Belgrade at the end of January for discussions with him and Nedić. They wrangled over NDH authority, until SE Command brought the initiative to an end. Such incidents made it plain that the German military on the spot were not free, like the Italians, to exploit the schism between the insurgents. The action in north-east Bosnia in January was limited and ephemeral. The insurgents had survived, in one way or another, but the population was disgusted with both sets. They had fought and plundered each other, not to mention non-Serb villagers, and then gone away, leaving the Serb peasants to the tender mercies of the NDH units that accompanied the Germans.

The Germans planned further anti-insurgent operations. They were dissatisfied—with the NDH regime, which they were coming to regard as the chief cause of the problem, and with the Italians who were not ruthless enough. They held a series of meetings with Italian and NDH commanders between January and April to prepare for joint operations code-named 'Trio'. There were disagreements and delays—over the area, over the overall command, over Italian intervention north of the line, over the Serb nationalists, over the participation of NDH troops, and the authority to be restored in the pacified areas. It was eventually decided to start with operations in eastern Bosnia, to disregard the demarcation line, not to negotiate with the chetniks in the course of operations, and not to allow NDH authorities back until pacification had been achieved. The ustashas feared losing part of Bosnia to Serbia, and part of Herzegovina to Montenegro. They exploited German-Italian differences, deliberately delayed the movement of Italian troops through transport problems, and tried to counter Italian influence by themselves approaching the chetniks.

Eventually 'Trio' was directed against all insurgents in the area between Sarajevo and the Drina. General Mario Roatta, who had just taken over at Supersloda from Ambrosio, appointed Chief of Army Staff in Rome, got Bader to consent again that those chetniks who gave themselves up without resistance should be treated as prisoners of war. Francetić's choice ustasha Black Legion jumped the gun, hoping to destroy Dangić before the Italians went into action. Intended for special purposes, it was made up of Croat and Muslim refugees from chetnik-controlled areas of east Bosnia, and was fiercely anti-Serb. An exasperated Bader then also went ahead. The chetniks, who were facing the ustashas, let the Germans through to get at the partisans. Ignoring the ustashas, Tito's best units descended on the rear of chetniks engaged against the Black Legion. The Germans suspected collusion. The chetniks were caught between the three. Dangić was arrested on the occasions of a visit to Belgrade. Many of his men were captured and sent to prisoner camps in Germany. There was turmoil as chetniks and partisans melted, went their own ways, and to one another, while ustashas indulged in another killing spree. As the partisans were squeezed out of their territory, a joint German-Italian pincer movement took possession of Foča on 10 May. It had already been evacuated by Tito and his command. The partisans' territory had been taken and their forces dispersed. Even though the rebels had generally avoided fighting, their losses had been huge. Long delays in planning had led to the forewarning of partisans and chetniks; there had been tension between Germans, Italians and the NDH; ustasha participation had made matters worse for Germans and Italians, chetniks and partisans alike.

In Herzegovina, not encompassed in 'Trio', Italian troops had operated in conjunction with chetniks, fully exploiting popular resentment against the partisans. Roatta was not going to get chetniks and partisans together by attacking the former as well as the latter.[16] He came to realise that the distance between Jevdjević and Mihailović was actually far greater than he had thought, that local chetnik commanders resented Mihailović's concentration on Serbia, and Birčanin's sitting it out comfortably in Split. The chetniks were getting the upper hand in most Serb-majority areas. The argument that operations had been directed first and foremost at communists, worked in their favour. It was then that the ustashas' fears of loss of territory came to coincide with the Italians' disillusion with occupation of the NDH. Unexpected losses due to the game of hide and seek in the Dinaric wilderness led Roatta to want to regroup his troops in bigger garrisons, just as the Zagreb government argued that it could take over again the civil powers that it had had to give up in Zone 3. On 19 June Pavelić and Roatta agreed that administration would be returned to the NDH in Zone 3 except where Italian garrisons were retained. Pavelić accepted the rights conceded to the population by the Italian military, including the presence of legalised chetniks labelled Volunteer Anti-Communist Militia (MVAC–*Milizia volontari anticomunisti*), and the retention of an Italian right to intervene again if necessary. Italian garrisons withdrew from most of Zone 3, thus creating a near vacuum in a broad belt of territory from Sandžak to westernmost Bosnia.

The geography of Bosnia made regular operations difficult. Unable to put down the rising there, the ustashas did not want foreign occupation troops to do it for them. They had thus got their local authorities to settle with many of the leaders of Serb bands in ad hoc arrangements, concluded with reservations and all too often transgressed, that nevertheless ended ustasha power in much of the uplands. But such concessions could not be afforded in the mainly Serb-inhabited 'Krajinas'—the marches between Bosnia and Croatia, because they could endanger the coast, or were too near the centre

---

16 He was not going to attack 'people who, for reasons of their own, prefer shooting at our enemies than at us', he wrote to Ambrosio on 3 March 1942, adding cynically: 'rather let them cut each other's throats [*si sgozzino fra di loro*]'.

of ustasha power. Ustashas and Italians sent periodic expeditions to ensure no insurgent territory emerged, thus causing tension between ustashas and Italians, as well as between villagers. Those whose settlements had been destroyed had no further reason to avoid a clash with Italian troops, and sought the protection of guerrillas. The partisans' influence had increased among the homeless and bereaved peasants of those western areas. Tito had practically lost Serbia; his attempt to subdue east Bosnia had misfired; the partisans had been forced out of Montenegro. He now fully realised there was no early prospect of restoring any influence in the eastern territories. On 19 June he announced to the Central Committee that they were going west, to that no man's land where the partisans had been more successful, and where they controlled a considerable free territory.[17] The cadres realised that the move away from Serbia was a far-reaching setback. The partisans from Serbia were reluctant to abandon a territory crucial to the outcome of the war, in order to go to a remote and backward region where the KPJ had never developed. Tito told his commanders that the Comintern supported his decision, which indicated 'the shortest route back to Serbia'. The force of some 4,000 partisans (over half of whom came from Montenegro) set off on what has been called their 'long march', by analogy with the Chinese communists' 'long march' from Jiangxi province in central China to Shaanxi province in the north-west in 1934–1935.

Meanwhile the Germans had decided to do something about the guerrillas that had extended their field of action in north-west Bosnia to the river Sava. 6–7,000 partisans centred on the Kozara mountain west of Banjaluka had effectively closed down some iron-ore mines and threatened important communications. Bader was again put in charge of an operation. Using the German division in the NDH and another brought in from Serbia, with added Domobrans and ustashas, he planned to encircle and destroy the guerrillas caught in the

---

17 'That decision [...] was proclaimed rather than proposed by Tito; he was apprehensive that it might be opposed. But nobody opposed it', Djilas wrote in his memoirs (*Wartime*, 183).

trap. Tens of thousands of Serb peasants had also taken refuge in the heights. In July, the Germans attacked from three sides, inflicting huge losses, as refugees, with women and children, massed up against the barrier put up by the attackers on the fourth side. Because the task was urgent and there were few troops available, orders were issued for 'immediate and ruthless measures' against insurgents, their accomplices and their dependents. The Germans actually wanted to dislodge a disloyal population from a region of communication arteries. The divisional history of the core German 714th Division describes it as 'a battle without mercy, without pity'.[18] Villagers were brought to collection centres, where ustashas sorted out the males over fourteen years of age and fit to work. Those selected were given the choice of working in Germany or being sent to concentration camps. There were more massacres as ustasha units combed the area. When the operation was concluded, the number of people killed as well as the number of those deported ran to tens of thousands. The Germans ascertained 12,000 insurgents killed in combat by 24 August, and 14,000 prisoners executed. According to their own reports, German casualties had been low: thirty-three killed, eighty injured, thirty-three missing.

However, they had largely left the Italians to deal with the rebellious areas. In July 1942 the Italian Second Army numbered some 240,000, yet the revolt of Serbs in the NDH had not been against them. Their territory was a haven for Serb refugees, and a supply base for armed bands. The military had extended their influence by tolerating, and coming to terms with, many of the Serb rebels, starting in annexed Dalmatia, and moving on to Serb areas of the NDH in the early summer of 1942. As they made arrangements with the occupation troops, the chetniks of the Italian zone were also anxious to acknowledge Mihailović as a nominal authority, for he had become a legend in the Serb parts of Yugoslavia. In the mixed-population areas, the events of 1941 had caused hatred of Muslims and Croats

---

18 Quoted by Jonathan E. Gumz, 'Wehrmacht Perceptions of Mass Violence in Croatia, 1941-1942', *The Historical Journal*, 44, 4, Cambridge, 2001: 1022.

among the Serb population, and a consequent revulsion from the Yugoslav idea. As they turned their back on Croats, Muslims and communists, the chetniks of these regions continued to idealise King Peter and the 'English', both of whom Mihailović represented. They feigned to ignore that he also represented a government committed to restoring Yugoslavia in alliance with the Soviet Union. They considered their arrangements with the Italians as a temporary expedient, and saw no contradiction in their double game. Mihailović provided legitimacy and an alibi. They felt that, if the Axis won the war, the Italians would not let them fall under the rule of Croats, and if the British won, there would be a return to an improved version of the old Yugoslavia. These local captains kept the communists in check; they made Mihailović's JVO appear more widespread; he knew that they would never oppose British troops and hoped that, by the time of the expected landing, they would effectively be following his orders. There was anyhow not much he could do but trust them or reject them. He took the risk of hoping for the best. After Grdjić had left Mostar for Opatija (Abbazia, in pre-war Italy) in March 1942, Birčanin asked him to go to Cetinje, to arrange for a link to Mihailović. Contact was made through Djukanović; Mihailović provided letters of appointment which empowered them to represent him in Cetinje and in Split respectively, letting them free to act as they thought best, and expressing full confidence in their understanding of the situation.[19]

Birčanin, who was made commander of the chetnik units of Bosnia, Herzegovina, Lika and Dalmatia, attempted to organise nationalist 'resistance' against ustashas and communists as part of the JVO. Army officers had made their way to Split, from Montenegro, or released from prisoner-of-war camps in Italy. They were sent to various chetnik groups, to command, counsel or coordinate. Some were more loyal to Mihailović, others to Birčanin. Most followed their own ideas, while a few were planted by Italian Military In-

---

19 We do not have the verbatim text of these letters, which survive only in reminiscences.

telligence (in Birčanin's entourage, for example). The officers made little headway; some of them were even killed in suspicious circumstances. Roatta used the MVAC in order to spare Italian lives, and to express his refusal to fight a war in the Balkans on German terms. Birčanin cooperated fully. In spite of a uniform Italian appellation, the situation varied in time and with Italian commands. In principle, the Anti-Communist Volunteers were armed, paid and fed auxiliaries incorporated with Italian divisions, taking part in the repression of communist insurgents. In Italian military terminology, they were considered distinct from 'chetniks', who were irregulars, some of them affiliated to the JVO, others with no control whatsoever, sometimes in rivalry among themselves. In fact, MVAC volunteers and chetniks were often the same people, moving from one group to another and not really worried by labels. Italian generals had a fair understanding of the different reasons for, and different grades of, collaboration. Their soldiers' morale was flagging; they disliked their German and ustasha allies more than the insurgents. Roatta's was a calculated political move—to counter ustashas and Germans, as well as Mihailović's attempt to bring the chetniks under his control. The chetniks (whatever their guise or appellation) could also be of use at the end of the war. If the Axis won, it was an advantage for Italy to have friends among the Serbs. Otherwise, it was an advantage to have friends who would probably not turn against Italian troops, and a link to Mihailović and the Allies, although political commitments were carefully avoided.

The chetniks were also a source of trouble. After 'Trio', NDH troops remained in eastern Bosnia, and even south of the demarcation line, in spite of Italian protests. Ustashas—now mainly local Muslims—returned to Foča, intent on retribution. The Serb population appealed for help to the nearest chetniks, and Jevdjević appealed to the Italian corps commander in Dubrovnik. Chetniks appeared from northern Montenegro, to clear the area. Having retaken Foča, they murdered and pillaged until the Italians intervened at the end of August. Jevdjević was a man of action, an organiser and an intriguer.

Since the summer of 1941, he had raised an armed band with which he had rescued villagers from the ustashas, rekindled chetnik morale in Herzegovina after Todorović's murder, negotiated the formation of MVAC units in exchange for food aid in famine-stricken Herzegovina, and generally steered his own course.[20] Elsewhere in Zone 3, as a result of the evacuation of Italian garrisons, returning ustashas resumed their unfinished business over the Serb population, and chetniks responded in equal measure. Outrages were also committed in Zone 2, and even in Zone 1, against villages alleged to be ustasha or partisan nests. Protests from the NDH increased, along with German demands that militias be disbanded. Mihailović and Birčanin met in July in Herzegovina. Birčanin's trip had been arranged for talks with Muslim notables. The Italians were not meant to know that a secret rendezvous had also been arranged with Mihailović. They met near Avtovac on 22 July. Jevdjević and Major Petar Baćović, Mihailović's newly-appointed commander for Herzegovina, and eastern and central Bosnia, were also present. Mihailović confirmed Birčanin's and other appointments, and repeated blandly that he was confident they were acting according to their best understanding of the situation. According to Italian records, Mihailović told the chetnik leaders that his government was pressing him to start guerrilla warfare against Axis troops throughout Yugoslavia; but that he had answered he would only consider it when the British and the Russians were nearer at hand, in view of the losses already suffered by the Serbs.

By the autumn Roatta was becoming worried. He summoned Birčanin and Jevdjević to his headquarters between 21 and 26 September, to question them, along with Grdjić, who seems to have acted as a general factotum. How many chetniks did they control? What were their long-term aims? How loyal were they to the Italians? Roatta read them the riot act. They were being helped exclusively

---

20 Mihailović is alleged to have said of him in January 1943: 'If only I could get hold of him, I would string him up from the nearest tree', while the head of the Intelligence Office at the Italian VIth Army Corps command described him as a gangster.

in their fight against communists, and had to stop anti-Croat and anti-Muslim actions. They could act defensively, but not offensively, without his authorisation. He was told that Birčanin had 'moral command' over all of them.[21] Asked specifically whether they were also under Mihailović's dependence in any way, they explained that his effective field of action was limited to Serbia and Macedonia, in agreement with Nedić. Mihailović was no more than a 'moral head', whose wishes were taken into account when they coincided with real Serb interests. Asked bluntly what they would do if events took an unfavourable turn for the Axis, and Mihailović ordered action against occupation troops, they said that they would take defensive action on the borders of what they considered to be Serb territory, but that no Serb would ever attack an Italian. More informally, they hinted to officers of Supersloda's Intelligence Office that, just as they would not turn against the Italians, so they would not oppose the British if they landed. Roatta noted: 'I no longer believe them'. It seemed to him that both they and Nedić were collaborating with Italians and Germans respectively until the time when they thought they could come out openly with Mihailović against the Axis.

All was not well between Birčanin and Jevdjević. Birčanin, whose health was fast declining, realised that he was caught between the Italians, who had gradually moved from tolerance to patronage of the chetniks, and Jevdjević, who wanted to take over. Jevdjević argued that his increasingly open collaboration was a patriotic act that allowed others to save face. Birčanin was believed to have kept contact with British Intelligence. Separately from his 'moral command' of chetniks, he was trying to get some sort of cooperation between Serb and Croat political personalities gathered in Split, in order to help refugees, calm Serb-Croat tension, gather support for Mihailović, and prepare for eventual action against the Axis. Split provided a favourable environment, with its Yugoslav-minded mid-

---

21 According to Roatta's report of 26 September 1942 to the Supreme Command in Rome, the MVAC numbered 12,320 volunteers, over eighty per cent of them Orthodox, and over half of them under Jevdjević.

dle class, its many refugees—Serbs, Jews (about 1,500) and Croats. General Quirino Armellini, commander of the XVIIIth Army Corps, who was reputed to be close to the Italian royal house and an anglophile, kept fascist organisations under close control. Italian military intelligence noted at the time a marked rise in Yugoslav feelings in the coastal region, and of sympathy for rebels in general, including Mihailović who was considered to be enjoying British support. Privately, Armellini's intelligence officers dismissed the work of the Split group as an ineffective 'salon resistance', whiling away the time in expectation of a British intervention, as the partisans were gathering strength. They were more worried by the rise in communist influence than by the suspected presence of British agents among Birčanin's anti-communists.

Contact between the western chetnik territorial commanders and Mihailović was not easy. Often without radio contact, they relied on couriers. Radio messages were read by the Italians and even more by the Germans. At his trial in 1946, Mihailović claimed that he had never ordered the elimination of Croat and Muslim villagers, and that much was hidden from him. Some of the commanders did not want him to know of the crimes that had been committed, but others proudly reported them to him, such as Djurišić, who having announced that he intended to flush out the Muslim militia on the right bank of the river Lim where Orthodox villages had been destroyed, then boasted about the Muslim villages that he had in turn destroyed. Mihailović was appalled by what he learnt, complained about it to his entourage, wrote threatening letters, but did not publicly denounce such action or report it to his government. The British, who were on the spot, generally knew what was happening, and Mihailović knew that they knew. He also believed that the British backed Birčanin, and he probably did not know the full extent of the chetniks' collaboration with the Italians. He gave their commanders formal positions within the JVO; he recommended promotions and awards on their behalf; he sent them pre-signed papers. On the rare occasions when he met them, he told them that he trusted them to do what was best in the circumstances. He had to be satisfied if they accepted his nominal command, which occasionally enabled him to act as mediator between them. It was all done in the hope that he would eventually be able to control them by the time that Allied forces arrived to liberate the country. Meanwhile, he was becoming dependent on armed groups whose policies and accommodations he could neither denounce nor condone.

Until spring 1942, Italian troops had been able to believe in the illusion of restored normality in their zone. Thereafter assassinations and mutilations were no longer actions committed between armed groups of the native population, but against Italian military personnel, particularly officers. Roatta reacted with his Circular 3C of 1 March which ordered the use of 'powerful means' in localities where operations were undertaken against armed rebels—including the taking of hostages, the destruction of houses, and the treatment as rebels of males wearing distinctive apparel captured near points of attack. The circular was meant to put an end to the Italian army's 'soft' reputation as the partisans' pressure increased. They had been the main beneficiaries of Roatta's partial withdrawal to the coast. Tito's well-organised and communist-led mobile guerrilla force had surged in the direction of least resistance, along the wooded mountainous watershed that marked the boundary between the German and the Italian zone, where nobody was really in charge, to join the 'free territory' in the west.

The 300 km march did much to restore the partisans' image. The region they went through had been fought over by ustashas out for Serb blood and chetniks eager for revenge, with Muslims in between, but the mixed population was on the whole neutral. The partisans had to be careful to remain outside German reach, and to avoid fortified Italian garrisons, but they benefited from the tripartite tension between Germans, Italians and ustashas. They withdrew when pursued, and made convenient arrangements with Domobran garrisons. They were generally greeted as protectors by the Serb population. Although mostly Serbs themselves, they were now usually more careful (certainly at leadership level) to prevent hatred of the usta-shas from turning against Croats and Muslims without regard to specific instances, which helped them infiltrate local NDH person-nel. By October a partisan corridor stretched from Herzegovina to the Krajinas. Tito decided to take Bihać, a market town of 15,000 inhabitants that still separated partisan territory east and west of the river Una. He ordered that it be taken before 5 November, to mark the twenty-fifth anniversary of the October Revolution, and it was captured in time, after a fierce struggle with its ustasha defenders. Bihać yielded an enormous booty; it provided a new 'capital' for the NOP and a venue for Tito's intended assembly of delegates from all the partisan-liberated areas.

It is usually said that the partisans had come to control a territory almost the size of Switzerland. Largely eradicated from Serbia and east Bosnia, driven out of Montenegro, the partisans were now reset-tled in the heart of the NDH, in Serb-inhabited regions where the ustasha terror of the previous year had wiped out traditional leader-ship. That left the local chetniks divided and vulnerable after the final parting of the ways with the partisans, the departure of the Italians and uncertain arrangements with NDH authorities. The NOP thrived on the anarchy of the ustasha state. Having penetrated the desperate struggle against extermination of the Orthodox Serbs in the NDH, it advocated religious and ethnic tolerance, in spite of and against the feelings of local partisans. In Bosnia in 1942, the partisans were on the side of those fighting for their lives, unless they were political ri-vals. Their reputation went ahead of them, and helped them through non-Serb areas. They attracted numerous uprooted young men and women who were eager to fight. Croats and Muslims in their turn came to escape conscription and the possibility of being sent to the Russian front. The KPJ took the adolescents of Bosnia out of their respective milieux, so that by the end of the year, they were no longer territorial militias defending their villages against other militias, but the Peoples' Liberation Army under Tito's command, with cadres made up of the original partisans who had come with him. It was a

129

force that had increased tenfold since leaving east Bosnia, according to German estimates.[22] It was half-way between a guerrilla force and a 'normal' army, with an asymmetric command structure that generally combined central control and local initiative. In Croatia, where the partisan struggle had hitherto been an almost entirely Serb affair, with combatants usually won over from the chetniks, the recruitment of at least some Croats allowed the units to be labelled as 'Croat'. Revolution was no longer mentioned; the NOP presented itself as an all-Yugoslav patriotic people's struggle. The KPJ was able to use non-Serb, and even local Serb, perceptions of chetniks as a propaganda weapon against Mihailović, who was anyhow no more than a distant and misunderstood symbol. Tito's movement made full use of the failure of chetnik leaders to use the growing disillusion of Croats with the NDH and generally to develop any appeal for non-Serbs. The best that the chetnik leaders could do was the occasional rhetorical and perfunctory endorsement of the Kingdom of Yugoslavia. The partisans' cause was associated with a new type of Yugoslavia.

Having found refuge and new sources of strength in an area that was at the time without strategic importance for the Axis, and ignored by Mihailović and the chetniks in the east who believed that the partisans had definitely collapsed, Tito now wanted a broader platform from which to rally non-communist patriots and to challenge the exiled government. He consulted the Comintern about creating 'something like a government'. The Soviet Union by that time had provided Tito with the 'Free Yugoslavia' transmitter in Russia purported to be in partisan territory; it had released arguments against Mihailović; but it continued to press for cooperation with all possible resistance groups, and to warn against premature public espousal of communism. Stalin thus approved the setting up

---

22 A maximum of 45,000 at the end of 1942. Post-war official Yugoslav sources say 137,000–150,000, which seems out of proportion with the manpower and arms available then in 'liberated territory'. On the other hand, Stephen Clissold totals no more than 24,000-32,000 (*A Short History of Yugoslavia from Early Times to 1966*, Cambridge, 1966: 220).

of an all-Yugoslav and broadly anti-fascist body, but he did not want an antigovernment to the exiled one.

The Anti-Fascist Council of the Peoples' Liberation of Yugoslavia (AVNOJ—*Antifašističko veće/vijeće narodnog oslobodjenja Jugoslavije*) that met on 26-27 November 1942 was completely of Tito's making, and carefully arranged. Revolutionary intentions were concealed behind the struggle against the invaders.[23] Fifty-four pre-selected participants were gathered, and prominence was given to a JMO senator, a HSS parliamentary deputy and a couple of Orthodox priests. Ivan Ribar, a non-communist but fellow-travelling Croat who had been vice-president of the Democratic Party and president of the Constituent Assembly in 1920, was smuggled out of Belgrade to be president of AVNOJ. Tito's inaugural speech said that they were setting up a political authority, as an expression of the unity of Serbs, Croats, Slovenes, Montenegrins, Muslims and all others, whatever their religion and nationality, to gather all forces in the fight against the fascist occupiers and their lackeys. In spite of Stalin's advice, he mentioned only the help received from 'our Slav brethren the Russians and all peoples of the USSR'. The resolution made AVNOJ the representative body of the liberation movement that harnessed all true patriots. It set up an Executive Committee, which was not called a government but looked liked one. It adopted the slogan 'Death to fascism—freedom to the people' and the red star on the Yugoslav flag, but did not spell out the aims of the KPJ. Tito had thought out the theory that NOP was sovereign over the whole territory of Yugoslavia, and that no armed force was entitled to be on its territory unless by agreement with the Supreme Commander of the Peoples' Liberation Army of Yugoslavia—himself.

---

23 'The positions which Tito initiated [...] were so broad that they could have been accepted by all opponents of the occupation—had the opponents not known that those positions originated with the Communists and so concealed ulterior motives. [...] It was as if, now that the revolution had found its vital concrete path, it could conceal itself', writes Djilas in *Wartime*, 208–9.

Wrapped up in some mystery outside the inner circle of the KPJ leadership, Tito was already the object of a cult, residing in a manor some 15 kms north of Bihać, in the company of the poet Vladimir Nazor, who had recently come out of Zagreb. He had satisfied the international demands of Stalin, whom he glorified in articles written in Bihać as the faultless human being 'without whom the sun would have been darkened'. However, he had not departed from the conviction that the fate of the communist revolution had to be determined during the war by destroying all groups not under the control of the KPJ, particularly as the KPJ leadership believed the British were conspiring with Mihailović and the chetniks against the partisans.

The Failure of the Policy of Forced Conversions in the NDH

The ustashas had placed their faith in Pavelić to obtain independence for Croatia on the best possible terms, and he had kept all negotiations to himself. At the beginning of 1942, when it was obvious that all had not gone according to his intentions, he called together a sabor to show that the NDH was nevertheless well in the historical continuity of the Croatian state. The assembly that met on 28 February 1942 was a formal gathering of selected individuals meant to represent the uninterrupted existence of a Croatian polity from the Habsburgs to the ustashas. They were survivors of the 1918 Sabor of Croatia-Slavonia, of Croatian Party of Rights representatives elected in 1920 to the Constituent Assembly of the Kingdom of Serbs, Croats and Slovenes, and of HSS members of the last Yugoslav parliament (excluding those who had 'sinned against the achievements of the NDH, or offended the honour and reputation of the Croatian nation', but including two innocuous Serbs), ustasha cadres, and two representatives of the German national group. Of 217 nominees, only 150 turned up, more than half of them ustasha notables. Their only duty was to hear the Poglavnik's speech and to adopt a motion invalidating the inclusion of Croatia in the state of the Serbs, Croats and Slovenes.[24]

By the summer, the ustasha régime controlled little more than the Zagreb region with a few larger towns where there were strong ustasha and German garrisons, but even there life was bleak. The cost of living increased by 335 per cent during 1942. The currency circulation almost doubled from 7.5 m kunas (the NDH *kuna* being equal to the old Yugoslav dinar) in mid-1941 to 14 m a year later. It would finish at 241,000 m in 1945. The ustashas' incapacity to govern, otherwise than by arbitrary disregard for life and property, was causing more and more Croats and Muslims to turn away from them. Domobrans virtually handed over local administration to local chetnik captains in exchange for dubious formal acknowledgement of the NDH, or provided arms, ammunition and recruits for the partisans. Although its troops partly occupied and administered the NDH, Italy had no political clout in Zagreb and was disillusioned with its involvement across the Adriatic. The Reich disposed of the economy, and even of the labour force, to the point of attracting all workers of 'Aryan descent' (meaning that Serbs could also come, and many thousands preferred working in Germany than remaining in the NDH), but its frustration was growing. Because of the spread of partisan and chetnik territory, Germany had to take stronger action to protect mines and communications. In November, it sent a second occupation division of reservists in training; it recruited the Volksdeutsche into the SS, and it started to set up Croatian 'Legionnaire' units with German cadres.

In July, the office of the Duke of Spoleto—absentee 'King-designate' of Croatia—noted that the situation had begun to reverse Croatian opinion away from Axis-sponsored independence, back to a renewed, albeit different, Yugoslav union. This went for Arch-

---

24 The Sabor would be summoned twice again during 1942—in April for the anniversary of the NDH, and in December, when it was dissolved after its president, an elderly ustasha returnee, had addressed a memorandum to Pavelić criticising certain policies and making proposals for the reorganisation of the assembly into a permanent body.

bishop Stepinac too, who had been shocked by the ustashas' policy of persecutions. From the beginning of 1942 he started to protest privately, to intervene on behalf of individuals and to help baptised Jews, Slovene refugee priests, Orthodox orphans. In May he went on to public criticism, through sermons, of forcible conversions, although the elderly Bishop Alojzije Mišić of Mostar, who died in March 1942, had gone much further in his outright denunciation of ustasha inhumanities. To Lieutenant Stanislav Rapotec, a Slovene Yugoslav army officer and secret emissary of the government in exile whom he saw several times that year, Archbishop Stepinac was eager to tell what he had done to help suffering individuals, Serbs, Jews, Slovenes and Croats alike. Pavelić resented him; some Germans regarded him as *Judenfreundlich*.

The HSS had lost its organisation and its bearings. Party notables in Zagreb had been imprisoned, interned or kept under surveillance, with a new wave of arrests of about eighty former members of parliament over the summer. Maček, released from internment at the beginning of the year, was sent off to his country house until January 1943, when he was allowed back in Zagreb. Although under house arrest, he could receive visitors. He told them that he believed the Western Allies would eventually land, that Germany would be defeated, that Yugoslavia would be restored, and that the Russians would not be allowed to play a part in the reorganisation of Eastern Europe. He advised against cooperation with the ustasha régime, but was not in favour of active resistance that could be dangerous. Croatian and HSS interests were well represented and cared for in the Yugoslav government in exile. In spite of the leader's optimism, as the HSS right had gone to the ustashas in April 1941, so the left turned to the partisans as 1942 went by. Yet various people were looking to the HSS for help. Increasingly disillusioned Domobran officers worried about the fate of Croatia after the war. Some of them were HSS sympathisers, but they were not politically minded, organised or well informed. Mihailović in December sent emissaries to Zagreb to contact HSS personalities and to enquire about the possibility of Domobrans accepting his Yugoslav command, with no result.

It was the German military around Glaise von Horstenau in Zagreb who most thought in terms of replacing the ustashas with the HSS, as they came to believe that the chief cause of unrest in the NDH was the policy of the current régime, and in particular its behaviour towards the Serbs. Their opinion came to be shared by General Alexander Löhr, who had taken over the Wehrmacht SE Command in August 1942. A former Austro-Hungarian officer, born of a German father and a Romanian mother in Hungary, and brought up as an Orthodox, he wanted the German field commander in the NDH to be entrusted with civil powers as well, just as his Italian opposite number. Hitler turned the idea down, with the argument that the ustashas should be allowed to 'rage themselves out'. Nevertheless, a gradual inflection took place in the attitude of the ustasha régime towards its Serbs. In his opening speech to the Sabor, Pavelić had explained that the NDH's objections were to a *Serbian* Orthodox Church, not to Orthodoxy as such. Propaganda now spoke of a 'communist-chetnik' plot (operated by Jews and freemasons) rather than a 'Serbian' plot. On the eve of the agreement concluded with Supersloda for the withdrawal of most Italian garrisons from Zone 3, emissaries tried and failed to get Jevdjević and Grdjić to acknowledge the NDH.

Pavelić was in fact admitting that by 'raging themselves out' against the Serbs, the ustashas had failed to get rid of them, and now risked a complete takeover by their Axis protectors. The policy of forced conversions had failed. Kvaternik Jr would later observe in his memoirs that the régime's Serb policy had 'reached a blind alley'.[25] The remaining Serbs who had not been converted to Catholicism[26] could

---

25 Eugen Dido Kvaternik, *Sjećanja i zapažanja. Prilozi za hrvatsku povijest* (Jere Jareb, ed.), Zagreb, 1995: 285.

26 When asked by Jozo Tomasevich in 1966 for his estimate of the number of converts to Catholicism in the NDH, Vladimir Bakarić (wartime political commissar of the partisan command in Croatia, and at that time leader of the League of Communists of Croatia) said: 'Guarded estimates indicate

be Orthodox Croats. The idea was probably a German one. After a
group of trustworthy Serbs had submitted a request to be allowed to
set up an Orthodox church community in Zagreb, Pavelić issued an
ordinance, followed by a constitution on 5 June 1942, which set up
a state-subsidised autocephalous Croatian Orthodox Church on the
territory of the NDH. The eighty-one year old exiled Russian Bishop
Germogen, who had arrived in Yugoslavia in 1922 and was a member
of the Episcopal Synod of the Russian Church Abroad, was brought
out of a monastery in Banat to be appointed 'Archbishop of Zagreb
and Metropolitan of the Croatian Orthodox Church'. In spite of
pressure from the Gestapo not to do it, the governing Synod of the
Serbian Orthodox Church in Belgrade condemned Pavelić's creation, but could not publish its decision. The Russian Church Abroad
immediately excluded Bishop Germogen from its synod and prohibited him from celebrating. The NDH government provided very
little help, and Germogen found very few priests. By the end of the
year, he had seventy-three, on paper at least, thirty of them Russians;
numbers thereafter dwindled until there were only five left in Zagreb
at the end. Another Russian, with most dubious qualifications, was
eventually found for the see of Sarajevo in 1944. Germogen managed
to obtain pensions for a number of priests' widows and orphans, but
the whole enterprise was little more than a propaganda exercise.

By the autumn there was a considerable drop in killings throughout
the NDH. In the case of Jews, instead of dealing directly with those
who remained, Pavelić's government asked the German authorities
to deport them. At the end of summer, 5,000 were rounded up and
transported to camps in Eastern Europe, which effectively started
a second phase of liquidation, but outside the NDH. The Finance

a figure of about 300,000 people' (Tomasevich, *War and Revolution in
Yugoslavia, 1941-1945. Occupation and Collaboration,* 542). Mark Biondich
quotes NDH archival material according to which a little fewer than 100,000
conversions to Roman Catholicism occurred in 1941-1942 (Mark Biondich,
'Religion and Nation in Wartime Croatia. Reflections on the Ustaša Policy
of Forced Religious Conversion, 1941-1942', *Slavonic and East European
Review,* 83, 1, London, 2005: 91).

Ministry paid the Reich government thirty reichsmarks per deported Jew as a contribution to its help in solving the Jewish question in Croatia. Germany started making enquiries from Italy about handing over the Jews who were in Italian occupation zones. Supersloda came up with a figure of 3,000. Government departments in Rome and generals in the field then began a long process of evading and delaying tactics. In compensation, the NDH turned systematically to the destruction of Gypsies.

The Muslims were considered to be 'pure Croats', but the ustashas and the Italians, having used them, abandoned them to Serb retaliation. Most of them anyhow rejected the idea that they were Croats. Apart from those who had been personally involved, they had not really adhered to the régime and did not approve of the violence against Serbs and Jews. From the end of 1941, personalities from their urban élite in Sarajevo, Mostar and Banjaluka criticised ustasha brutalities in statements submitted to the Muslims in government. They deplored that ustashas made use of 'rabble', inviting retribution from Serbs; that they failed to protect Muslims from chetniks; and that they designated as 'communists' those who protested against the maltreatment of Serbs. Some complaints were also addressed to German or Italian authorities. For the Germans, the 'Gothic origins' ploy was tried, and the idea was mooted of a 'region of Bosnia' as the best guarantee for the Muslims' security. In August 1942 Muslim religious and cultural organisations sponsored a big meeting in Sarajevo urging Muslims, Orthodox and Catholics to work together to end religious discord. They again protested at the ustashas' failure to protect Muslims from chetnik atrocities. Some of the chetnik commanders in east Bosnia had, right from the start, resented the indiscriminate action undertaken against Croats and Muslims, and tried to work with 'honest Croats' and 'Serb Muslims', but the massacres in Foča and elsewhere did not incite many Muslims to join them. Even Mihailović's more conciliating gestures towards Muslim mayors and his inefficient rebukes to chetnik commanders were of little avail until he was approached by one of these mayors, Ismet

Popovac, who advised him to try and recruit a prominent Muslim to his command to make up for the lack of a Muslim minister in the exiled government. Popovac was backed by a group of local JMO politicians, and by Mustafa Mulalić, a JMO politician in Belgrade who eventually went out to join Mihailović. Their efforts and those of a few Muslim Yugoslav army officers managed to persuade a number of their coreligionists from south-east Bosnia, north-east Herzegovina and Sandžak to seek security with chetniks and to form Muslim units against the ustashas. But there were still chetnik commanders intent on continuing their anti-Muslim work, and no chetnik organisation was ever set up in Sarajevo, even among the local Serbs. Popovac, who had also tried to enlist Italian aid for a Muslim anti-communist volunteer militia, was eventually murdered in Mostar (by communists or by chetniks).

In late 1942, when the partisans took over the predominantly Muslim area of Bihać, Muslim villagers began to join the partisans. However, most JMO politicians thought it best to retain all options and not to align with any of the warring parties, until November when a group turned to Germany, asking for an autonomous area in Bosnia protected by the Wehrmacht, and where ustashas would be banned. They threatened to emigrate massively to Turkey 'if this insane [ustasha] régime continues', and sent an appeal to that effect to the Turkish National Assembly in Ankara. Muslim self-defence units also appeared. The best known were formed and commanded by two agricultural traders turned warlords—Muhamed Hadžiefendić's 5–6,000-strong Volunteer Legion that did not acknowledge the NDH, in the Tuzla region of north-east Bosnia, and Husnija (Huska) Miljković's force raised in the Cazin area of north-west Bosnia, that eventually grew to 3,000, and that went back and forth between partisans and Domobrans. All this prompted Himmler to use Muslim disillusionment with the NDH to German advantage by getting Hitler to agree to the formation of an SS division of Bosnian Muslims, the first SS division composed of non-Germans.

Zagreb was full of rumours in the latter half of 1942 that the Germans wanted a new government with HSS participation. Löhr and Glaise pressed Hitler to have an incompetent Kvaternik *père* and a bloodthirsty Kvaternik *fils* removed before a fundamental reorganisation of NDH forces took place under German control. Pavelić gave in when he visited Hitler in Ukraine in late September. Slavko Kvaternik was allowed to resign for health reasons on 10 October, and to retire to Slovakia with full honours and on full pay. With him went his son Dido. Pavelić used them as scapegoats for the failure of the armed forces and for the terror. In spite of the fact that the ustasha régime was increasingly chaotic and that support for it was dwindling, Hitler wanted neither to let the Italians sort out the mess nor to replace the Poglavnik. He would muddle through with Pavelić, but under much tighter German control. The violence and chaos of Axis-protected ustasha independence, HSS passivity, the sectarianism of chetniks and their accommodations with occupying forces and local authorities alike, were turning the young of all three communities of the NDH to the partisans. The very idea of Yugoslavia, which had formally survived the collapse of April 1941—through the Allies, the government in exile, Mihailović and the KPJ, seemed to have been further destroyed in the conflagration that raged in the mixed central regions, but older reflexes, aspirations and outlooks resurfaced in 1942. The communists were internationalists; they knew how to use Yugoslavia's 'national problem'; they benefited from the turn of events.

Slovenia Divided between God, Satan and an Uncommitted Centre

Although Nazi plans for ethnic reconstruction were abandoned by the summer of 1942, the expulsion of the intelligentsia and of the politically unreliable, the mass enrolment of the population in official German organisations and continued reprisals for even minor offences (1,367 executions in 1942), meant that there was not much resistance in northern Slovenia. Ljubljana, seat of the Italian *Pro-*

vincia di Lubiana, continued to be the centre of political activity. Partition having stripped it of its economic importance, it was full of unemployed and refugees, with a whole spectrum of secret organisations. The executive of the Slovenian section of the KPJ was there, the only secret organisation with any discipline, and so was Colonel Vauhnik, with an intelligence network apparently working for the British. There was tension between High Commissioner Grazioli, who headed the Italian civil authority, and General Mario Robotti, the commander of the XIth Army Corps. Robotti complained of the importance given to fascist organisations, but considered that Grazioli's policy was otherwise too lenient.

Ljubljana was a nest of subversion. Partisans were spreading out in wooded hilly areas. Acts of sabotage and attacks on isolated Italian military personnel were on the increase. On 19 January 1942, Robotti obtained from Mussolini that the province be declared an 'operational area'. He decided to cut Ljubljana off from the rest of the province, and to disarm its population. Orders were given to control movements in and out of the city, search all premises, and arrest all those found in possession of weapons. Between 24 February and 14 March, 18,887 men were taken away for questioning; 878 of them were interned; sixteen were eventually sentenced to death by military war tribunals and executed. Slovene gendarmes, policemen and prison guards were disarmed. Further searches were made in surrounding villages. All premises were searched, including cafés, cinemas, schools, hospitals and churches. Not much was found by way of weaponry and subversive material: several pistols and bayonets, a few Yugoslav flags (including one with a red star), portraits of King Alexander and King Peter II hidden behind portraits of King Victor Emmanuel III and of Mussolini in schools, a portrait of Stalin, a couple of Yugoslav army officers' uniforms, printing material, several radio receivers and transmitters, Yugoslav army maps, a circular to Yugoslav officers reminding them of their duty to fight for King and country. A country house near the city yielded sixteen shotguns, thirteen antique swords and five antique pistols.

In September work started on the erection of a permanent barricade around Ljubljana. Robotti was a zealous enforcer of Roatta's Circular 3C. The idea was even discussed at Supersloda to organise camps in Italy to house up to 20,000 evacuees from operational zones, and to transfer property from rebels to the families of Italian soldiers killed in action. Grazioli objected that such German-type brutality would in fact drive a generally passive rural population to the partisans. The Supreme Command in Rome reminded Roatta and Robotti that confiscation of property was contrary to existing legislation. 'It was only an idea', Roatta explained to Ambrosio on 26 June, as he told Robotti that the full rigour of Circular 3C should be applied only in 'unusual' situations.

There was a new cycle of operations in the second half of July. In addition to his two divisions, Robotti was assigned two more for the task (from Herzegovina and Montenegro). There was another roundup in Ljubljana, of potential cadres and recruits for subversive organisations—officers and non-commissioned officers, civil servants, teachers, students, unemployed, young men of fighting age, and suspected sympathisers 'communist and nationalist alike'. The former Yugoslav military cadres were those living at home as prisoners of war on parole. Many of those rounded up had been involved with the rather inefficient efforts to coordinate a potential guerrilla network linked to Mihailović's JVO. By the end of July, about 9,000 people (including 1,000 officers and NCOs) were sent to internment camps in Italy.[27] The Italians had overestimated both the number of armed partisan combatants (at 8,000-10,000 when there were probably no more than 3,000 at the time) and the potential of a JVO underground movement. The anti-insurgent operations consisted in a series of short, sharp actions aimed at surprising, encircling and destroying partisan bands in the wooded hills between Ljubljana and the Croatian border. They were accompanied by the dropping by

---

27 Supersloda data indicate that in April 1943 there were 18,838 Slovene internees in Italy. Perhaps as many as 400,000 Slovenes may have gone through Italian camps in 1941-1943.

air of 15,000 leaflets guaranteeing safe-conduct to those who gave themselves up with arms and ammunition. The partisans had as usual anticipated the move. Most got out of the way. Italian army statistics note 867 partisans killed and 501 surrendered, with Italian losses at thirty-six dead and 106 injured.

Disappointed by the lack of cooperation from the Slovene élite and the spread of armed resistance, the Italians had reacted by retaliating against all forms of resistance, real or potential, and by playing up the communist bogey. However, the partisans had become dangerous, not only to Italian military personnel but also for all those who wanted to remain outside the Liberation Front (OF) in their opposition to occupation. At the beginning of 1942, the OF had expelled non-communist groups. Although it did not yet come out with a communist programme, it claimed the monopoly of opposition to foreign occupation. After Mihailović's first representative in Slovenia, Colonel Jaka Avšič, had gone over to the partisans, the communists turned against their rivals and did all they could to hinder the officers' attempts to set up a JVO network. However much they distrusted each other, the different party legions had all considered themselves to be part of the JVO. They had not engaged in military action, but they gathered intelligence and distributed leaflets. Officers in touch with Mihailović's Supreme Command were trying to coordinate in anticipation of future action when the Allies landed. In equal anticipation of an Allied landing, the partisans considered 'bourgeois' forces as rivals to be liquidated; their 'Security and Intelligence Service' listed officers opposed to the OF as one of these groups. Villages were caught between partisan attacks on the Italians, OF pressure on villagers to join the partisans through playing up the danger of reprisals, and effective reprisals by occupation forces.

The Slovene People's Party (SLjS) initiated consultations between non-communist groups on how to stand up to communists. The leading figures were the former Ban Natlačen, General Leon Rupnik (chief of staff of the First Group of Armies in April 1941, who had been released after a brief spell in captivity) and Bishop Rožman. The result was the setting up of the underground Slovenian Alliance (SZ, *Slovenska zaveza*)—a co-ordinating body intended to embrace all political tendencies. It named a three-member executive to represent the Liberal, the Catholic and Socialist tendencies, but the communists did not join it. It advocated the union of all Slovenes within a reorganised federal Yugoslavia, and condemned the communists' solo action as aimed to win power after the war. Its driving force was the SLjS, which had links with the Yugoslav government in exile and the Holy See. The Slovene ministers in the government called on the SZ to follow Mihailović. However, the SZ was handicapped by its belated appearance and the lack of an armed organisation. Rupnik wanted to obtain from the Italians more administrative autonomy and a native security organisation. Mihailović's new representative, Major Karel Novak, resumed the attempt to organise a JVO network in Slovenia. The SLjS, which secretly owed allegiance to Yugoslavia, the exiled government and Mihailović, did not want Novak to act as an independent intermediary. They had all come to believe that the communists were more dangerous than the transient enemy occupation, which they could anyhow not get rid of without Allied support. The Italians were at first opposed to the creation of Slovene units; the internment of officers seriously handicapped the project and further weakened Novak's influence. Meanwhile the SZ had begun quietly to organise village guards (*vaške straže*), often through parish priests, for self-defence against partisan attacks. When they were approached for arms, the Italians realised they could put to good use the basically conservative spirit of the rural population reacting to the increasing communist orientation of the partisans, and generally confuse all the non- and anti-communists.

In July, Rupnik accepted the position of *podestà* (government-appointed mayor) of Ljubljana; the Italian command began to organise an MVAC for the Ljubljana Province, with full support from the Church. From a nucleus of 800, it expanded to about 2,000 in November, and would reach a peak of 6,134 in July 1943. In August, Roatta had been to see Bishop Rožman to tell him that Catholic forces in the province should abandon their neutral stance in the struggle between the forces of 'civilisation and religion' and the 'bolsheviks'. Soon afterwards, the Bishop wrote to Robotti, stating his readiness to work with the occupation authorities for the restoration of order. He suggested releasing reliable young officers in an unobtrusive manner. The SLjS designated the officers and NCOs to be sent home. The rank-and-file were mostly refugees from German northern Slovenia, with some Serbs from the NDH, and no more than 1,800 from Ljubljana Province. At first used as interpreters, guides and informers, the guards were used in combat against the partisans, as auxiliaries to Italian units, from September. As the MVAC extended to the informal village guards, the overlap was not clear. Guards infiltrated partisan areas, and partisans turned into guards at the end of operations. By November, the destruction of the MVAC/village guards had become the top priority of the partisans.

The Catholic Church was the only organised autonomous force that survived, and Bishop Rožman of Ljubljana the most important personality in the province. He was, like Archbishop Stepinac, a traditional prelate, although his anti-communism was probably even more elemental. In the absence in London of Miha Krek, the leader of the Catholic SLjS, he had political as well as moral authority, acknowledged by what was left of the pre-war political establishment and by the Italian authorities alike. This was even more the case after the assassination of Natlačen in October by the partisans' Security Service. Rožman himself rarely mentioned the OF by name in public, condemning violence in general terms. However, from the autumn, the press, which remained fairly free in spite of Italian censorship, generally identified the struggle against the communist-dominated OF with the defence of the faith. 'Either with God or with Satan; there is no third way', wrote the widely-circulated *Slovenec* on 3 November 1942. Generally speaking, the controlling force behind the MVAC was the SLjS's Slovene Legion. The Catholic party saw the militia as the only reliable opponent to partisan terror, and strongly resisted Novak's efforts to keep some 'illegal' underground units who, while not fighting occupation or partisan forces, would attract recruits to potential JVO units.

Civil war flared up in the autumn, when both anti-communist 'defenders of the faith' and communist-controlled 'liberators' went out to win the uncommitted centre of Slovene opinion, or to force it to come out with a clear choice. The communists had particular problems with the clergy and the liberal bourgeoisie. In the autumn, Edvard Kardelj, Tito's lieutenant for Slovenia, issued instructions to kill priests, officers, intellectuals and kulaks. Catholic priests were the communists' most committed ideological opponents: seventeen of them of them were killed during 1942 as 'traitors to the people'. Slovenia's urban Liberals posed another threat; untainted by collaboration, they could play a part with the Anglo-Americans if the OF collapsed. They had to be 'neutralised'. Partisan bands, which seemed to have been dispersed, gathered again in late September in the south of the province on the NDH border and on the old Italo-Yugoslav frontier, when insurgents crossed over in order to spend what they thought would be a quieter winter in Slovenia. When it was noticed that 9,000 partisans had assembled in the wooded hills of Gorjanci, Robotti launched another operation in mid-October, with four Italian divisions from Slovenia and the NDH, German troops and ustasha battalions on the other side of the border. The offensive had been preceded by the closure of Ljubljana University and another roundup of intellectuals, most of who were released at the end of operations. The partisans were pushed out of a large part of their 'liberated territory'; thousands were killed, sent to concentration camps, or deserted.[28] In the course of the offensive, the partisans' use of terror against all opponents, real or potential, had led to the nadir of their popularity. The OF realised it had to change gear and decided it had to show that it was not faith-

---

28 In his victorious order of the day of 9 November, Robotti compared the achievements of his soldiers to those of their comrades in Libya and on the banks of the Don. He announced a rounded off grand total of 7,000 losses for the partisans (killed in combat, executed and captured), a figure that is probably inflated, as against forty-three Italian dead and 139 other casualties.

less. The only priest who joined the partisans in Slovenia before the capitulation of Italy was Fr Metod Mikuž. He was appointed religious adviser to the partisan command of Slovenia in time for Christmas celebrations in partisan territory.

At the very end of 1942, opinion in Slovenia was in a state of confusion. Even the civil war had subsided as a result of the last Italian operation and of the OF's change of tactics. The OF had not managed to set up a real 'liberation front', nor had the educated élite yet gathered into a real 'anti-communist front'. Everybody believed that the Western Allies would soon land. People seemed to think that Mihailović and the KPJ were secretly working together on a deception plan to confuse the Italians, or that one of the two would eliminate the other, before the landing. A very muddled public opinion still had a large uncommitted centre.

The conquerors had both destroyed Yugoslavia as a state and set its components against each other. An infernal cycle of massacres had been started by the ustashas against the Serbs of the NDH. The latter had risen in self-defence, as chetniks and partisans who had gone on, there and elsewhere, to try and eliminate each other and their supporters, while facing brutal periodic anti-insurgent operations organised by the Wehrmacht.[29] The occupation used repressive methods, mainly on the Serb population, but without sufficient manpower, that created an environment favourable to the propagation of a revolutionary war. Both Mihailović, who represented the exiled Yugoslav government in London, and the KPJ, which was part of the Communist International, believed that the German Reich would eventually lose the war and that Yugoslavia would be restored in one way or another. The communists fought a revolutionary war in a

---

29 According to German military sources, German anti-insurgent operations in Serbia and the NDH between August 1941 and August 1942 resulted in 49,724 killed in combat and in reprisals.

shifting pattern, but with a fanatic drive to power. It took them time to realise—not necessarily everywhere at the same time—that they had to appear as a broader patriotic movement in order to acquire and retain the support of non-communist followers, but their object was always to destroy all those who opposed the transformation of their war of liberation into one for the establishment of KPJ rule. For that reason, they endeavoured always to force their domestic opponents into extremes, and to cause conflict between and within them. In 1942 their military skills were still in infancy, but when they held a territory they quickly learnt how to set up what Djilas later described as 'the germ of a government'.[30] Tito enjoyed strong outside support from the Soviet Union, which besides being the bastion and the centre of communism, was also Russia, the elder Slav brother. Even when it could not provide material aid, it gave moral and propaganda backing. Even when it was not satisfied, it did not say so publicly.

The communists' opponents were divided and localised. The outright separatists, who had wanted the destruction of Yugoslavia and who had placed themselves under the protection of the Axis Powers, were inimical to one another, and only enjoyed what limited authority was granted to them by their protectors. In principle, General Mihailović was the representative in the occupied and partitioned homeland of the legitimate government of Yugoslavia exiled in Allied London. His authority rested on an illusion of strength at the end of 1942. In fact he was a commander with no troops under his direct command, who controlled a resistance network in Serbia, and who believed that the communist-led partisans had been practically defeated because this is what he could ascertain from where he was. Further west from eastern Bosnia and Herzegovina, in the Italian territory, in the rest of the NDH and in Slovenia, he did not really know what the situation was. Fed hopeful information, he was confident that he would eventually control the spontaneously generated and self-appointed local chetnik commanders. The Allies—the Western Allies—would do the rest. Mihailović and all those who acknowledged his command,

---

30 Djilas, *Wartime*, 93.

however formally, reasoned that the real struggle against the Axis was being fought in Africa and in Russia, and that meanwhile there was not much they could do to help. They readied themselves for the final battle—against the communists, and against the retreating occupiers when the Allies eventually appeared.

The British, who had practically built up Mihailović, continued to back him until the middle of 1942, on the grounds that he was the most suitable rallying point for all Yugoslavs opposed to the Axis and loyal to the Yugoslav ideal. Simon Trew shows how, by the beginning of 1943, the emphasis had shifted to his being the only alternative to communist chaos in Yugoslavia.[31] How much did the Allies really know then about the situation in Yugoslavia? The Yugoslav government found it difficult to maintain independent links. Mihailović and his government usually had to communicate through British channels. Rapotec had been sent out from Cairo by the command of Yugoslav troops in the Middle East in coordination with the British Special Operations Executive (SOE), on a mission to get a clearer picture of the situation. Between January and July 1942, he was in Split, Zagreb, Mostar and Belgrade. He returned to Cairo with codes, microfilms and messages from a variety of sources, and very realistic views of the kaleidoscopic situation he had found. But not much of what he had to report was passed on to London, as if it were not to the liking of those who debriefed him. The Americans still left the Balkans to the British who, from January 1942, sent in more SOE missions, to Dalmatia and to Bosnia, to see who was resisting. Tito did not like them. He believed the British wanted to force the struggle against the occupiers at whatever cost and to their own benefit, or worse, that they were out to encourage the chetniks against the partisans. However, he was clever enough (after having consulted the Comintern) to use these British missions to tell them extensively about the active resistance of his partisans and the dastardly collaboration of his opponents. At least in Cairo, SOE knew of the Italian connections of local command-ers who acknowledged Mihailović, and of links between the JVO in

---

31 Trew, *Britain, Mihailović and the Chetniks*, 187.

Serbia and the Nedić administration; they did not disapprove, or at least did not worry about it. SOE was a subversion agency rather than an information agency.

There were other sources of British intelligence, particularly in the western territories of Yugoslavia, of which less is known than of SOE, and there was the decrypting of enemy signals. This was far from being systematic or all-revealing since, to quote Sir Michael Howard, 'some of [the signals traffic was read] most of the time and most of it some of the time'.[32] The British at that time had a fairly balanced, albeit very incomplete, view of the situation. Decrypts indicated that the partisans were active in areas known to be outside Mihailović's control, in central and northern Bosnia, in northern Croatia and in Slovenia. There was knowledge of the feelings of many Italian officials in the Yugoslav lands, the realisation that Mihailović avoided serious clashes with the occupation forces as he conserved his forces to strike when the time was right, and the understanding that Axis reprisals caused more damage to the country than the partisans caused to the Axis.

The Soviets, who had their own sources of information, from Tito's reports, from their legation in Sofia and from independent informers, operated a drastic change of policy in mid-1942, when their media turned against Mihailović, accusing him of having been in touch with the Nedić government and with the Italian military. The change was linked to discussions held on the Anglo-Soviet Treaty and the urgency of the second front. It was an interesting coincidence that the Soviets publicised their charges against Mihailović in *Soviet War News* on 12 August, the day when Churchill arrived in Moscow to explain to Stalin that there would be no second front in Europe until 1943. If the Western Allies could not yet provide necessary diversions of German troops on the scale required by the Soviets, they had at least to get more German troops in the Balkans. Mihailović and his movement remained important, but he had to be

---

32 Michael Howard, in a review article of Anthony Cave Brown's *Bodyguard of Lies*, in *The Times Literary Supplement*, 28 May 1976.

better controlled and incited to greater activity immediately, while the partisans' value in keeping Axis troops busy in areas far away from Mihailović's sphere could no longer be ignored. Some at the Foreign Office may have secretly hoped that the partisans might be wiped out, and accepted that they had not. Some in the Intelligence Service may have already formed the opinion that the partisans were likely to play a leading rôle in fixing German troops, and become the dominant force at the end of the war.

The war moved on at the end of 1942. With Allied victories at Stalingrad and in North Africa, interest in the Balkans increased and the mood in the peninsula changed. Everybody seemed to be expecting—fearing or hoping as the case may be—an Allied landing in the near future, preferably on the Adriatic coast. Reading their signals at least gave some idea of what the Germans feared the Allies would do, and made it possible for the Allies to play on these fears through deception.

1. Belgrade, 27 March 1941. Demonstrators with portraits of King Peter heading for central Belgrade. On that day a military coup proclaimed Peter II of age, thus bringing to an end the regency and the government that had adhered to the Tripartite Pact two days earlier. Hitler immediately gave orders for Yugoslavia to be destroyed 'with merciless brutality'.

2. Guerrillas leading German prisoners, somewhere in German-occupied Serbia in September 1941. Received in London by the Yugoslav government in exile, the photograph was captioned as 'Serbian chetniks leading German war prisoners' (specifically through the village of Koštunići, near Ravna Gora).

3. The German military go into counter-action. This photograph, similarly received in London at the time and apparently taken by a hidden bystander, shows the rounding up of hostages in a town in Serbia in October 1941.

4. Cazin, northwest Bosnia, July 1941. As the ustashas lost control of vast tracks of their Independent State of Croatia, Italian forces were slow to withdraw, and then returned to specific areas, to end the insurgency in the hinterland of Italy's new Dalmatian coastline. They launched a propaganda campaign to convince the population they had come as protectors.

5. Drvar, western Bosnia, September 1941. Most of the insurgents, who had risen against the ustashas, were not interested in taking on the Italians. However, in Drvar, a small industrial centre where the communists had set up a well-organized base, Italian troops moved in and took away captured insurgents. Tito would set up his headquarters in Drvar in February 1944.

ДОЛЕ КРАЉ

6. Belgrade, 14 January 1945. Demonstrators with portraits of Marshal Tito and 'Down with the King' banners heading for central Belgrade. Back in liberated Belgrade, Tito had made final arrangements in November 1944 with Šubašić, the last prime minister of the government in exile, for King Peter to delegate his prerogative to a regency, and for a joint government to organise the transition to a postwar régime.

4

THE ALLIES DO NOT COME;
THE ITALIANS WITHDRAW
1943

In Expectation of an Allied Landing

With the Allied victories at Stalingrad and in North Africa at the end
of 1942, interest in the Balkans increased; the mood in the peninsula
changed. An assault on 'Fortress Europe' was expected and prepared.
The Italians knew they could not defend both Italy and the Balkans,
and wanted to repatriate troops. However, the Germans saw Italy
as more difficult to invade, whereas the Balkans were an area where
the Western Allies would want to block the Reich's supplies and bar
the way to communism. Yugoslavia's partisans had by then found a
safe base in the Independent State of Croatia (NDH). Along with
pro-Allied anti-communist armed groups, they became a concern
for the Germans, who wanted to destroy all native enemies, real
and potential, before an Anglo-American landing. Allied planning
undertook to feed such fears; deception operations were designed
to divert attention from real invasion plans. Massive anti-insurgent
action in the Balkans was, for Germany, a way to keep Italy involved
and a response to Allied 'deception'. Mihailović looked forward to a
landing, to trigger the general rising that he believed was an essential part of Allied plans. Tito dreaded it, as a reactionary factor that
would team up with Mihailović to frustrate the Peoples' Liberation
Movement (NOP). There is anecdotal evidence that Birčanin in Split
was told as early as September 1942 to husband his resources and to
provide information on troops, installations, communications and

shipping, in anticipation of a landing. At his trial, Mihailović stated that Colonel S.W. Bailey of Special Operations Executive, when he had been parachuted to his headquarters in December 1942, led him to understand that there would be a landing and that the partisans were to be eliminated. With or without encouragement, Mihailović wanted Tito roundly defeated before the landing, by any means—and vice versa.

The Germans needed to have full control of NDH forces, which Pavelić had to accept. Hitler also wanted to subordinate the Italian Supersloda to the German SE Command. More 'political' than his predecessor Ambrosio, Roatta had realised that he could not pursue a policy that antagonized the German ally. For a start, he spoke German and thus did not have to speak French to the German generals. He also set himself to improve relations with the NDH government and to tone down the pro-Serb tendencies of his staff and commanders. His rhetoric was tough. However, he immediately faced a German proposal to take over more territory. Without reinforcements his only way of minimising the military problem was to split the rebels. Hitler did not trust Roatta: the commander of Supersloda had equipped rebels whom the Allies acknowledged as part of a resistance movement; he intended to reduce again Italian-occupied territory and let these rebels take over in anticipation of an Allied landing. In December at a series of top-level meetings, the Germans brought home to the Italians the dangers of their relations with chetniks. Hitler said there was no alternative to destroying all 'chetniks' (meaning all insurgents) with the utmost brutality. He then imposed the most determined cycle of operations in the Yugoslav lands, to take place in January-March 1943; the Italian Supreme Command entrusted General Löhr and his SE Command with coordinating the action.

Hitler's Directive 47 of 28 December 1942 instructed Löhr to pacify the region once and for all, and to destroy all bands in cooperation with the Italian Second Army. Löhr's plan would be carried out in several phases: operation 'Weiss I' to surround and destroy the partisans in western Bosnia and Lika; 'Weiss II' to push the survivors into a trap further south where they would be annihilated, at the same time as the chetniks of the Italian zone were disarmed; finally 'Schwarz' to destroy all armed bands in Sandžak and Montenegro. Four German divisions and associated NDH units would press from the north, while three Italian divisions would block the way to the south. In total contradiction to what had been agreed (and seen by them as a humiliation), Italian generals speeded up deliveries of arms to the MVAC before the start of operations. They wanted to place them on the partisans' anticipated routes, so as to bear the brunt of the fighting and to widen the gulf between chetniks and partisans. Hitler had insisted with Mussolini that all bands had to be destroyed with their dependants and supporters. Berlin saw it in the light of the expected landing, which would have enabled Mihailović to emerge as head of a nationwide rising in the rear, threatening communications and mines. German Military Intelligence assessed him as being first at that time, among the various armed movements of the ex-Yugoslav lands, in terms of leadership, armament, organisation and activity. He headed a Serb-based pan-Yugoslav movement; he was part of a government in the Allied coalition, with British liaison officers attached to him. Italian Military Intelligence was rather less sanguine. Mihailović's movement was anti-communist and anti-Axis, but its wait-and-see attitude reduced its vitality and sapped its prestige. Eventually, by the end of February, Mussolini promised that he would deal with the danger.

He replaced Roatta with Robotti as part of a general 'changing of the guard' in February 1943.[1] Robotti had been tough in Slovenia, but did not consider any more than Roatta that he had enough troops to handle communists and nationalists at the same time. Both sensed the danger that the chetniks, if they suspected they were about to be dropped, would make common cause with the partisans. Roatta

---

[1] Ambrosio replaced Marshal Ugo Cavallero as Chief of the General Staff of the Supreme Command. In June, Roatta returned to the post of Chief of the Army General Staff.

had received Jevdjević again to test him on his reliability. Jevdjević had assured him that both Mihailović and the Yugoslav government in London were opposed to the partisans; that the Allies wanted all insurgent movements to unite around the most important and the most 'Yugoslav'; that all attempts to bring together Mihailović and the communists had failed; that the chetniks, whatever their present differences, would form a coherent armed force by the end of the conflict. If the Axis won, they would at least have preserved their land from bolshevism, and could encourage Germany and Italy to accept the existence of a small Serbia. If the Allies won, they would create a greater Serbia, and there would be no objection to Italy holding on to some non-Serb districts. He also spoke of the close links Tito had with the NDH administration and army. Roatta refused to discuss politics; he did not accept Jevdjevic's statements at their face value. However, he needed the chetniks' cooperation; they were better than the Domobrans who increasingly provided recruits and weapons for the partisans, not to mention the ustashas who created more rebels than they eliminated. He tried to keep 'his' chetniks under stricter control, by confusing their commanders as to his intentions, and by sending some of their more 'Mihailovićist' officers back to prisoner-of-war camps in Italy. Although he never shared longer-term thoughts with them, he was encouraged by Jevdjević and Birčanin to think that anti-communist Serbs could be useful friends whatever the outcome of the war.

Fed up with Italian equivocations, the Germans actually went ahead in December. The Italians were told that they were expected to execute not only rebels, but also passive populations who had contacts with chetniks, and that they were to use their own chetniks to ensnare and kill Mihailović. On 16 December Hitler had given orders to shoot everybody caught in insurgent areas. Glaise convinced Löhr and General Rudolf Lüters, the newly-appointed commander of German troops in the NDH, to shoot only those actually suspected of being rebels. Eventually the Germans passively accepted that the Italians would use the MVAC alongside their own troops, and that no NDH armed units would be sent into Serb-inhabited territory. The fate of the non-combatant population and that of the chetniks was not settled. Weiss I was not a success. For the Italians, it postponed their intended contraction, caused disproportionate losses, resulted in conflicts with the NDH authorities, and disturbed their almost cosy relationship with the chetniks. They suspected that the Germans had deliberately pushed rebels towards the coastal region, and even planned the operation as a cover to take over territory. The chetniks turned out to be the stumbling block between German plans and Italian behaviour on the ground. The Germans saw Italian generals as being monarchists rather than fascists, and suspected them of trying to set up links with Yugoslav monarchists, for a new post-war Italo-Yugoslav understanding, and a channel to the British. They complained that Italian generals pursued a different policy from that which Mussolini had accepted.

In the spring of 1943, the partisan command had already made preparations to go back to Montenegro, thence to penetrate into Serbia, to destroy the chetniks before the Allies landed, and to be nearer the advancing Red Army. Weiss merely anticipated Tito's move. The withdrawal was carried out in haste, in winter weather. Bihać fell on 29 January 1943, and the partisans' territory was mostly taken over, with numerous casualties, especially among the civilian population. By exploiting the bad coordination between the Axis partners, and the NOP's infiltration into the NDH apparatus, Tito managed to get out of the Germans' way. Not only was the main partisan hospital and some 3,000 other wounded also evacuated, but the population at large was encouraged to withdraw as well, rather than face retribution. An operational group of the best and most experienced units had been formed to push through. The partisan command of Croatia was left behind, to deal with the local chetniks. It played on the Croats' anti-chetnik feelings, and specifically on anti-Mihailović prejudices, as more Domobran officers sought contacts with both movements. In Lika, partisans concentrated on fighting chetniks, while in Kordun, ustashas and Croat communists settled accounts, with local Serbs caught between the two. Although the partisans had not been eliminated, Weiss I was said to have been completed by 15 February. The partisans had been dislocated, but they remained a cohesive force. The Germans pressed for accelerated action (and the disarming of chetniks by the Italians) in the next phase.

Coincidentally, Mihailović had also made ambitious plans for a 'march on Bosnia' to destroy the partisan concentration, and for subsequent operations when the Allies landed. The chetniks of Herzegovina, northern Dalmatia and Lika—including the MVAC—with help from Montenegro would set up a corridor through the Italian zone to the partisans' 'soviet republic', encircle and destroy it. This would give Mihailović more control of the Adriatic hinterland, and create a bridgehead for the Allies. Muslims and Croats would be induced not to act against the Yugoslav Army of the Homeland (JVO), and even to join it. The Italians would be neutralised by vague promises, encouraged to surrender, disarmed if necessary. After the landing, operations would move on to capture Split and Sarajevo, and then push further west and north, with help from Serbia. The plan was finalised in early December at Mihailović's headquarters in Montenegro. Operations were to start on 5 January 1943. Major Zaharije Ostojić, who had come from Cairo with the first SOE mission, was put in charge, with an operational command in Kalinovik, eastern Bosnia. The plan had many flaws. For a start, Mihailović's design to create a united movement had come to little. The further west he sent his nominees, the more they were ignored, sent packing, and even eliminated. Most Serbs in the NDH had either rallied to the partisans, or made arrangements with occupation or NDH authorities to survive in a power struggle with the communists, and were determined to pursue retribution against Croats and Muslims. In Slovenia, as a result of the arrest of officers by the Italians, and of the communists' determination to brook no competition, there were only a few hundred men responding to the JVO command. Even back in Serbia, Mihailović had little more than a staff, cadres, and command fiefdoms with, at the time, little substantial armed following.

The British, the Italians and the Germans overestimated his influence. He himself had acquired an exaggerated sense of his authority. He did not understand that a revolution was under way. He was the representative of his legitimate monarch and government. He believed that the Western Allies could not possibly assist the communists, and so needed him. He could not dissociate himself from those who had tied themselves to occupiers, as his armed strength derived largely from their following. He probably did not even want to, for he believed that they would prove their anti-Axis worth as soon as the Allies landed. Apart from underestimating the partisans' strength, he overestimated the number of chetniks that he could muster and direct. He had faith in his ability to outmanoeuvre the Italian generals by getting the chetnik commanders to extract intelligence, supplies and ammunition for anti-communist operations that would be directed by him and for his benefit, as he prepared to disarm Italian troops as soon as the Allies landed. Various stratagems were tried to threaten the Italians with feigned partisan attacks. Mihailović's nominal subordinates did not follow his orders; they had their own local agenda. They wanted time to obtain supplies, ammunition and transport; they tried to conceal the extent of their deals with the Italians. They quarrelled among themselves, and denounced each other. Tension developed between them, and between them and Mihailović. Having nominated Jevdjević for a high military decoration for services at the time of the 1941 massacres in the NDH, Mihailović did not want the award gazetted, and almost came to the point of repudiating him. Most of this was known to the Italians, whose Military Intelligence deciphered radio messages between Mihailović and his commanders, intermittently from November 1942, and more regularly from March to July 1943. In February 1943, the Germans contributed their stack of intercepts to convince Rome of Mihailović's blatantly pro-Allied sympathies.

The chetniks' attitude towards Muslims and Croats was full of contradictions. Mihailović had issued orders to prevent the looting and killing of innocent villagers, as he tried to exploit alienation from the NDH, obtain Muslim cooperation and establish Domobran contacts. He tried to set up Muslim units under Major Fehim Musakadić and a few other Muslim officers. However, chetnik commanders on their way to western Bosnia wanted to clear their rear of threats from, among others, pro-ustasha, pro-communist, pro-Italian or simply anti-Serb Muslims. With or without orders issued in (or above) Mihailović's name, they destroyed and killed, forcing Muslims to flee in fear. Djurišić reported how many hundreds of militiamen, and how many thousands of old men, women and children he had killed in the region, but Mihailović was unable or unwilling to stop the massacres. He had to prevent the partisans from getting into areas where he expected the Allies, and for that he needed the cooperation of all chetniks. Caught between Mihailović's orders, the Italians' demands, and their own interests, the chetnik captains had performed poorly. Their relations with the Italians had suffered.

As the Germans locally were mainly concerned with mines and rail communications through Sarajevo, and the Italians with holding on to some key points such as Mostar, the partisans were let through to the chetniks for mutual elimination before they were all rounded up. Tito's men suffered great losses but they got through to the river Neretva by mid-February. Mihailović's intended march to the west had come to nothing. His orders were now to stop Tito's forces from crossing the river. Ostojić radically changed his tune towards the Muslims, presenting his men as brothers coming to defend them from the communists, but he complained that the chetniks were prone to drifting home with their loot, and not very keen to confront the proletarian brigades. Unable to secure a crossing of the river, Tito ordered the capture of Italian-held Prozor which blocked the way. The town fell to the partisans, and its garrison, which had refused to surrender, was put to death, except for the drivers, who were spared to transport the booty. Italian prisoners were more generally turned into a 'lower class' of underfed hard-labour workers.[2]

At the end of February, 15,000 chetniks were massed on the Herzegovinian heights above the Neretva between Mostar and Kalinovik, to meet the partisans being pushed into the steep valley by the Germans. Mihailović had issued a call-up in his capacity as War Minister. Ostojić asked Jevdjević to obtain more supplies from the Italians. As they refused, Ostojić wanted to declare war on them. 'I cannot ask the Italians for arms *and* declare war on them', Jevdjević lamented.[3] After a bloody battle that raged from 27 February to 7 March, the partisans got across. They were surprised by the chetniks' disarray. Mihailović decided to go and take over personally to try and salvage the situation.

In the early months of 1943, the entanglements between the different sides became increasingly complicated. Not only did Italian commanders not believe in large-scale pacification operations, but there were also Germans who had come round to the opinion that the insurgency in the NDH needed a political solution, and the partisans' Supreme Staff were engaged in negotiations with them. In the summer of 1942, at the time of Tito's 'long march' to the west, the partisans had captured a group of German mining technicians from Mostar. They belonged to the Nazi Organisation Todt which ran the bauxite mines in the Italian zone, and were led by Hans Ott, a mining engineer who was also an Abwehr officer. His suggestion that they might be used for an exchange deal had lead to the despatch of an emissary to Zagreb. Glaise von Horstenau, who wanted to test the ground for more than a simple exchange of prisoners, talked to the emissary. The possibility was evoked (though it is not clear who first mentioned it)

---

2 The partisan leadership had heard of the Red Army destroying German garrisons in Russia that had refused the surrender terms offered to them (Djilas, *Wartime*, 218–4).

3 Documents quoted in Kosta Nikolić, *Istorija ravnogorskog pokreta*, II, 123–4.

of the partisans being allowed to withdraw to some area nominally held by the Italians and which was of no importance for the German war effort, where they could deal with the chetniks, while they in turn left the Germans free to mine and export the minerals they needed. Negotiations and prisoner exchanges went on. Glaise was backed by the German minister to Zagreb, Kasche, and by German economic agencies in the NDH, in the hope of a *modus vivendi* south of the river Sava that freed the mines and the Zagreb-Belgrade railway. The partisans' Supreme Staff broached the idea that they should get combatant status according to international conventions.

The following March, in the middle of the greatest fighting around the Neretva, contact was made again after the capture of another group of Germans, including a Major Arthur Strecker, the son of a Vienna university professor who knew Löhr and Glaise. Tito suggested trying again for a prisoner exchange and regular belligerent status. Caught between Germans and chetniks, in expectation of the Allied landing that would turn Mihailović's JVO into the only legitimate force, he was in need of a respite, to get out of the trap, and concentrate on destroying the chetniks. Strecker was sent off to the nearest German divisional commander to ask for delegates to be received for talks. They were Koča Popović, Spanish civil war veteran and commander of the First Proletarian Brigade, Djilas and Vladimir Velebit. The latter was a young communist lawyer from Zagreb, the son of a Yugoslav general and the grandson of an Austro-Hungarian general, who spoke excellent German and who had been involved in previous contacts. They were instructed to deal with the question of prisoners. They were to state that international war rules should be applied to the Peoples' Liberation Army of Yugoslavia (NOVJ, *Narodnooslobodilačka vojska Jugoslavije*). They were to request a suspension of hostilities during negotiations, for humanitarian reasons, but also because the partisans considered the chetniks to be their principal enemy. There followed a longer period of talks, during which there was a de facto ceasefire that lasted for more than six weeks.

Operation Weiss was grinding to an inconclusive end. German commanders were worried by the bauxite mines and the Zagreb-Belgrade rail link; they needed to rest their troops; they did not really want to have to enter the Italians' zone as they had to give their allies some satisfaction in return for their cooperation. Approaches were also made to Mihailović, to obtain undisturbed rail transit from Belgrade to Bulgaria and to Greece, in exchange for thinner occupation coverage. These were turned down by Mihailović, who suspected an attempt to exploit the crisis of confidence between him and the Allies. Löhr approved an informal ceasefire with the partisans while the talks went on. Tito issued orders to stop activity against the Axis in order to concentrate on Mihailović's chetniks, whose captured officers were to be shot on the spot while other ranks were to be disposed of secretly unless they joined the partisans. While Popović had returned to report to Tito, Djilas and Velebit went on to Zagreb, where they were interrogated by German officers supervised by Ott. Velebit was also received by Glaise, who had known his father. Djilas and Velebit went again to Zagreb at the end of March. In the meanwhile, Velebit visited (occasionally disbelieving) partisan commands in Slavonia and in eastern Bosnia, with orders to suspend operations against the Germans, particularly rail communications, to release prisoners, and at times to join Tito's main force.

During their second stay in Zagreb, the partisans' plenipotentiaries again insisted on the recognition of their regular status, and on the futility of further hostilities between them. In fact they asked to be left to fight Mihailović. It is not clear which side first raised the question of what the partisans would do if the British landed, but the emissaries certainly told the Germans they would fight the British if they landed without authorisation.[4] In their determination

---

4 The talks were first referred to in the 1950s, on the basis of their own sources, by Wilhelm Höttl (Walter Hagen, *Die Geheime Front. Organisation, Personen und Aktionen des deutschen Geheimdienstes*, Linz & Vienna, 1950), General Rudolf Kiszling *(Die Kroaten. Der Schickalsweg eines Südslawenvolkes*, Graz & Cologne, 1956) and Stephen Clissold *(Whirlwind. An Account of Marshal Tito's Rise to Power*, London, 1959). In the late 1960s, Ilija Jukić

to take over power, the Communist Party (KPJ) leaders would not have hesitated to oppose the British, if that became necessary. The talks and the ceasefire enabled the partisans to act against the chetnik force that was blocking their way, without in fact making any concrete long-term concessions. The Italians at the same time stopped their logistical help to the chetniks. It made sense for the Germans to suspend hostilities against the partisans while the latter were busy fighting the chetniks, in anticipation of a landing. Glaise and Kasche asked their respective superiors to agree to substantive negotiations. Ribbentrop and Hitler overruled them, and on 29 March 1943 further contacts were forbidden. Mihailović was the first to hear that Tito had been making some arrangements with the Germans, and informed Bailey who reported the information on 22 March; it was not taken seriously. Italian Military Intelligence came to know. Tito had mentioned the exchange of prisoners to the Comintern, but Moscow was quick to understand that more was afoot. It expressed strong dissatisfaction and asked for an explanation. Tito, taken aback by the lack of confidence shown in him, argued that he was receiving no help and had to think of captured fighters and refugees. His guard had been slackened. There had been no formal ceasefire, and when the inconclusive Weiss turned to Schwarz in mid-May, he understood that the respite he had obtained had become a trap.

---

provided hard evidence from German Foreign Ministry sources (*Pogledi na prošlost, sadašnjost i budućnost hrvatskog naroda*, London, 1965) and Ivan Avakumović from captured German military documents (*Mihailović prema nemačkim dokumentima*, London, 1969). The American diplomat and scholar Walter Roberts caused an international incident in 1973 by providing a reconstruction of the talks (*Tito, Mihailović and the Allies, 1941-1945*, New Brunswick NJ). Djilas then told his story in 1977 (*Wartime*). In 1967, the Yugoslav historian Mišo Leković had been officially commissioned to write a full report on the talks, but could not publish his findings until after Tito's death (*Martovski pregovori*, Belgrade, 1985). Koča Popović's version appeared in 1989 in conversations with Aleksandar Nenadović (*Razgovori s Kočom*, 2nd ed. Zagreb), and Velebit's in 2001 (in conversations with Mira Šuvar, *Vladimir Velebit, svjedok historije*, Zagreb) and 2002 (*Tajne i zamke Drugog svjetskog rata*, Zagreb).

Chetnik commanders were aware that their turn would come. German troops were pursuing them, and destroying their bases in eastern Bosnia. Löhr's problem was how to reconcile Hitler's directive to regard them as enemies with insufficient manpower to deal with all rebels, and avoid clashes with chetniks deployed and commanded by Italians against retreating (or advancing) partisans. Anxious to protect the bauxite mines, the Germans had reached a *modus vivendi* with the Italians in the Mostar area: the Italians accepted the presence of German troops, and the Germans accepted the use of chetniks by the Italians, but they soon also clashed with chetnik units there who issued leaflets calling on Serbs to free themselves from the Axis. The chetniks had not been able to prevent the partisans from getting to the Neretva valley, that linked Sarajevo to the coast, but Mihailović still controlled the mountains to the north-east of the river, and his influence extended to the south-east and the Adriatic hinterland. If he could prevent the partisans from getting across, he hoped they would be destroyed by the Italians. However, by late March the Italians did not mind the partisans being diverted into Mihailović-controlled territory, so long as they did not come down to the coast. Rival chetnik commanders followed their own wishes or those of their Italian suppliers rather than Mihailović's; or spent time clearing Sandžak and northern Montenegro of Italian-armed Muslim auxiliaries and of Muslim settlements. The partisans threw themselves against the Herzegovinian and Montenegrin chetniks waiting for them. They eventually crossed the narrow gorge, and the chetniks beat a fighting retreat to the right bank of the Drina. Mihailović's presence had not been able to shore up the defences. As Tito prepared to cross the Drina on 29 March, he repeated orders not to attack Germans, and not to undertake any sabotage on railways. At the same time, Jevdjević considered approaching the Germans for help (indirectly through the Italians), and the Germans were themselves attacking other chetnik units in their rear.

The chetnik defences of Herzegovina had disintegrated, and the Montenegrins were forced back into Montenegro. During the first half of April the partisans' Supreme Staff and their main operational force had broken through into the 'chetnik state' of Montenegro, but they had no military organisation there. The Germans believed that, even if Tito's main force had not been destroyed, it had been so weakened that, pushed into the wilder parts of Montenegro, it would not survive. As Serb irregulars fought each other, Löhr had actually moved on to Operation Schwarz. The aim was to destroy the Montenegrin chetniks, capture Mihailović, and finish off the partisans. Preparations were to be kept secret from the Italians. Incidents would be engineered to justify moving into Italian-occupied territory. An air attack was envisaged on Mihailović's headquarters. 'Brandenburg' units (special operations forces formed in October 1939) disguised as chetniks would be used to capture him (the 'soul of the resistance movement in Serbia'), his staff and his archives (perhaps in order to find something about Allied landing plans). Since 20 April, Mihailović was back at Lipovo and planning to return to Serbia. On 13 May, Löhr informed the Wehrmacht Command of attacks by chetniks, and German forces moved into Herzegovina and Montenegro. The Italians protested and participated in Schwarz with great reluctance. Mihailović managed to leave in time and make his way back to Serbia, but thousands of chetniks were captured.

The situation in Montenegro had never been so confused. The partisans had let the Germans through to attack the chetniks, but exchanged prisoners with the Italians and cooperated informally on issuing passes to civilians; they sometimes sided with chetniks, who were more often than not with the Italians. As he was about to leave, Mihailović met 'his' Montenegrin commanders, and quarrelled with Djurišić. Did the Germans try to induce Djurišić to be 'legalised' in order to help them destroy partisans and 'illegal' chetniks? Did he offer to go and fight on the Eastern Front as a token of his anti-communism? He appears to have mentioned to Mihailović the short-term possibility of assisting the Germans against the partisans, which Mihailović did not even want to contemplate. The fact remains that Djurišić was defending his 'chetnik capital' of Kolašin from a partisan onslaught from the south and the west, when the Germans arrived from the north and the east, and that by making a stand there he contributed to Mihailović's escape. On 14 May, the Germans entered Kolašin with tanks; they captured and disarmed Djurišić and some 2,000 of his men. In spite of extensive searches for him, Mihailović, his staff and the British mission made their way through Sandžak with the help of JVO units from Serbia, and were back on Kopaonik mountain in western Serbia on 24 May.

Lüters had assembled all the troops he could muster, including ethnic German SS and native irregulars. The intention was to turn guerrilla weapons against guerrillas and to terrorise the population, and it was all done in order to disarm and capture Italian-controlled native militias. As Italian troops withdrew from most of the NDH, remaining only in the coastal area and in annexed Dalmatia, Italian generals could but warn the chetniks generally, evacuate individuals, abstain as much as possible from Schwarz and tell them all that they would be regarded as enemies if they resisted the Germans. As many chetniks had lately gathered in towns, without the knowledge or against the will of Italian commanders, they were easily captured, but they were sent to prisoner camps so as not to provoke all-out hostilities. The Italians had roughly classified chetniks as *nostri* ('ours'), Mihailović's and those in between. They protested but had to follow suit, protecting *i nostri* as much as they could, and interning Mihailović's. The Germans and their auxiliaries then turned to pursuing the partisans, and caught up again with them in the mountains of northern Montenegro, where they intended to block them.

In spite of his losses, Tito had been on the verge of realising his objective of defeating the chetniks and moving back into Montenegro when he was surprised by the resumption of the German offensive. His knowledge of what the Germans were doing was sparse until they appeared between the Piva and Tara valleys, and attacked from 17 May with heavy weapons, tanks, planes and special operations detachments. He was furious at the Germans who had lied to his emissaries, and at the latter who had been taken in. He had to work his way back to Bosnia, through mountains slashed by gorges, exposed to the full onslaught of Axis operations after he and the Germans had done their best to destroy the chetnik screen. This time, he had to leave the wounded for the Germans to pick up. The hungry and decimated Italian prisoners who had been used as slave labour were executed. In their struggle for survival, thousands of partisans were killed, more died of disease, and more were captured. Tito, his staff and a force halved to less than 10,000, managed to extricate themselves by crossing the gorge of the Sutjeska, a tributary of the Drina. By the end of June, they were back in the relative safety of the uplands of eastern Bosnia, on NDH territory. The Germans did not pursue them. They had failed again to capture Tito or Mihailović.

It was on 28 February, just before Mihailović's departure for Kalinovik that the 'christening speech' incident took place at Lipovo,[5] when at the end of a long meal following a christening, Mihailović brutally expressed his bitterness about 'perfidious Albion', who required Serbs to fight to their last drop of blood without adequate assistance, so that his main source of supply to date had been the Italians. Since the fall of France, the Serbs were left without any real friends. However, more serious was the statement—as reported by Bailey—that he would turn against the Germans and Italians only after he had dealt with the 'partisans, ustashas, Muslims and Croats'. Mihailović then departed without saying where he was going. The incident signalled a breakdown of confidence between the British mission and Mihailović's staff, and caused angry responses from both the British and the Yugoslav government. The British and Mihailović, and even the exiled government in London and its War Minister at Lipovo, were disappointed in what they expected of each other. Allied deception plans had successfully deceived everyone but, far from uniting native anti-Axis forces, they had given fresh impetus to the civil war.

---

5 This has been analysed by Heather Williams, *Parachutes, Patriots and Partisans. The Special Operations Executive and Yugoslavia, 1941-1945*, London, 2003: 110–12.

The Casablanca and Washington conferences in January and May had decided that Mediterranean operations would take priority over the cross-Channel landing in France, delayed until late spring 1944. More plans, and more guerrilla activity in the Balkans, were called for to cover real intentions and deceive Hitler, but also to demonstrate to Stalin that the Anglo-Americans were doing all they could to relieve pressure on the Soviet Union in spite of the delayed second front. Stalin feared his allies might let the Russians fight the Germans to mutual exhaustion, and the Western Allies could not exclude the possibility that Stalin, once he had turned Hitler out of Russia, might leave the West and Germany to fight it out. By exploiting the situation in Yugoslavia, Britain could force Germany to keep troops there that could otherwise be used on the Russian front or in north-western Europe; it could lead Hitler astray on the location of the assault, and give some satisfaction to Stalin. Churchill, who had known since the autumn of 1941 of the action of 'partisans' in areas where Mihailović had little or no organisation, was no longer prepared to accept arrangements with the Italian military. Liaison with Mihailović was increased, but his movement had been so praised and so inflated by British propaganda that the reality seen by SOE officers was below expectations. At the same time, Mihailović and his officers were puzzled that the reinforced British presence did not signal large-scale parachuted help. The 'christening speech' expressed the growing suspicion, fanned by both communist and German propaganda, that Britain was just using Yugoslav (i.e. Serb) flesh and blood to further its own ends.

Bailey had been sent to report back on the situation before further decisions were taken. He had arrived when preparations were being made for the march on Bosnia, and understood that it was not possible to reconcile chetniks and partisans as they tried to occupy the same territory. He had expected Mihailović to disperse the partisans, and then turn to vigorous action against the Axis. However, by April it was clear to British Military Intelligence that it was Mihailović who had suffered a major reversal at the hands of the partisans. Eventually, it was decided to send more missions to Mihailović's units, but he was told in May that all existing arrangements with the Italians must cease, while future exceptions had to be cleared with Bailey. The guerrillas operating in areas outside his control would also be contacted. As far back as the summer of 1942, the green light had been given to SOE to contact the partisans, but it was not before April 1943 that missions began to arrive to them in eastern Bosnia. The man chosen to go to Tito's command was Captain F.W.D. Deakin, who was not an old Yugoslavia hand, but an Oxford don who had been research assistant for Churchill's historical works. His mission was dropped in May just as the partisan force was extricating itself from the German trap. Tito reaped the advantages of British impatience with Mihailović, and of the first favourable impressions of British officers, but the communist leaders were highly suspicious. They asked the Comintern to check and double-check on the mission. Yet they realised that its presence was politically useful in a region only just vacated by Mihailović, as it conferred legitimacy in the eyes of the local population. Tito and his lieutenants did not want to be recognised as merely an additional or more active guerrilla movement aiding Allied strategic objectives. They wanted to be formally associated, and they wanted Mihailović clearly rejected, before the impending landing.

In Expectation of Italy's Withdrawal

The Italian military estimated the numbers of chetniks in their zone of the NDH at over 20,000, and almost as many in Montenegro, before Weiss, falling to 3,000 and 5,000 respectively, after Schwarz. Two thirds of them were MVAC. Through them Mihailović had been able to obtain much larger quantities of armament than from British drops, but tightly-controlled Italian supplies did not enable chetniks to carry out extended operations on their own, and the partisans anyhow captured or otherwise obtained more from the Domobrans. The British did not mind, and Mihailović was careful to stress to chetnik commanders who did have Italian contacts that they did so on their own responsibility. Italian field and staff officers suspected that their generals wanted to find a direct line to Mihailović, in order to get to the Allies. At the turn of the year, feelers were indeed put out, by Roatta and Pirzio Biroli, and simply forwarded by Mihailović.

Trifunović Birčanin died in February 1943; his death decapitated whatever organisation the JVO had ever had in Dalmatia and in the Italian zone of the NDH. Jevdjević and Djujić were rivals for his succession. The Serb and 'Yugoslav nationalist' Croat intellectuals and businessmen in Split who had tried to act as his political advisers and whom Italian Military Intelligence dismissed as 'the Yugoslav drawing-room resistance', were worried. They appealed to Mihailović to send a personality who could take over in his name and repair the situation. He sent Colonel Mladen Žujović, who in civilian life had been a lawyer and a prominent member of the Serbian Cultural Club (SKK). Žujović arrived in April under an assumed name, with an ambitious remit—to wind up the policy of collaboration with the Italian military and to set up a real underground JVO organisation in order to receive the Allies, to stop the drift to the partisans, to seek out willing Domobran officers and HSS politicians, and set up a Yugoslav political committee for Dalmatia, Kordun, Lika and western Bosnia. Whatever his instructions and his intentions, he had to adapt to circumstances, and generally act as local actors wanted him to. All he managed to do was meet some Croat officers and politicians, keep a state of mutual toleration with the communists in towns, and recruit a few hundred young Croat volunteers who were sent to chetnik units in Lika and Bosnia. Local chetniks did not like his interference or his new line. In June, the Italian police arrested Mihailović's delegate, whose identity it had discovered (or known since his arrival), along with most of the Yugoslav officers living in Split. Was it because local chetniks wanted to get Žujović out of the way, or because Italians wanted to contact Mihailović? Did he see any Italian general? Italian sources have not yielded any such evidence. Žujović was released after Mussolini's fall, and went into hiding. In mid-July, Italian Military Intelligence had intercepted radio-messages between

Ostojić, Baćović and Mihailović. The chetnik commanders reported that Djilas had approached them on behalf of the partisans' Supreme Staff, to see whether they would agree to common action against the occupiers, in view of the fact that a new government in exile was about to be formed without Mihailović. Mihailović, suspecting an attempt by the communists to neutralise or to separate these chetnik commanders, had reacted angrily, threatening to exclude them from the JVO if they pursued such contacts.

As part of the 'changing of the guard' in February 1943, Bastianini was recalled to Rome to become under-secretary for Foreign Affairs, and replaced as governor of Dalmatia by Francesco Giunta, an old Triestine fascist irredentist, who nevertheless decided to put an immediate end to any more 'prestige' spending in a territory that Italy might have to give up. Italy was by then waiting for Mussolini to go and the war to end. Its occupation troops were left without motivation or adequate means. Yet few deserted; it was after the Allies had landed in Sicily on 10 July and Mussolini had been removed from power on 25 July that morale suddenly collapsed. Germany had been making preparations to cope with Italy's withdrawal, and continued to fear an Allied invasion. The Comintern had ceased to exist in May, as a gesture to reassure the Western Allies, but relations between Moscow and communist parties continued through the International Department of the Soviet Communist Party. Tito still referred to it as the 'Comintern'. On the eve of the landing in Sicily, the 'Comintern' had advised him to go slow, in order to preserve his forces for action at a later date. On the morrow of Mussolini's fall, Mihailović gave instructions for action to begin in the Italian zone as soon as the capitulation had been announced—to disarm the occupation troops and avoid sharing the booty with the communists, to occupy the coast in order to help the Allies when they landed and to block their contacts with the partisans. General Giuseppe Pièche, on a roving mission for the Ministry of Foreign Affairs, wrote that the Jews were 'the only people who, generally speaking, had not caused us trouble'.[6] The Italian authorities had tried to limit the number of those seeking refuge in their zone, and managed to resist increasingly pressing German demands to hand them over. From the end of 1942 they had begun to assemble Jews, to show that something was being done. In February 1943 they started to move as many as they could to the island of Arbe (Rab), which was pre-war Italian territory in the upper Adriatic. Robotti, when appointed to Supersloda, was told by Mussolini to invent all the excuses he could, but not to hand a single Jew over to the Germans.[7]

In early May, Italian troops had resumed control of Montenegro in a manner of speaking. They were back in their urban strongholds. The Germans retained some control over a broad belt of eastern Montenegro from Sandžak to Albania. The remaining chetniks returned to their clan bases, in spite of Mihailović's attempts to form flying brigades to cover the approaches to Serbia. Once back in Serbia, he had told the rival commanders to avoid any further contacts with either Germans or Italians, and again sent the Slovene Perhinek as his delegate to sort things out. Perhinek found that they were only interested in defending their patch from the communists, and returned to Mihailović. The Italians then finally turned against them or at least against 'Mihailović's', fearing an attack in their rear on his orders. Mussolini directed Pirzio Biroli to issue an order on 28 May to offer a reward of 1 million lire for the capture of Tito, and half a million for Mihailović. The arrangements with Djukanović were denounced. An operation was launched to clear north-eastern Montenegro of chetniks. Many 'nationalists' were arrested, interned or disarmed. The outright pro-Italian secessionist Greens in the Cetinje

---

6   23 October 1942, quoted by Davide Rodogno, *Il nuovo ordine mediterraneo. Le politiche di occupazione dell'Italia fascista in Europa, 1940-1943*, Turin, 2003: 455.

7   By 25 July 1943, there were 2,661 Jews on the island of Arbe. On 19 August, confusing directives were given by the Foreign Ministry that, in the event of a withdrawal, they should be left free to go or to stay, but not allowed to move to Italy in large numbers. Most eventually left or were freed by the partisans, but some 300 were deported by the Germans.

area were listened to again, so that they were used by the communists as a channel to feed Italian suspicions of chetniks, after a resumption of executions of communists in reprisal for the executions of Italian prisoners by the partisans.

What was Pirzio Biroli up to? Mihailović's chetniks believed he was 'a friend of the English [*engleski čovek*]'. Lüters thought that he was still in touch with the chetniks, and probably with the British. Called back to Rome for consultations, he was contacted by a young relative and fellow cavalry officer, on behalf of the underground Partito d'Azione, who told him that in view of Mussolini's imminent fall, he should stop all operations against guerrillas and set up secret contacts with Tito. Pirzio Biroli excused himself on the grounds that he was an old-fashioned soldier who could but carry out orders. On 20 July, a few days before Mussolini's fall, he was replaced in Montenegro by General Curio Barbasetti di Prun. As all awaited the final outcome, the Italians ceased to be either protectors or providers.

In the mixed Slav-Albanian and Orthodox-Muslim areas straddling Montenegro and Italian-extended Albania, the situation had worsened. Responding disproportionately to Tirana-backed provocations, chetniks had gone on the rampage, wrecking the relatively successful attempts of Italian civil administrators backed by the Cetinje Governatorato and the Rome Foreign Ministry to hold a balanced peace between ethnic groups. In March Jacomoni was replaced as King's Lieutenant in Tirana by General Alberto Pariani, and in May the Germans assumed control of most of the region. It was the turn of Albanian authorities and militias to turn to violence.

In Italy's Ljubljana Province, General Gastone Gambara had succeeded Robotti as commander of the XIth Army Corps. A nucleus of active partisans remained, against considerable odds—Italian military operations, the anti-communist Catholicism of the peasantry, the distaste of urban people of all classes for guerrilla warfare. Italian control of Ljubljana had become too efficient, along with MVAC domination of the surrounding countryside, for the Liberation Front's (OF) communist leadership to operate in and through the city. Early in 1943 it had moved south to the Kočevski Rog uplands. Disagreements with the remaining non-communists in the OF—Edvard Kocbek's Christian Socialist group and the Liberal left—were formally 'smoothed out' in such a way that the Front was fully turned into a 'front' organisation for the Communist Party in Slovenia. At the same time, the KPJ adopted a new strategy for Slovenia. It adapted its Yugoslavism locally to the cult of Slovenian 'statehood'. It maintained a tenuous link with the Catholic Church through Kocbek and Fr Mikuž,[8] and moved towards a more moderate approach to the MVAC and the clergy rank-and-file. It also benefited from the presence among the partisans of the enthusiastic and eccentric Major William Jones whose SOE mission had arrived in May.[9]

Mihailović's JVO was also reactivated in Slovenia, through his Belgrade cell and with money received from the government in exile by way of Switzerland. Novak had a staff. It issued propaganda and gathered intelligence, sent out through Vauhnik, essentially on German military plants in northern Slovenia. From February 1943, he also began to set up military units, popularly known as the Blue Guard. As regular Yugoslav army officers were being sent home again to Slovenia from Italian prisoner-of-war camps, Novak got some of the younger ones to come out as cadres for the 300-400 men he eventually turned into an organised underground force. The Italians seemed to know, and not mind, considering them as a Western fifth column and one that, for the time being, was not attacking them. Mihailovićist propaganda explained it as preparing, in agreement with the Yugoslav government and the Allies, for the forthcoming large-scale movement to be undertaken by the Anglo-Americans.

---

8 Metod Mikuž had been formally but discreetly suspended *a divinis* by the Church authorities in June 1943.

9 He signed all correspondence and leaflets as ' W.M. Jones, D.C.M. and Bar, Major'—the usual form to indicate an additional award of the Distinguished Conduct Medal, but a mysterious cipher to Italians and Yugoslavs alike, especially when translations were attempted.

Novak's relations with the Slovenian Alliance (SZ) were difficult. He pressed the Alliance to allow more MVAC to join his units and to start action against occupation troops. He tried to influence directly the cadres of the MVAC in Ljubljana Province—some 6,000 by August 1943. But the SZ did not want to release men, and sabotaged Novak's work. Its propaganda portrayed Slovenia as being caught in the cross fire between occupation troops and communist partisans, and stressed the need for strong self-defence units against the communist-led OF. The overall attitude was that there was no point in opposing the Italians at a time when they were obviously on their way out, if not about to turn to the Western Allies who would come to Slovenia and certainly not support the communists. With the fall of Mussolini, competing forces jockeyed for position. Partisan attacks on occupation troops were reduced, but were successful in diverting Novak's intended move south in the direction of the expected landing. The Germans used the pretext of a partisan attack on a German train to move a division through Ljubljana Province to the rail approaches to Udine, Gorizia and Trieste.

Italy had practically given up on the NDH. For the military, what 'pacification' it had achieved had been cancelled by the ustashas' insistence to return to 'pacified areas'. Even the German military realised that the ustasha state no longer helped German interests, that its armed forces were turning into an arsenal for the communists, and that it would be better for everyone (as Glaise told Pavelić in January) if all concentration camps in the NDH were closed and their inmates sent to work in Germany. Löhr ventured to ask Hitler that Pavelić be removed, the Ustasha Movement disbanded, Kasche recalled, and Glaise appointed as special Reich plenipotentiary with executive authority and command over all troops. What Hitler decided on 10 March was to entrust Himmler with extensive powers to ensure lasting pacification. This was the culmination of the SS leader's long struggle against the Armed Forces Command, to add the Balkans to his organisation's sphere of interest, with authority over all the Volksdeutsche. His appointed plenipotentiary for the NDH was SS

General Konstantin Kammerhofer, an Austrian nazi who ensured that public security was fully subjugated to German requirements.

In addition to the SS 'Prinz Eugen' division of Yugoslav Volksdeutsche, set up in 1942 and now brought to the NDH, Kammerhofer established a German gendarmerie. It would be recruited by voluntary enlistment, with a core of 6,000 ethnic Germans, topped up with Croats taken from the NDH army and police, and anybody else to fill the quota of 20,000. It would swear allegiance to Hitler, and be used in areas of engagement to be determined by the German authorities. Pavelić had to accept. He had been received by the Führer on 24 April 1942 and subjected to a lengthy monologue, which emphasised the need to pacify Croatia so as to secure German bauxite supplies and communications, and free German troops for more important tasks. Hitler's anti-Serb remarks had encouraged Pavelić to return immediately to a higher level of terror, which had been reduced since November. German officers on the spot acted to stop ustasha violence. When in August General Lothar Rendulic was transferred from Russia to the command of the newly-formed second Panzer Army for the NDH and Serbia, he too saw that the ustashas were an obstacle to fulfilling Hitler's brief—to control with as few German troops as possible. With twenty more Wehrmacht divisions he would be able—he said—to 'kill everybody in this country',[10] but he did not have them, and Hitler wanted no change in the NDH, beyond strengthening its armed forces under German guidance. The situation on the eve of the Italian armistice was such that Pavelić's writ was effectively reduced to the Zagreb region, and that the Germans had to raise troop levels in one way or another, to insure against the imminent Italian withdrawal and the fear of an Allied attack.

Italy's economic position in the NDH had been weak from the start. Its zone was the poorest; penetration was successfully resisted

---

10 Quoted in Peter Broucek, ed., *Ein General im Zwielicht. Die Erinnerung Edmund Glaises von Horstenau*, III, Vienna, 1988: 272. Rendulic was yet another Austrian, of Croat lineage which he did not like to admit.

by the ustashas and even more so by the Germans. Its exploitation of it had consisted of the export of timber, tobacco and some foodstuffs, that benefited corrupt officials, and was compensated by the necessity to bring in other foodstuffs to feed the population of food-deficit areas. By 1943, Germany took eighty per cent of NDH exports, and provided seventy-seven per cent of its imports. The cost of maintaining German occupation forces was the cause of ever-rising inflation. From the beginning of 1943 Germany had agreed to bear these costs, from NDH advances that would be deposited in Germany, but that could only be made in the first instance by printing notes, and redeemed essentially for military supplies. However, most catastrophic was the situation in territory controlled by guerrillas, where much of the housing was destroyed, where there was not enough food, and where typhus killed more than civil war, military operations and repression.

The ustashas had used Muslims in their anti-Serb actions in Bosnia and Herzegovina. Serb armed bands had retaliated ruthlessly. Muslim refugees had fled for safety to towns, or to ustasha-controlled areas; they had also joined the ustasha Black Legion, for pay and for revenge. In eastern Bosnia, and in north-east and north-west Bosnia, the conflict had been particularly brutal. There, the ustashas had first organised Muslim units to help them carry out their anti-Serb policy, and then to defend Muslim villages once their action had produced an anti-Muslim backlash, before making arrangements with various local chetnik bands. Muslims had quickly come to realise that the ustasha régime, once it had used them, was incapable of protecting them. The sympathies of Sarajevo's Muslim élite shifted. In November 1942, some Muslim notables appealed to Hitler, they denounced ustasha policies and asked for the formation of a Bosnian Guard under German authority. The outcome was to give some shape to Himmler's dream of a link between National Socialism and Islam. He obtained Hitler's approval for the formation of a Muslim SS division. Again Pavelić had to agree. The SS enlisted the support of Amin el-Husseini, one-time mufti of Jerusalem, who came to the NDH in April 1943 to help with the recruitment. Bosnia's Muslim promoters thought of it in terms of a move away from the NDH, towards some sort of autonomy under German protection. For the Germans, it was essentially to get more natives to pacify the NDH, and a propaganda tool for the Middle East. An intense recruitment drive, run by the SS from Sarajevo, obtained 12,000 men by the end of April, and the 13th SS Division was formed (eventually named 'Handschar')—sixty per cent Bosnian Muslims, with Yugoslav Volksdeutsche making up the rest, including most of the officers and NCOs. The minimum target of 20,000 was reached with some difficulty by the end of the year.[11] The capture and execution by the partisans of Major Musakadić practically destroyed Mihailović's attempt to set up Muslim units of the JVO. However, a number of small, independent, local Muslim armed formations appeared in the summer of 1943.

By the spring of 1943 the NDH state structure suffered from war weariness, but after the landing in Sicily, its leadership took courage with radical propaganda and a final phase of liquidation of Jews. It called for absolute obedience, absolute solidarity with Nazi Germany, absolute opposition to all who thought of a revamped Yugoslavia—government in exile, Allies, chetniks, partisans and the HSS. After a relative lull in its persecution of Jews, it rounded up and handed over to the Germans another few thousand individuals who were sent to death camps in the Reich. The armed forces remained large on paper—110,000 in the Domobranstvo and gendarmerie, 40,000 in the Ustasha Militia—but disintegration had set on as early as the summer of 1941, when Glaise had noted that soldiers felt anti-insurgent operations as civil war. Draft evasion and desertion were rife. There was increasing tension between Domobran and Militia officers. The

---

11 The recruits came from existing militias, from ustasha units and even from the Domobrans. In August they were sent for training to Germany, thence to southern France. The mutiny of a unit at Villefranche-de-Rouergue in September was brutally put down. The recruitment, training and use of that division caused tension between Croats and Muslims, as well as between Croats and Germans, not to mention anti-Serb behaviour.

special police spied on untrustworthy 'Yugoslavs', arrested, imprisoned, executed or otherwise liquidated those who were detected or denounced as having contacts with insurgents. Many had been Croat Peasant Party (HSS) supporters. In their desire to distance themselves from the régime, and to avoid ending up on the losing side, they were ready to cooperate again with the HSS and with the Western Allies. A network gravitated around Colonel Ivan Babić, who had been one of the organisers of the pre-war HSS Guard. He tried to contact Krnjević, the HSS deputy prime minister of the government in exile, through the Vatican and Switzerland, and in April 1943, no less a military personality than General Ivan Prpić, Chief of the General Staff, sent a report on the contribution the Domobrans could make to an Allied landing. They got no answer, but because they had no understanding of the situation and of the policies of the Western Allies, they somehow got the impression that they should go on trying, and expect instructions.

Archbishop Stepinac retreated into an obsessive preoccupation with the fate of Catholic Croatia. In March he wrote to both the Italian Minister and the Apostolic Legate to tell them that Italy would be held responsible 'before God and history' if it did not support Croatia's thirteen-century long struggle for the Christian civilisation that was common to both Italy and Croatia. He protested against the inhuman behaviour of Italian troops in Herzegovina, where they had even allowed cases of 'passage from Catholicism to schism' (converted Serbs reverting to Orthodoxy?). Anxious to deny allegations made by the government in exile that the Catholic Church in Croatia had condoned measures against the Orthodox, he accepted, in reports to the Holy See, that atrocities had been committed, but they had been reactions to what Serbs had done in the interwar period. In a guarded defence of the NDH government, he stated that it had not known about the atrocities. Furthermore, the régime had also taken salutary measures—against abortion (which had been carried out mainly by Serb and Jewish physicians) and pornography, Freemasonry and communism; religious education in schools and the salaries of priests had been increased. He had managed to obtain that Jews in mixed marriages with Catholics be spared from deportation, and when a group of Slovene priests were sent to Jasenovac and executed there, he wrote to Pavelić that their murder was 'a shameful stain [...] just as Jasenovac camp as a whole is a shame for the Independent State of Croatia'.[12] By August, fearing what would become of Croatia following the defeat of Germany, he is reported to have told a priest about to leave for Rome that a temporary communist government would be better than a chetnik régime.[13]

Maček and others in the HSS leadership believed in an Allied victory. They too assumed that the Anglo-Americans would land on the Dalmatian coast, and expected support as a democratic and anti-communist force. Early in 1943, August Košutić, vice-president, Ivanko Farolfi, acting secretary in Krnjević's absence, and Ljudevit Tomašić, who had had British contacts before the war, reactivated the leadership in Zagreb to conduct business in Maček's absence. They started some illegal papers and leaflets, to popularise Maček as the only personality whom the Allies trusted and who could rally Croatian public opinion, but who was temporarily incapacitated as a prisoner of the ustasha régime. They sent out a delegate to the Italian-occupied coast, to try and link up with the Allies. All he could do was to be in touch with both the Peoples' Liberation Movement (NOP) and the JVO, and to organise some underground HSS help for Allied troops when they landed. In Zagreb, the interim leadership cultivated contacts with friendly Domobran officers. The idea was that the HSS would be in a strong bargaining position at the end of the war if it had control of the NDH army as well as Western support. The ustashas acknowledged the influence of the HSS. On the eve of the Italian armistice, they even tried to get into their government a few of the politicians close to Maček, to strengthen their

---

12 Quoted by Fiorello Cavalli, *Il processo dell'arcivescovo di Zagabria*, Rome, 1947: 279.

13 According to the exiled ustasha writer Vinko Nikolić, *Pred vratima domovine*, II, Munich, 1967: 322.

own position. Maček and his friends were not willing to compromise their position at a time when they expected the Allies. In fact, they continued to wait and see.

At the turn of the year, Košutić and Farolfi had seen emissaries from Mihailović, who had also been in touch with Domobran officers. Mihailović, with backing from his government, wanted the HSS to set up a military organisation to work with the JVO, and to take over at the time of liberation. He expected to be acknowledged as commander of all Yugoslav armed forces in the homeland, and assumed that Maček could simply 'deliver' Croatia. Košutić explained that Mihailović did not have a good image among Croats, that it would be helpful if he disowned those chetnik groups responsible for the killing of innocent Croats, and that the HSS was anyhow well organised to take over. Intelligence was exchanged, but the HSS leaders avoided a broader arrangement. They hoped to get a link to the Western Allies through Mihailović, asked Krnjević for advice, and obtained no answer. Like Archbishop Stepinac, most Croats considered Mihailović's movement as more dangerous than Tito's, for chetnik massacres in mixed areas were laid at his door. They did not want to be made collectively responsible for ustasha crimes. They feared that a Yugoslavia restored in its pre-war form would initiate large-scale retribution, and even accept a deal with Italy at Croatia's expense. The NDH administration and army were already much penetrated by Tito's NOP. When Mussolini fell, an NDH diplomat told an Italian colleague in an offhand way: 'We are ustashas by day and partisans by night'. Many Domobran officers cooperated locally with the partisans, supplying intelligence and equipment, and exchanging prisoners. With a lull in military action in expectation of Italy's withdrawal, the partisans' leadership in Croatia concentrated on political action. Andrija Hebrang, the newly-appointed secretary of the Party Central Committee for Croatia, was saying openly that the primary aim of the movement was political, and that the immediate danger was the HSS leader. Fearing Maček's links with the Domobranstvo and with the West, the communists tried to separate

Pavelić's armed forces from the HSS. Talks were initiated at high level in June, involving General Prpić once again. As nothing was achieved, communist propaganda appealed to soldiers to go over to the partisans, and attacked 'Maček's clique'.

Over the summer, Tito's men had worked their way back across Bosnia to their earlier bases. In spite of extensive losses from operations and disease, the partisans' permanent force of KPJ militants and uprooted peasants was so much more mobile and so much better welded than anything anti-communists could recruit territorially, that it could recuperate and grow again. In NDH territory, the demoralisation of the régime facilitated the NOP's reorganisation. As an essentially political movement, it had better propaganda skills. The NOP projected among non-Serbs an image of Mihailović as the bearer of Serb vengeance, and among Serbs, projected an image of him as an agent of the British who exploited them. To encourage Domobrans to come over to the partisans, they were assigned to units operating on home ground, and their cadres were guaranteed rank and immunity. All opponents of the NOP were collaborators. The Soviets were helping with propaganda, if not with arms, and the British too, on the eve of the Sicily landing, were giving signs of beginning to prefer Tito.

As the KPJ strengthened again in Croatia, it tended to put more emphasis on Croatia than on Yugoslavia. This was because the Croats of Bosnia, and even more so of Herzegovina, were still under ustasha influence and totally hostile to the partisans, whereas Croats looked to the HSS the more one went to the core of Croatia. Serb partisans did not understand the leadership's 'liberal' attitude towards Croats crossing over from the Domobrans, which did not apply to Serbs coming over from the chetniks, or the appointment of Croats to command positions in Serb areas and Serb units. The KPJ knew how to pander to local nationalism when convenient. In Croatia, where it had first used Serb feelings, the local Central Committee began to assert some of its old nationalist outlook as it freed itself from dependence on the Serbs. It created unease among Serbs, who had suffered from the ustashas, and who had been the first to join the partisans.

With Mihailović's return to Serbia, his movement rapidly recovered its unquestioned dominance in the region. In the meanwhile, Nedić had seized the chance to undercut him by submitting to the German occupation authority the draft of a fundamental law which would have structured Serbia as an idealised, traditional yet corporatist, peasant national community, within the orbit of the great German Reich. The Germans considered it 'untimely' and left it at that. Bader's reprisals order of 28 February 1943, although it reduced the 100:1 ratio to 50:1, was in fact a return to a policy of executing hostages to be taken from among 'DM supporters', 'communists' and all those who 'helped bandits'. The Gestapo took care of the first category. Nedić's police was given a free hand with the second. Otherwise Nedić could only step up crude propaganda against those whose influence he judged to be the strongest in Serbia—Mihailović and his backers in the government in exile. They were deemed to be the principal enemies of the Serbian people, in the service of the Anglo-American capitalist plutocracy, manipulated by the Jews who wanted to destroy Germany, the last obstacle to their domination of the world. Having failed to catch him in Montenegro, the Germans continued their search for Mihailović in Serbia. Operation 'Morgenluft' was carried out in July, with orders from Himmler to use all means to locate, capture or liquidate him and his headquarters. Once again a reward was offered, published in the collaborationist press on 21 July 1943 and placarded throughout Serbia, of 100,000 reischsmarks in gold for whoever delivered Mihailović or Tito, dead or alive. Crudely-produced peasant posters then appeared awarding 1 dinar in paper for Hitler's head. All through the summer, with the help of Bulgarian troops and of Ljotić's Volunteers (sometimes disguised as chetniks) the Germans continued to mount actions against Mihailović's armed men, with waves of arrests and executions of sympathisers—some 3,000 between February and August according to German police records.

There was in July a reorganisation of the German military command structure in the Balkans, in view of the impending collapse of Italy. Field-Marshal Maximilian von Weichs, who had directed the German onslaught on Yugoslavia in April 1941, became overall Commander SE, taking in also the Italian area, with headquarters in Belgrade, thus emphasising 'the overwhelming importance of Serbia for the entire conduct of the war in the south-east'.[14] At the same time, a fourth Bulgarian division replaced one of the German divisions in Serbia. Bulgarian troops were judged good at dealing with guerrillas, whose mentality they shared and whom they managed to keep down until late 1943. Further south, in Yugoslav Macedonia under Bulgarian rule, neither Mihailović nor Tito had any great success as yet. The approach of Tito's delegate Tempo was to organise a distinct communist organisation for Macedonia, on the lines of existing arrangements in Slovenia and Croatia, to negotiate with Bulgarian, Albanian and Greek communists for a joint resistance committee, and to press them to accept the principle of a union of all Macedonians. The result was in June a declaration by the new Macedonian Central Committee calling for a united and independent Macedonia, with no reference to Yugoslavia, for which Tempo was sharply criticised.

Mihailović was now receiving some arms drops from the British, and disarming SDS detachments. He mobilised in certain areas, undertook sabotage, and skirmished with Bulgarian troops and with the few partisans left in Serbia, but generally avoided Germans. He realised that he was not strong enough to carry out greater operations on his own, and feared reprisals. Local actions were meant to keep his men on their feet and to prepare them for greater action to come. Mihailović's orders were for resistance 'on hold', to keep occupation troops and their auxiliaries blocked in towns, to 'clean out' Ljotićites and communists. Others in the service of the occupation power were

---

14 Hitler's Directive 48 of 26 July 1943, in Walter Hubatsch, ed., *Hitlers Weisungen für die Kriegsführung, 1939-1945*, Frankfurt am Main, 1962: 222.

told that, for the time being, their only way to save themselves was to go out 'to the woods' (the resistance), before it became too late and they had to share the fate of traitors. Propaganda was increased against Nedić, described as the greatest traitor of all. Since the spring, most of Serbia wished for and believed in Germany's defeat, but also feared reprisals, and the better-off peasantry, the middle classes and the intelligentsia feared communism as well. The Germans knew it all through their intelligence, and wanted to destroy Mihailović's organisation in time.

The peasants were unwilling to part with their produce at low official prices, so that their passive resistance to delivery quotas could be encouraged. In 1943, the Germans, who were in need of greater food supplies, once again assigned the collection to their district Kommandaturas, who called on the assistance of Serbian auxiliaries, the German police, and even German troops. They continued to recruit labour for Germany. As there were not enough 'volunteers', prisoners of war were also used. Removing military personnel from Serbia had the added advantage of reducing the number of potential recruits for the resistance and the expected uprising. They bargained with Nedić in May to release elderly and sick prisoners of war in exchange for able-bodied workers on the basis of one for two. By the autumn there were 45,000 civilian workers and 94,000 prisoners of war from Serbia working in the German economy. The Germans also needed labour in Serbia, particularly for the mines operated by the Todt Organisation. The Bor mines employed 40,000 workers in 1943, and needed 10,000 more. One of the main inducements to work away from their localities had been the food rations given to them and their families, but more drastic steps were now needed, such as drafting able-bodied men in areas favourable to guerrillas. There was passive resistance here too, and drafted workers deserted to guerrillas. In the summer a battalion of soldier-miners was brought in to increase production and discipline. Foreign workers were used. The Hungarian government bartered Jews for deliveries of copper ore. Then there were Polish and Bulgarian workers, captured Greek partisans and eventually, after the Italian armistice, Italian prisoners of war. From the summer of 1943, Bor became a large concentration camp for workers, protected by Bulgarian soldiers.

Where there were no occupation troops, the JVO controlled the local administration, which took orders from it, or acted as cover for Mihailović's parastatal 'Free Serbian Mountains'. Mihailović attempted to control his commanders, enforce discipline and fight abuses, in meting out justice to collaborators and communists, in demanding voluntary contributions, and even in taking unauthorised initiatives. Captain Nikola Kalabić had tried and failed to bargain with the Germans just before Mihailović's return from Montenegro. The SDS, except for the top command structure, was increasingly sympathetic to the JVO. The local clergy was relied on to keep up patriotic feelings, counter communism and provide references. Since the collapse of the state and the massacres perpetrated in the NDH, the general attitude of the Orthodox Church was to preserve the faithful and what remained of its structure from further persecution, and to survive the war as best it could. Such a position reinforced Mihailović's fear of losses.

The advisory committee had become inactive. Vasić, who had wielded most influence, was an authoritarian who clashed with Mihailović's more wishful-thinking and easy-going attitude. Once (and perhaps still) a republican and a sympathiser of the USSR, he had been opposed to any collaboration with the communists and to the Italian connection as well. The chetnik defeat on the Neretva was the final proof that it had all gone terribly wrong, and Vasić had left the Supreme Command. Thereafter he was practically kept in confinement. Mihailović became sensitive to criticism that his Serbian-centred movement left Croats with the NOP as the only way out of the NDH, and that his resistance to 'politics' led to authoritarian tendencies among younger officers. General Trifunović and another commander, Captain Zvonimir Vučković, also influenced his decision to contact traditional political parties, and to extend such contacts to Croatia. Back in March, Mihailović had asked his

Belgrade centre to approach what personalities of the old political parties could be found—in particular Živko Topalović, the leader of the small Socialist Party of Yugoslavia, and the judge Branislav Ivković of the Democratic Party. Topalović, the first to be seen, was very outspoken in his criticism. He argued that, by allowing the systematic denigration of politicians, Mihailović was condoning the tendency to military authoritarianism; that the talk of grouping all Serbs in a separate territorial 'Serbia' in post-war Yugoslavia, when the Serbs did not in fact form an integrated nation, sounded like an echo of Nedić's call for all 'Serbs to rally'. Fearing that the war would end with either a chetnik military dictatorship or a communist dictatorship, the hitherto passive Serb politicians who had remained at home realised that they would have to resume their political activity, albeit clandestinely.

As the only party leader available on the spot, Topalović undertook to set up a committee of politicians to discuss with Mihailović, who encouraged the move. Talks dragged on, as they were conspiratorial, and because of resistance by the Moljević circle at headquarters. It wanted the political parties to adhere to what it saw as a 'Ravna Gora Movement' expressing the new views coming out of the resistance. The party politicians demanded the express reaffirmation of a Yugoslav framework, a federal state, parliamentary government and social reforms, improved relations with the Western Allies and a renewed attempt at reconciliation with the partisans. A Ravna Gora Movement could join a united political front alongside the traditional parties. In April, the Belgrade committee produced proposals for economic and social reform—the nationalisation of mines, forests and principal industries, worker participation, the resettlement of poorer peasants on the holdings of expelled ethnic Germans, Hungarians and Albanians, the spread of cooperatives. Two youth groups, of generally urban students, set up within the JVO in the summer, expressed the new political division between more right-wing and more Serb-minded adherents of the SKK looking to Moljević and more left-wing and more open-minded adherents of the Democratic Party looking to Vučković and to Mihailović himself.

In spite of such developments, it was clear that Mihailović had not understood all the changes that had occurred since 1941, in the Allied camp and throughout Yugoslavia. What intelligence he received was limited, and interpreted through his wishful-thinking. He had no real political advisers. Even the government of which he was formally part was not able to give him frank and independent advice. Communications usually went through British channels, and in so far as they did not, they were handled by a group of younger Yugoslav officers with the government in London. They were Serbs, friends and classmates of Mihailović's officers at home, and they shared the same grievances against the political class. They insisted on the sovereignty of the Yugoslav government, to be defended against British interference. Mihailović was shocked that the British, after the chetnik defeats in Herzegovina, wanted him to concentrate in an area of Serbia where his movement was strong, there to undertake greater sabotage action on German communications, while they also paid attention to the partisans in order to step up activities in other regions. Unwilling to accept that he was no longer seen as a factor of unity for a future Yugoslavia, he stuck to the idea that any real action was linked to a 'D-Day' in his own country. All he could do for the time being was to prepare for the arrival of the Allies in the Balkans. Not only did he see the situation in Serbia as being favourable, but he considered it to be quite good even in other regions. He estimated that there were still tens of thousands of chetniks under arms in Montenegro that he could consider as part of the JVO. Further west, it was a question of destroying the communists, of attracting Muslims and Croats, of destroying Pavelić's régime and of launching the general rising. He was in touch with officers of the NDH General Staff, and estimated that Slovenia would rally to his propaganda, which was now all Yugoslav.

After the Withdrawal of Italy

Marshal Badoglio, the new Italian prime minister, negotiated secretly with the Allies. Secrecy, fear of German moves before arrangements were complete, and equivocations, led to what the Italians thought was an anticipated announcement of the armistice. The initial 'short armistice', signed on 3 September, simply brought hostilities with the British and Americans to an end as they landed in southern Italy. It was made public on 8 September. The King, government and Supreme Command immediately left Rome for Allied-held territory in the south. Orders to react to attacks from anybody else, to act against Germans if provoked, and eventually to consider them as enemies, reached Italian commands in the Balkans days late, if ever. In spite of plans to transfer troops from Yugoslavia, the bulk of Italian forces remained in their original areas, effectively under German control. Most learnt of the armistice from broadcast announcements; and so did partisans and chetniks of all sorts, along with the SOE missions who had not been informed in advance. Stefano Gestro, the historian of what was to become the Italian 'Garibaldi' division that fought with the Yugoslav partisans and who served in northern Montenegro at the time, writes that the armistice was received by Italian troops like the sound of the factory siren at the end of a day's shift: it was time to go home.[15]

However, a unified Italian command that decided what course of action forces across the Adriatic should follow practically ceased to exist. Every unit had to muddle through on its initiative, and many disintegrated. The Germans dropped leaflets calling on them to hand over their arms and return home. Most Italians were taken by the Germans to prisoner-of-war camps in Germany. Some resisted briefly; some managed to return home. Italian soldiers had come to hate the Germans, and most would have preferred to give their arms to guerrillas, and leave. Some did fight with the partisans, but those

---

15 Stefano Gestro, *L'armata stracciona. L'epopea della division "Garibaldi" in Montenegro, 1943-1945*, Bologna, 1964: 35.

Italian generals who wanted to continue as an Allied force found it difficult to cooperate with communist-led guerrillas who, anyhow, did not want whole regular units. Guerrillas moved in with intent to disarm them, regardless of the armistice provisions, with British liaison officers in assistance. The partisans were bolder and usually at hand. The chetniks were disoriented, and only in northern Montenegro did they have an SOE mission within reach of an Italian division. The partisans disarmed four Italian divisions and parts of nine others. They obtained much more from the great military depots in the coastal towns. The bulk of Italian weaponry went to Tito's NOV.

Evidence from German decrypts suggests that Italian commanders approached chetnik and partisan commanders in the NDH, offering arms in exchange for the guerrillas covering their withdrawal. Jevdjević wanted Mihailović to ask the British that the Italians be allowed to hold the ports until the Allies arrived. Mihailović had instructed Baćović and Lašić to contact Italian commanders in their areas for possible initial joint action against the Germans, the Italians providing arms and supplies, in exchange for which the JVO would ensure their repatriation, all in view of the imminent Allied landing.[16] No such landing was seriously contemplated, but Allied commanders were keen to exploit all opportunities to involve the enemy on the other side of the Adriatic once they had invaded Italy.

From the beginning of 1943, Churchill had once again become caught up in Yugoslav affairs, and British sympathy for Mihailović gradually declined. It is most likely that intelligence received by the Chiefs of Staff and the Prime Minister from decrypts of German

---

16 Davide Rodogno quotes from the diary entry for 8 September 1943 of the Italian Foreign Ministry official Luca Pietromarchi, according to which he suggested to General Gambara to take the initiative of action against the Germans, in agreement with both Tito and Mihailović, in order to keep control of the ports (op. cit., 487). Badoglio claims that he was encouraged to use British channels to tell Italian troops to join the partisans (Pietro Badoglio, *L'Italia nella seconda guerra mondiale. Memorie e documenti*, Milan, 1946: 140).

wireless messages was the primary reason.[17] It indicated that chetniks claimed as part of Mihailović's JVO were compromised in their relations with Italian occupation forces more than was deemed acceptable, and that Tito's partisans were the most important anti-Axis element outside Serbia. The Yugoslav government in exile was losing prestige. Endemic discord prevented it from being able to provide leadership for those pro-Allied moderate Yugoslavs at home, wedged between fascists and communists, who looked to their exiled leaders. Disunity led eventually to the end of all-party government in August. A new government of civil servants took over under the diplomat Božidar Purić, who kept on Mihailović. They were dependent on the confidence of their twenty-year-old King who wanted a cabinet to approve his marriage to Princess Alexandra of Greece, and on the toleration of an increasingly impatient British Prime Minister.[18] Distance, the lack of detailed knowledge, a confused understanding of the situation in Yugoslavia, and good communist propaganda on behalf of Tito further contributed to an opinion being formed in British decision-making circles, that to support the partisans could help remove Soviet suspicions of Western intentions. Both the desire to fix around the Mediterranean as many Germans as possible while the 'Overlord' landing was being prepared, and the need to give the Soviet ally some satisfaction pending the long-awaited second front in Western Europe, pointed to the need to back Tito, in addition, or as an alternative, to Mihailović. Helping Tito could also make him responsive to British influence.

What started in the summer as a policy of 'backing both sides', with strengthened missions each to be headed by a brigadier for a

---

17 See Nicholas C. Brashaw, 'Signals Intelligence, the British and the War in Yugoslavia, 1941-1944', Ph.D dissertation, University of Southampton, 2001. Brashaw argues that, since Churchill could not reveal the source of his decrypts, the report later provided by Brigadier Maclean enabled the Prime Minister to justify his decision to turn away from Mihailović, previously extolled by the British as a hero of the European resistance.

18 See Margaret Anne Kay, 'The British Attitude to the Yugoslav Government-in-Exile', Ph.D dissertation, University of Southampton, 1986.

full assessment of the situation, turned into the Churchillian quest to find 'who was killing more Germans', and led to the no less Churchillian conception of a postwar Yugoslavia ruled jointly by the King and the communist guerrilla leader. The brigadiers arrived after the Italian armistice. Although suspicious of the British, Tito had taken advantage of their exasperation with Mihailović. In August, Deakin had already reported from NOV headquarters in Bosnia, on the basis of evidence supplied by Velebit, who had been attached to him as liaison officer, of the 'close, constant and increasing' collaboration between Mihailović and the Germans. Fitzroy Maclean—late of the Foreign Office, Conservative MP, Captain in the SAS duly promoted to Brigadier—was Churchill's choice as head of the strengthened mission to Tito. After eighteen days at NOV headquarters in late September-early October, he made his way out again, via Italy, to Cairo, to meet the Prime Minister on his way to the Tehran Conference. He was the first British liaison officer to return from Yugoslavia with a full report. He assessed the partisans to be the most important political factor. They were expected to reconstruct the country on the ruins of the old order, under a totalitarian and Moscow-oriented régime; they refused to cooperate with Mihailović whom they considered as a traitor, along with the exiled government and Maček. Only armed intervention on a large scale could prevent them from taking power after the German withdrawal. To concentrate on the partisans and establish satisfactory relations with them would produce immediate military benefits, reduce Soviet influence and end the civil war. Otherwise his report was widely inaccurate, based entirely on partisan sources—regarding the number of armed partisans, the losses inflicted on Germans, and the situation in Mihailović-controlled areas with which he had no contact.[19]

---

19 The figure of 220,000 partisans was reduced to figures varying between 100,000 and 180,000 in subsequent accounts. E.M. Rose of the Foreign Office Southern Department minuted that if the figures for resistance forces in Serbia were true, the partisans would already have 'mopped up' Mihailović's men there.

The Brigadier at the head of the strengthened mission to Mihailović was Charles Armstrong, a regular officer with no experience of irregular warfare who wanted no truck with political matters. The report that he produced with Bailey was a carefully weighed analysis of the problems with Mihailović's movement and of the ways to overcome them. It was considered impractical to bring Armstrong out of Serbia, and his report arrived in London too late for Eden to take with him to Cairo. Churchill only had the partisans' case presented to him by Maclean and Deakin, but the presence of Armstrong and Bailey would probably have made little difference, for his mind had already been made up. At Tehran, he argued in favour of the Yugoslav partisans. Stalin was unmoved by Churchill's enthusiasm for them, and interested in the Anglo-American invasion of north-western Europe above everything else, but agreed that they should receive the greatest possible support in order to mislead the enemy. Tito had benefited from the desire of Churchill, Roosevelt and Stalin to find common ground in an uncertain area before the important hurdles had been overcome.

The enthusiasm of Italian troops in Montenegro on hearing the news of the armistice soon evaporated, as the Germans cut off their means of communication, moved in from the NDH and Albania, and dropped leaflets calling on the 'freedom-loving people of Montenegro' to fight against their 'cowardly Italian' occupiers and those 'in the pay of bolsheviks and capitalists'. General Djukanović asked that the Italians hand over power to him; they refused. General Ettore Roncaglia, the commander of the XIVth Army Corps, gathered his divisional commanders and ambiguously called on them to accept a German takeover. No clear decision was taken. Germans, chetniks, partisans, Muslim militiamen and the Albanian military all wanted to take their weaponry. On 15 September, the Germans entered Podgorica and captured Roncaglia.

General Giovanni Battista Oxilia, of the 'Venezia' Division in Berane, had argued that he could use his contacts with chetniks and their British liaison officer, to ask the British to bomb Podgorica airport, already a German base, and to call on all anti-German factions to organise common action. In the circumstances, pressed on all sides, he tried to keep a delicate balance, as he attempted to establish a radio link with the Italian Supreme Command. Perhinek arrived to discuss joint action, but Oxilia did not want to extend it against the partisans, and the chetniks started to take Italian arms. Bailey, who had also come from Serbia to assist with the parley, managed to obtain an agreement: the JVO would take over the civil administration of the area; 'Venezia' would hand over some weapons to the chetniks, and fight the Germans. At the end of the month, the partisan corps of former Spanish Civil War veteran and NOV General Peko Dapčević crossed into Montenegro from Bosnia, avoiding the Germans, to disperse the chetniks and take over Italian equipment. It first blocked Kolašin to force the Italian garrison there to hand over and break with Lašić, the chetniks' commander who was himself trying to take over. After a five-day battle, the Italian garrison withdrew, the partisans took over, and Lašić went to Berane, to disarm the Italians there and prevent the town from falling to the partisans. General Djukanović came to berate Oxilia for having a foot in each camp.

In the end, Dapčević won the day, after alternating negotiations and ultimatums with accusations of breaking the armistice. The reported presence of unidentified British officers helped Oxilia realise that the partisans, rather than the chetniks, were the Allies' preferred Yugoslav force. He agreed that his division would join Dapčević's corps to fight with the partisans against the Germans. The partisans entered Berane, but not before 4,000 chetniks had left with a quantity of arms given to them by the Italians. A much reduced 'Venezia' infantry division and a good part of the 'Taurinense' Alpine division further south at Nikšić were by then the only Italian troops left as regular fighting units. They eventually formed the 5,000-10,000-strong 'Garibaldi' division fighting with the NOV, while all other disbanded smaller units and soldiers joined the partisans as individual recruits. Tito's Supreme Staff gradually turned them into guerrilla units, cleared of fascist and other unacceptable officers, and given political commissars. Relations were, to say the least, far from fraternal as former occupiers became exploited auxiliaries, carriers and cannon fodder.[20]

By 20 September, the Germans were in control of the coast, of Cetinje, and of a few communications centres and links, leaving the rest to internecine warfare between chetniks and partisans. They left one division in what became the Feldkommandatur Montenegro under the German General in Albania and Montenegro, with an auxiliary National Administrative Council, made up of individuals well disposed to the Nedić government in Serbia, but whose authority barely extended beyond Cetinje. Once Italian food supplies had stopped, the population soon faced near starvation. Djukanović and Stanišić, who had asked to take over from the Italians on the day the armistice was announced, and had been sent away, did not want to cooperate with the Germans. After a useless appeal to the partisans to join him against the Germans, Stanišić with Djukanović and the National Committee for Montenegro—most of the 'nationalist' leadership—went to Ostrog monastery, a seemingly impregnable mountain retreat that had been Stanišić's headquarters. They were caught up on 15 October by a strong besieging partisan force coming from Herzegovina. Ostrog fell to the communists after a four-day siege; Djukanović and his committee were executed; Stanišić and a few others committed suicide. Lašić, who was in the north, formally took over what remained of JVO forces in Montenegro. They were generally left undisturbed, as by the end of October, they had lost authority, except locally. The partisans, once more in control of large parts of Montenegro, had even held an 'assembly of representatives of the people of Montenegro' at Kolašin, once the 'chetnik capital'.

---

20 According to Giacomo Scotti, a Tito sympathiser who after the war went on to reside in Yugoslavia, where he edited the Italian-language daily *La voce del popolo*, Yugoslav sources are silent about the execution of several Italian high-ranking officers by the partisans after the armistice, for acts committed earlier (*Ventimila caduti. Gli italiani in Jugoslavia dal 1943 al 1945*, Milan, 1970: 12–13).

A new development was Djurišić's arrival in Serbia in November. He appears to have escaped from (formerly Polish) Galicia and made his way to Belgrade, where he was arrested again, before being asked by Nedić to form a Montenegrin Volunteer Corps, to be sent to Montenegro to fight the partisans. The mysterious episode was not to the liking of all Germans. Djurišić was pledged to Nedić, but in his characteristic way he also once again claimed allegiance to Mihailović, on whom he counted to contact the Western Allies. He arrived in Sandžak, where he rallied a new chetnik concentration around Prijepolje.

The Italian armistice increased optimism in Serbia, where Mihailović was considered to be the representative of the victorious Allies. Propaganda against him was received with disbelief and indignation. Tito's appeal was still negligible. Posters appeared saying 'The English are coming'. Mihailović himself was unable to accept the change in the British attitude. At the time, he was in the Zlatibor mountainous corner of south-western Serbia, and he tried to obtain some Italian weapons from northern Montenegro. With his newly-formed mobile combat units and the local chetniks that he rallied, he attacked German positions in eastern Bosnia. He had been exhorted by the British and his own government to step up anti-Axis activities, and refrain from fighting the partisans, in return for maximum support. The British wanted to test him, and keep the Germans guessing. He was encouraged by the recent arrival of Brigadier Armstrong with more British liaison officers, and by the availability of eager recruits for his permanent detachments. By late September, operations had reached Višegrad on the Drina, an important point on the Sarajevo-Belgrade line well garrisoned by NDH troops with German backing. Mihailović sent emissaries (a Croat and a Muslim) for talks with sympathetic Domobran officers who wanted to defect. However, the possibility of a peaceful handover of Višegrad was sabotaged by other chetniks. Although the railway bridge over the Drina was destroyed, along with several minor bridges on the Užice-Višegrad line, the operation was not otherwise successful. In pursuing the Germans in the direction of Sarajevo, the chetniks had crossed into partisan territory, and were attacked in their rear by other partisans from Montenegro. Caught between partisans and Germans, who counter-attacked, the chetniks had to retreat back across the Drina. Mihailović moved his headquarters further north into Serbia. There was sabotage action elsewhere, in eastern Serbia on Danube shipping and on the Morava valley railway. Radio Free Yugoslavia in Soviet territory and the BBC attributed the action on the Užice-Višegrad-Sarajevo railway to the partisans. A discouraged Mihailović drew the conclusion that he should return to his old ways.

The JVO 'parastate' continued to spread in the vacuum produced by the diminishing authority of the Nedić administration, but in a disorderly fashion and mostly under the influence of Moljević's 'Ravna Gora' tendency. Self-appointed committees supervised rural teachers and priests. Brigade commanders appointed 'legal officers' to take over the work of district courts. The Supreme Command berated commanders for arbitrary and unauthorised actions. It also issued injunctions against gambling, prostitution, drunkenness and immoral behaviour. It issued reminders that its authority extended over all armed forces on the territory of the Kingdom of Yugoslavia that were fighting against 'the enemy'. The communists were top on that list. Mihailović realised that the Germans expected them to try and get into Serbia, which would lead to fighting with the 'nationalists', and allow the occupiers to destroy both factions more easily. Muslims and Croats were to be attracted. A real Croat had been a welcome addition to Mihailović's entourage at the end of the summer. He was Vladimir Predavec, son of a pre-war HSS vice-president. He had taken refuge in Belgrade, where he had been in touch with other refugee Croats, with the JVO secret command and with General Trifunović. A rise in optimism among Mihailović sympathisers was followed by a rise in weariness towards all armed formations among the peasants, whose private security came before any patriotism or ideology. The Germans were still taking hostages and making arrests, even if in much reduced numbers. In September, a special Gestapo operation captured Major Žarko Todorović and most of the person-nel of the JVO underground command in Belgrade, which was also nominally responsible for the 'northern territories' (the provinces north of the Danube and Sava, with Croatia and Slovenia), and sent them to various camps. Mihailović replaced him with General Sve-tomir Djukić, who had been living in the capital 'on parole'.

By the end of the year the situation had quietened down again. The partisans had failed to break through from Bosnia. Locally, the Germans had interpreted the attempt as meaning that there was no imminent threat of a landing in Dalmatia, but Hitler still believed there was. Following the Italian withdrawal, the Germans had had to take over responsibility for the whole of south-east Europe. They managed, by reducing controls to essentials, by coordinating their structures, and by belatedly accepting the Italian argument that they could not rely on military means only. By November, they had ac-knowledged that Tito was their most dangerous opponent. Hermann Neubacher, a highly-educated Austrian Nazi, once mayor of Vienna, was appointed Special Foreign Affairs Representative for the South-East, with residence in Belgrade and entrusted with the task of guid-ing national anti-communist forces. He considered it a mistake to have dismembered Yugoslavia in the first place, and then even more so to have subjected the Serbs to a reign of terror that had aroused hatred of Germany. He wanted to adopt more reasonable policies in Serbia so as to make it the hub of the anti-communist approach, and favoured the removal of the ustashas from power in the NDH. He had support in the Foreign Ministry and in military circles, and found some ready allies in the German General's Civil Administra-tion staff and in Military Intelligence in Belgrade. In October, he submitted his suggestions to Ribbentrop: the creation of a greater Serb federation of Serbia, Sandžak and Montenegro, with a federal government given real executive powers, Nedić as president and the German military authority reduced to a controlling rôle.

Ribbentrop passed the proposals on to Hitler in December. Neubacher was going too far, and nothing came of his proposals, although he was responsible for measures that altered the occupation régime in Serbia. The reprisals quota was removed, and the execution of hostages became a rarity by the end of the year. Neubacher had a hand in Djurišić's liberation after he had been arrested on his arrival in Belgrade. He tried to unite available anti-communists in Montenegro, but Krsto Popović's independentist 'Greens' would not hear of links with Serbia. He found it even more difficult simultaneously to court Serb anti-communist feelings and work with Albanian anti-Serb nationalism. In Zagreb he made indirect contact with Košutić to explore the possibility of a new government, but with no success. Though the good offices of Military Intelligence, he managed between mid-November and the end of the year to conclude secret arrangements with four of Mihailović's commanders, including Captain Nikola Kalabić and Major Vojislav Lukačević. These were cessations of hostilities concluded for periods of five to ten weeks, to facilitate the transport of produce, to stop attacks on mines and bridges, to prevent clashes with Muslim militias. Some of them envisaged joint action against the partisans if arms were provided. They did not prevent sporadic clashes, and the Germans came to the conclusion that they had done nothing more than strengthen the chetniks and facilitate their penetration of the Nedić administration. The four officers, who felt wedged between communists and Germans with dwindling supplies, had probably signed the agreements to tide themselves over a difficult period. Optimistically, they interpreted them as a sign of German weakness. However, the Germans saw it, more realistically, as a sign of weakness of Mihailović's movement. Nothing much was achieved by these secret deals, except that their existence was revealed by decrypts to Churchill, who also read the full text of the Lukačević treaty, which considerably affected the British attitude.

In giving his approval, Weichs had stressed that he doubted that such 'collaboration' could be trusted or extended, and that Mihailović had not given up his determination to pursue the struggle against Germany. Mihailović had not been involved, and there is no evidence that he approved, although British Military Intelligence thought it was possible ('very possible', said Deakin) that he was 'conniving'. Publicly, he denounced the agreements as being false, and as being intended to muddy his reputation with the Allies. Less publicly, he described them as unauthorised acts of treason. On 8 December, he ordered that there should be no contacts, let alone agreements, with the occupiers. Neubacher tried to get in touch with Mihailović himself, but failed because of opposition within German circles, and obstacles set up by Nedić, who feared competition. Nedić was actually the weakest element in Neubacher's plans. He was by then mistrusted by most Serbs, not fully trusted by the Germans, and no longer trusted even by the upper reaches of his own government. Most of the local administration sided with Mihailović, and so did most of the SDS. Even Ljotić's Volunteers had to resort to conscription by the end of 1943. Neubacher was not able to overcome the incoherence of German policy towards Serbia, or push through a strategy that could make up for its decreasing ability to solve problems by force only.

Euphoria had greeted the Italian armistice in Dalmatia. For a moment and in some places all seemed to participate—Italian soldiers and local civilians, partisans and nationalists. The Italian general in command of the XVIIIth Army Corps thought of inviting the partisans to join his troops in fighting the Germans. The commander of the 'Bergamo' Division in Split gave them arms, after arms had been sent to Djujić's chetniks. The partisans wanted to take over, and demanded that the Italians join them, or at least hand over all their equipment and leave. After a week, the commander of the partisans' first Proletarian Division, NOV General Koča Popović, came accompanied by Deakin and secured the consignment of Split, of Italian arms and stocks, and the departure of Italian troops for Italy. He held the city for ten days, and evacuated it after German air bombardment and the arrival of the SS 'Prinz Eugen' Division. Over 9,000 remaining Italians were captured and taken to prisoner camps in Germany; five generals and seventy-six other officers were executed. For a short while, the coast from Sušak to Split was practically in the hands of the partisans, who acquired volunteers, but also drafted, and settled accounts with Italians and native opponents. The pro-Mihailović committee in Split had anxiously tried to ask him whether he would be sending troops to defend Dalmatia from the Germans. It had organised several hundred armed volunteers, which the partisans demanded should join the NOV. Some did. Others went off to Djujić. One unit tried to take over some islands on behalf of the JVO and await the British there; the survivors who made it to Bari included a mixed collection of chetnik personalities, from Grdjić to Žujović.

The ustasha régime had also reacted euphorically, as it proclaimed the 'final act of the thousand-year struggle' of Croatia on the Adriatic. Pavelić annulled the offer of the crown to the House of Savoy, abrogated the Rome Agreements with Italy, proclaimed the incorporation of Dalmatia into the NDH, and announced an amnesty for all those Croats who had joined the insurgents because of Italian brutalities. Croatian territorial demands extended south to Kotor, and north to Fiume and Istria, but the régime was unprepared for the Italian withdrawal. The Germans had made contingency plans, and advanced to the coast. Pavelić was told brutally that the situation was such that the NDH government was not to make any demands: the coastal area was a German zone of operations. A series of operations was launched against the partisans who had taken control again of large tracts of the NDH. The coast had to be secured, along with the mines of Bosnia, the agriculture of Slavonia, and the railway lines from Austria to Zagreb and Belgrade. The Germans extended their hold over more than the NDH. The Italian provinces of Udine, Gorizia, Trieste, Pola, Fiume and Lubiana became the operational zone Adriatisches Küstenland (Adriatic Coastland), under Friedrich Rainer, the Gauleiter of Carinthia.

However, they did not have enough troops to replace the Italians. As NDH forces were considered useless, ethnic Germans were increasingly drafted into the SS. A Cossack cavalry division, organised and trained in southern Russia, had been deployed in the Srem and

Slavonia plain region since March 1943 to protect the Zagreb-Belgrade railway. Made up of Red Army prisoners of war and deserters, and of recruits from occupied Soviet areas, it contained Turcoman, Azeri and Kalmuk horsemen beside Cossacks. From October, their range of action was extended, driving fear into the population with their undisciplined behaviour. Dutch and Scandinavian SS were also brought to the NDH, generally treated as occupied territory. Ustasha protests, that districts or villages were declared guerrilla nests so that the German military could take all able-bodied males to work in the Reich, were rejected outright. The Germans managed to recover their balance, and by the time the Allies had definitely turned to Tito in the wake of the Tehran Conference in November, their anti-insurgent operations had once again drastically reduced all resistance in Yugoslavia. Nevertheless, their hold of the coast was precarious, and they were unable to secure all the islands.

A balance was restored in the western regions, between German control and NOP free territory. However, the geographical distribution of forces had enabled the partisans to gather most of the Italian arms before the Germans moved in. This was the first time that an underground movement had been able to arm itself properly. It meant that Tito's NOV thereafter had the means to grow significantly, particularly as it would go on to obtain more Italian weaponry by courtesy of the Western Allies in Italy. By the end of the year, the new Supreme Command of the Italian forces allowed by the Allies complained that too much was being taken from them in Italy to send to the Yugoslav partisans. Morally, the Italian bequest of arms was also important to Tito's movement, and so was the support forthcoming from BBC broadcasts. One may even ask whether these broadcasts did not do for Tito morally as much as Italian arms did militarily. Yet the communist leadership, full of what Djilas describes as 'dogmatic ideological distrust' towards the British,[21] did not know what to make of their support. Tito was furious that he had not been given advance notice of the armistice, which would

---

21 Djilas, *Wartime*, 348.

have allowed his forces to take even more, and grumbled that not enough aid was being sent to the partisans from Italy. The feeling of elation that followed 8 September and Allied support nevertheless meant that many people, who wanted to be with the Allies in what had been the Italian zone, joined the partisans. There was a new wave of desertions from the Domobrans, so much so that the maverick pro-German Croat 'national socialist' Stjepan Buć suggested that 'our army should be disbanded immediately'. The local chetniks, and the hopes Mihailović had placed in them, disintegrated once Italian support was removed.

On the other hand, Tito's Supreme Staff had not expected the Germans to be strong enough for renewed extended anti-insurgent operations from many sides. The partisans had to abandon territory, and concentrate on some areas. Popular support and Mihailović's influence upheld the chetniks in eastern Bosnia, and there were other chetnik pockets in the NDH. There were few Muslim partisans as yet. The fall of Tuzla in north-eastern Bosnia, in the first days of October, was an important factor which helped the communists in their appeal to Muslims against the competing claims of Serbs and Croats over Bosnia. The whole Domobran garrison—2,200 soldiers and seventy-four officers—went over to the partisans with its commander, Colonel Sulejman Filipović. A Muslim and a former regular Yugoslav army officer, he issued an appeal to the Domobrans to join the partisans and was made an NOV general. Some of the independent armed Muslim movements then split as part of their adherents went over to the partisans.

The difficulty of the KPJ-led movement in western areas was that its strategy before 1941 had been directed principally against Serb hegemony, counting on the support of non-Serbs, but that in the war Serbs became the partisans' strongest potential base. In the more homogeneously Croat rural areas, where ustasha influence had been weaker, and where massacres had not assumed frenzied proportions, chetniks had not taken root, and Croats had been slow to join the resistance. In order to attract Croats and HSS supporters more particularly, the communists tried both to divide and to win over the HSS interim leadership, and placed great emphasis in their propaganda on 'Croatia' at the expense of 'Yugoslavia', which caused tension among Serb cadres of the party in Croatia. The Serb-inhabited Kordun region south of Zagreb had been the nucleus of the communist insurgency in Croatia since 1941, and had suffered most from ustasha and anti-insurgent operations. By the summer of 1943, its population was worn out, looking for ways to survive the last phase of the war, and showing signs of turning away from the NOP. The emphasis on Croatia, the appearance on political committees and in military cadres of many turn-coat Croats, affected Serb partisans whose main task was increasingly to fight against Serb chetniks. The moving over to the chetniks of a number of leading partisan figures from Kordun frightened the NOP leadership. The KPJ's cleverly modulated federal programme and national policy, its willingness to forgive past misdeeds for new converts, and the wholesale acceptance of Croat recruits did attract more Croats, but it worried the Serbs of Croatia. Many anyhow believed that Tito's movement would be forced to change under Western pressure.

The interim HSS leadership in Zagreb around Košutić was in occasional, if controlled, contact with Maček, who was kept under house arrest. The line that its propaganda stuck to was that, when the time came, and when called upon by Maček, its only legitimate representative, the whole nation would rise under him to ensure the freedom of Croatia. Meanwhile, it worried about how the Croatian nation would get to the end of the war with as few victims as possible, and it maintained links with some high-ranking Domobran officers, whose help would be essential at that crucial moment at the end of the war. Košutić had been approached by Mladen Lorković, one of those more moderate ustashas who had come to believe in the possibility of an Allied victory, to see whether the HSS would not enter a new coalition government for the NDH. He had also been approached by Glaise and by a representative of Neubacher's, about the possibility of an alternative HSS government. Košutić cautiously suggested a non-political government, but he passed a message on to the exiled government through Istanbul to inform it of the approaches: the HSS was willing to resume talks with Mihailović, and to send a representative to Istanbul for consultations with the Yugoslav government and the British. By that time, the HSS no longer had ministers in Purić's reduced and non-political cabinet, and there was no response.

Even more radical proposals had been formulated by the German military. A tour of the NDH depressed Weichs who saw that, apart from Zagreb and German-occupied areas, the rest was either Serb free territory (chetniks) or Tito's Soviet territory (partisans). He too called for much greater German involvement and drastic overhaul. After a conference with Hitler on 29 October, there was no real change, except for a unified command. Weichs was in despair, as he pointed to the danger that the impotence of the NDH represented. Pavelić had taken fright. A few days before the Italian armistice, he had actually appointed a new government, which was not very 'new', but it was no longer presided by the Poglavnik himself. The non-committed personality chosen by Pavelić to be prime minister was the forgotten Nikola Mandić, who had been vice-president of the Sabor of Bosnia-Herzegovina under Austria-Hungary and Deputy Governor during the First World War. To ward off German criticism of the armed forces, Glaise's candidate, General Friedrich Navratil, was made Minister for the Armed Forces. The army was duly reorganised into smaller and more mobile units, under German control—some 170,000 men, according to a report by Kasche in October. The Ustasha Militia was increased to 45,000, mostly tough young volunteers fanatically eager to fight for their beliefs, unaffected by the general change of mood. There was no political re-ordering of the state machinery, and different German agencies continued to follow different and often conflicting policies.

Immediately after the Italian armistice, individual German commanders were willing to see whether they could make use of some of the chetnik detachments, to help them secure some areas. Ap-

proached by the Abwehr agent Hans Ott, who had conducted negotiations with Tito's command, Jevdjević in Herzegovina offered the
services of 5,000 men. Djujić had once vehemently told an Italian
liaison officer that he would side with the British as soon as they
landed, but as they had not come, and the Italians had gone, he too
looked for cover with the Germans against ustashas and communists.
The Germans did not trust him, and there resulted conflicts with and
between local chetnik captains in northern Dalmatia. Orders from
SE Command, to put an end to such contacts and to arrest prominent chetniks, were not obeyed everywhere. Moscow duly passed on
to Tito intercepted messages referring to talks between chetniks and
Germans, to be used in propaganda. Strangely enough, Kasche, the
pro-ustasha German diplomatic representative in Zagreb, had been
in favour of trying to win Jevdjević over, and pleading for a new deal
with the partisans as well. His idea was that such deals sapped the
political and moral base of the insurgents, separated Croat from Serb
partisans, and caused discord between Serb insurgents. He wanted
to expand what the military had been doing yet again. Glaise had
been negotiating, through Ott, with Marijan Stilinović, a delegate of
Tito's Supreme Staff. By the end of December, they actually reached
agreement about treating captured partisans as prisoners of war, and
about exchanging prisoners. Since Weichs did not want to formalise
the recognition of the NOV as a belligerent party, the deal was not
actually signed, but Glaise nevertheless applied it, on the basis of
Weich's general decision to suspend reprisals, and on Hitler's unpublished order of 31 December not to execute captured partisans.
However, the SS and the Ustasha Militia did not feel themselves
bound by any such arrangements.

One brutal incursion by the SS in a village west of Zagreb was the
direct cause for the sermon delivered by Archbishop Stepinac on 31
October, in which he evenly distributed his denunciation of 'injustice
and violence committed in the name of theories of class, race or nationality'. 'Class' clearly related to communism, yet his own brother,
who was with the partisans, had been caught and executed by the

Germans, and the Archbishop was by then refusing ustasha requests to instruct the clergy to deliver anti-communist sermons, for fear of endangering the population. The Education Minister attacked in the press 'that high Church dignitary who has recently in his sermons passed beyond the limits of his vocation, and begun to meddle in affairs in which he is not competent.' Mandić and Lorković warned Stepinac against going too far.

In Slovenia too, particularly in Ljubljana Province, the Italian armistice had been greeted with joy, mixed, however, with apprehension of the German reaction. Most Slovenes shared a belief in the final defeat of Germany, and pro-Yugoslav feelings, in spite of all local national manifestations. German troops had already started moving through the province. More of them, essentially SS, came after 8 September, to secure the railways. Italian troops, that had been entrenched in towns, were disarmed. The province was placed in the Adriatic Coastland operational zone, as the partisans had taken control of much of it. Over the summer, they had had talks with the Italians, demanding that they should turn against the Germans, or at least hand over their arms and leave. Arms had been given to them locally. Within a day of the armistice, they had obtained much more, helped by the claim that they were the only recognised Allies in the region.[22]

The 'counter-revolutionaries' (as the Slovene historian Bojan Godeša calls the anti-communists) varied in their degree of anti-communism, in their relations to the Italian régime, and in how they wanted to organise post-war Slovenia, but most of them were preparing for the arrival of Western forces. They recognised the ultimate legitimacy of the exiled Yugoslav government, and even of General Mihailović. The SLjS-dominated Slovenian Alliance (SZ) planned to take over the MVAC who, with the units led by Mihailović's officers, would meet the Anglo-Americans. Both sides now considered that 'who is not with us is against us'.[23] Equipped with Italian artillery,

---

22 William Jones, *Twelve Months with Tito's Partisans*, London, 1946: 101-4.

23 Bojan Godeša, *Kdor ni znami, je proti nam. Slovenački izobrančeni med okupatorji, Osvobodilno fronto in protivrevolucionarnim taborom*, Ljubljana,

the partisans attacked, destroyed or dispersed their hesitating opponents, who had no unified command structure, no reliable means of communicating, and no Anglo-Americans to back them. After the destruction of his 'Blue Guard' nucleus in Grčarice, a dispirited Novak withdrew from the SZ and left for Italy. He was eventually replaced as Mihailović's 'shadow' commander for Slovenia by Colonel Ivan Prezelj, who had been working with Vauhnik. The MVAC, renamed the Slovene National Army, had concentrated an important number of men in and around Turjak castle, 20 kms south-east of Ljubljana, in preparation of a move to the coast. The partisans attacked and captured the castle, and killed all the 'White Guards' (as they called them) they could find in it ('to demoralise them', said Edvard Kardelj, Slovenian communist ideologue and vice-president of Tito's National Liberation Committee). There is controversy over the number of prisoners executed in both instances, as there is over the terror committed by the partisans against the Italian population in the Slovenian Littoral and Istria before the Germans took over.

After consulting Bishop Rožman, the Germans appointed Rupnik, who had been mayor of Ljubljana under the Italians, to be titular head (*načelnik*, prefect) of the province. The Bishop had assured him of his full moral support, as something had to be done to stop the civil war. The German occupation was more severe than the Italian, but there was no 'germanising'. The real authority belonged to SS General Erwein Rösener, who set up a Command Staff for the Suppression of Bands whose priority was to clear Istria and the coast, and to secure the main railway lines. Sweeping operations first cleared most of the territory the partisans had briefly held across the old Italo-Yugoslav border, and by mid-November, they were also driven from much of the territory they held in Ljubljana Province. Rupnik was allowed to set up the *Slovensko domobranstvo* or Slovene Home Guard, a volunteer force that numbered initially 1,000-2,000 mostly ex-MVAC village guards. The cadres were also from the MVAC, ex-Yugoslav army officers associated with the SZ. As Rösener as-

---

1995: 298.

sumed greater control, in order to use the Home Guard against the partisans for German security ends, so Rupnik's authority over the force diminished. As the communist-dominated OF left Ljubljana for liberated territory and as towns were held by counter-revolutionaries, divisions sharpened and accounts were settled more harshly. Yet confusion still prevailed among anti-communists. Many joined the Home Guard (particularly ex-Yugoslav regular officers) in order to protect and supply what remained of illegal, Mihailovićist, 'chetniks'. Rupnik's new Slovene Domobrans were generally in favour of the Western Allies. Partisans or the German police were believed to be responsible for mysterious liquidations, and there were rumours of a partisan-German compact to repel an Allied invasion.

Tito regarded Macedonia as potentially favourable terrain. He realised the KPJ could benefit from the population's alienation from both pre-war Serb-Yugoslav rule and wartime Bulgarian rule. However, the Bulgarian administration had managed to penetrate the KPJ organisation right up to Niš, thus successfully countering its work in occupied areas. Tito's delegate Tempo had worked from the western portion of Macedonia annexed to Albania, where conditions were more favourable. Italian control was lax, Serbs had been revolted by the excesses of Italian-backed Albanian nationalists, and Muslims feared Serb chetnik vindictiveness, but it was only after Italy's withdrawal that the partisans acquired a real foothold. A newly-created NOV command for Macedonia controlled parts of western Macedonia for most of the remainder of 1943. As Macedonian partisans demanded a statement concerning the national aims of the struggle, a manifesto was issued calling for an uprising against all enemies—Bulgarian occupiers, Mihailović's Serb hegemonists, Albanian hegemonists and Vancha Mihailov's Macedonian fascists[24]—in brotherly union with other peoples in Yugoslavia. The language appeared to intend that Macedonia would remain in Yugoslavia, yet it expressed support for

---

24 The Macedonian revolutionary nationalist of the 1920s was in Zagreb where the Germans thought of using him to enlist volunteers from Macedonia into the SS.

a union of all Macedonia and, eventually, a Balkan federation. There were reactions against it among activists in Skopje and elsewhere. Since September, an SOE mission had been attached to Tempo's headquarters. He had been warned by the Central Committee of the KPJ to be wary of the British. Although very suspicious of them, he still paraded them through villages to show that the partisans had the backing of the Western Allies. In traditional Macedonian fashion, he also organised a meeting of priests from partisan-controlled territory to discuss the eventual setting up of an independent Macedonian Orthodox Church. The British presence proved useful in countering Mihailović's movement, which had spread among the Serbs in the areas north of Skopje, and in western Macedonia. Djurić's small Vardar Corps, mostly made up of Serb refugees from Bulgarian and Italian-Albanian rule, fought against partisans and held meetings.

As Albanians of all hues wanted to keep the new borders, it was all but impossible for Mihailović to link up with potentially pro-Western Albanians, and the KPJ found itself in the strange position of being patron and guide of the small Communist Party of Albania while meeting stiff resistance all round. Slogans of self-determination for Kosovo were allowed to appear in its statements. A conference of local delegates for Kosovo that met on the last day of 1943 in the village of Bujan near Gjakovë (Djakovica) agreed to set up a regional People's Liberation Council for Kosovo and Metohija. It acknowledged that the area had 'a majority Albanian population that wishes union with Albania', that the only way to obtain it was 'through a common struggle with the other peoples of Yugoslavia against the occupiers and their lackeys', and that it had 'the right of self-determination, up to and including secession'. With such limitations and contradictions, the scope for action by Yugoslav partisans was slight in Kosovo. The Germans pandered even more than the Italians before them to Albanian nationalism. Their trusted agent in Kosovo was Xhafer Deva, who became Interior Minister in the Albanian government, who raised volunteers to fight 'Serb bandits', and who launched a new wave of expulsion of Serbs.

The idea of a united Yugoslavia was kept by the representatives of the pre-war régime—the King, his government and Mihailović, by Tito and the KPJ leadership, as well as by an increasing number of Yugo-slavs. The old ideology of 'integral' Yugoslavism had obviously failed to achieve its goal, and yet, disseminated as it had been throughout the 'twenties and 'thirties, 'Yugoslavism' *tout court* surfaced after the very idea of Yugoslavia seemed to have collapsed. As the partisans had moved back and forth across Bosnia, the KPJ launched its reunification on totally new ideological, social and political foundations. Its Peoples' Liberation Movement filled the power vacuum that gradually expanded. It was still Serb-based, but it was not based in Serbia, and most of those who wanted to get out of the enemy camp or out of the past, turned to it.

Once the Germans had established their control over what was essential to them, large areas of Bosnia and of inner Croatia were allowed to slip back to the Peoples' Liberation Army (NOV). Help was now forthcoming from the Allies in Italy. Jajce, in central Bosnia, with its imposing fortress, had been taken by the partisans in late August 1943, and was their new 'capital'. It seemed to Tito that the time had come to complete the setting up of a counter-government that had been started at Bihać, and to formalise it with a second session of AVNOJ—the Anti-Fascist Council for the Peoples' Liberation of Yugoslavia. He acknowledged that the broad masses, especially in Serbia, were not yet ready to renounce the monarchist tradition at a stroke, that he first needed to legitimise his counter-government through international recognition, and that he had to be careful not to complicate Soviet-British relations. The second session of AVNOJ was opened on 29 November 1943, with 142 communist and fellow-travelling participants, and in the presence of British and American liaison officers, who probably did not understand the speeches. The oratory denounced twenty years of oppression under a handful of greater-Serbian hegemonists and traitors, whose leaders were still enjoying the support of 'our Allies'.

AVNOJ was presented as the coming together of various 'national' movements associated with particular territories. A series of motions were adopted that virtually set up a new state, called the Federative (sic: *Federativna*) Peoples' Yugoslavia, 'on the basis of the right of every people to self-determination, including the right to secede, or to unite with other nations, in compliance with the true will of all the nations of Yugoslavia, confirmed in the course of the three-year long common peoples' liberation struggle which has forged the inseparable brotherhood of the nations of Yugoslavia [who wish to] remain united in Yugoslavia'. In spite of the convoluted jargon, the KPJ clarified its concept of a federal Yugoslavia as a community of equal nations, to the extent that it mentioned Serbs, Croats, Slovenes, Macedonians and Montenegrins, and 'the people of Serbia, Croatia, Slovenia, Macedonia, Montenegro and Bosnia and Herzegovina'. No decision was made as yet concerning the status of Bosnia and Herzegovina, although Muslims were mentioned as a separate ethnic-religious category. The definition of Macedonia and Montenegro was difficult enough. Most Montenegrins, even among the partisans, considered themselves to be part of the Serbian nation even as 'Montenegrins'. The question of Macedonia touched on other Balkan nations, and there were only a few Macedonians at Jajce. Even more delicate was the question of Kosovo. It was easier to lay claim to unredeemed territory to the north-west of Yugoslavia's pre-war international borders. AVNOJ assumed legislative functions, and gave Tito's National Committee the character of a provisional government. The question of the monarchy was left to be decided by the people after the war. Meanwhile, King Peter II was forbidden to return and the exiled government was denied any rights as Yugoslavia's legal government. The top rank of marshal was introduced in the partisan army. On the proposal of the delegation from Slovenia, it was attributed to Tito, who was already the object of a cult subsidiary only to that of Stalin.

The International Department of the Central Committee of the Soviet Communist Party continued to let him act as he knew best for Yugoslavia, within broad guidelines, so long as he did not upset Stalin's Anglo-American Allies. When it came to the Jajce decisions, Tito had informed Moscow in a way that would minimise the chances of their being downgraded at the last moment. He had announced the proposed transformation of AVNOJ into the base for a new government, with no mention of the King and the exiled government. He simply claimed that he had been told, by the head of the British mission, that London would not continue to support them. Stalin was initially irritated, as he feared the AVNOJ decisions, which coincided with the Tehran Conference, would complicate his negotiations with the Western Allies. Much to his surprise, the Jajce decisions encountered no resistance, as the Anglo-Americans came to accept Tito's view that his movement was not just the more effective, but the only resistance movement.

The Yugoslav communist leader had correctly calculated what he could get away with. His NOP had mobilised in Bosnia and Herzegovina a substantial amount of Serbs, Croats and Muslims who began to see the partisans as potential saviours from the mutual destruction that had been going on for over two years. Sectional nationalism was associated with the Axis Powers that had destroyed Yugoslavia, and were now losing the war. In the backward and mixed-population central-western regions that had suffered so much, the new order of 'brotherhood and unity' of ethnic communities was proving especially attractive. The KPJ had come to acquire sensitivity to the point of view of the different nationalities, while being committed to Yugoslavia. It harnessed various local and national feelings to its cause, largely disguising the real agenda. Its slogans on the rights of self-determination, with even the mention of secession, are apt to be misleading; the Yugoslav communist leadership never really believed they would be exercised. Their unwavering confidence was probably their most important asset, and it came from their fanatical faith in the victory of the Soviet Union. Tito's ethnic background and his past were at that time still shrouded in mystery. Part Croat, part Slovene, a communist who had spent most of his adult life abroad, he was a genuine internationalist. He was not afraid to face the reality of ethnic differences within Yugoslavia. He was ready to turn it into the starting point for the building of a new order, which was still based, at that time, on some degree of give-and-take between the KPJ's revolutionary aims and the constituencies upon which support could be mobilised. He had made a break with the old order and with the patterns of national belief inherited from the past. Increasingly, the NOP, even if lead by the KPJ, seemed to the Allies the only movement that could reunite the peoples of Yugoslavia.

5

THE KPJ LIBERATES, CONQUERS
AND RESTORES YUGOSLAVIA
JANUARY 1944-MAY 1945

Tito's moves, from Jajce to Belgrade,
via Bari, Vis and Moscow

A major Allied landing on the Yugoslav coast remained a fear for
some and a hope for others, although it was never really an option.
From the end of 1943, Tito's movement became the main benefici-
ary of British support forthcoming from Italy. Military considerations required pinning German troops in, and then hindering their
withdrawal from, the Balkans. Relations with the USSR called for
action that could count as a British contribution to the war effort, to
offset the long postponement of the second front in Europe. Political
considerations led to the belief that British influence could be maintained in a restored Yugoslavia, through support for the most active
domestic movement. The Yugoslav communists had been active, and
radically so, because they were carrying out their own revolutionary
plan, for long unobserved. Heather Williams notes that, as the war
against Nazi Germany and its allies became also a war for a 'brave
new world' in conjunction with the heroic Soviet ally, 'a situation
developed in which all the cards were stacked in favour of Tito and
the Partisans'.[1]

In February-March 1944, the German estimation of the number
of partisans was just over 100,000, of whom 80,000 were in the
NDH; they themselves claimed to be between 200,000 and 300,000.

---

1   Williams, *Parachutes, Patriots and Partisans,* 247.

The formation of a 'partisan government' at Jajce had left a deep impression on the population of Bosnia. *Marshal* Tito, President of the National Committee for the Liberation of Yugoslavia, posed as a statesman at the head of an ever more formal organisation, yet his Peoples' Liberation Movement (NOP) and Army (NOV) were not all that secure. They lorded over western Bosnia, parts of eastern Croatia and most of inland Dalmatia. The chetniks had strong popular support in eastern Bosnia. Muslims increasingly evaded NDH military call-up; they resisted more or less overt chetnik terror, covert partisan repression and ustasha ruthlessness. In spite of the 'Tuzla effect', evaders and deserters still provided manpower for various independent armed groups that protected Muslim villages and carried out anti-Serb forays. Nedžad Topčić led the 'Muslim Green Cadre'. He cooperated at times with the Domobrans, at other times with the chetniks; he maintained ties with the partisans, was watched with increasing suspicion by the ustashas, and was in touch with the SS. Muhamed Pandža, with his 'Muslim Liberation Army', sided with the partisans for a while, until arrested by the ustashas, when he expressed his loyalty to the NDH. Huska Miljković, with his 3,000-strong 'Muslim Army', was courted and threatened by ustashas and communists alike, before going over to the partisans, keeping command over his own men, until the ustashas had him murdered.

Muslims were drifting to the NOP, but also, and perhaps increasingly, turning to ideas of autonomy for Bosnia under the Germans. The return from training in France and Germany of the SS 'Handschar' Division reinforced the trend, as the unit was hardly more than a well-equipped ethnic militia, to be used locally. On 30 April, 15 Muslim personalities from Sarajevo presented a blunt memorandum of grievances to the NDH prime minister. The more resistant the Muslims' attitude became in all areas, the greater ustasha pressure against them, leading to incarcerations and executions by the autumn. The KPJ in Bosnia was still predominantly Serb, accusing the majority of Muslims of opportunism, or at the very least of gathering on a purely Muslim platform. It was not until the eve of the second session of AVNOJ (the Anti-Fascist Council for the National Liberation of Yugoslavia), in November 1943, that an 'Anti-Fascist Territorial Council' was set up for Bosnia and Herzegovina, said to be 'neither Serb nor Croat nor Muslim, but Serb, Croat and Muslim', and not until 1 July 1944 was the territory defined, on the basis of the freely-expressed will of its peoples, as a federated unit in the new Yugoslavia.

The NOP also had problems with the Communist Party in Croatia, as the dissatisfaction of Serb partisans increased. They had to show that they were fighting for the freedom of Croats and Serbs, under the Croatian flag, with Croatian names and Croat political commissars, in regions such as Krajina that were exhausted by the war, and where they were still the majority of combatants. The belief in an imminent Allied landing that would not allow the setting up of a communist régime, and memories of the days when the old Independent Democratic Party, rather than the KPJ, had been the Serbs' party in Croatia, in alliance with the Croat Peasant Party (HSS), also contributed to the defection to the chetniks in April of Joco Eremić, the commander of the partisans in the Kordun area, with part of his fighters. As it came at the time of Abwehr probes to see whether partisan fatigue and discontent could be exploited, the Croatian communist leadership decided to hit back at the rebellion before it got out of hand. Having got hold of a group of defectors, it staged a Stalin-type show trial (the first of its kind) in a village school in free territory, which resulted in executions and numerous sentences *in absentia*. Frightened by what could follow, the central KPJ leadership called the Croatian leadership to order, and sent Kardelj and Djilas to sort things out. In September, Vladimir Bakarić replaced Andrija Hebrang as KP secretary in Croatia.

The Germans had to be satisfied with controlling mineral deposits, the coast and vital communications, leaving the rest to guerrillas. Until the end of 1943, they managed with a couple of low-grade Wehrmacht divisions, German-supervised NDH units, Volksdeutsche and foreign SS, and various contacts with guerrillas. The Allied presence in Italy, increased support for Tito and the fear of an Anglo-

American landing induced the German High Command to mount again a series of brief anti-insurgent operations between January and June 1944, to wipe out the guerrillas in particular areas, in order to clear land and sea communications. Although not as thorough as before, they nevertheless forced Tito out of Jajce in January, and almost captured him in May. As a German expedition advanced on the NOP 'capital', Tito, with the National Committee, Supreme Staff and British mission, evacuated it on 7 January 1944 (incidentally the old-style Orthodox Christmas). After a fortnight on the move, they all settled at Drvar, a small town in an easily-defended valley in western Bosnia, where they had four months' respite. It was there that they received a Soviet military mission,[2] which joined Brigadier Maclean, Churchill's son Randolph and an American liaison attaché. It was from there that they sent out their own missions *via* Bari (Djilas to Moscow, Velebit to London). They decided that the new Yugoslavia which had 'originated' (*nastala*) by the will of the people of 'Serbia, Vojvodina and Sandžak, Croatia, Slovenia, Macedonia, Montenegro, and Bosnia and Herzegovina' would be called Democratic Federative (*Federativna*) Yugoslavia. A slackening of German operations, linked with further Abwehr talks on prisoner exchanges (supervised as ever by Hans Ott), allowed the KPJ leadership to concentrate its energies on domestic rivals. In anticipation of a re-entry into Serbia, it mounted expeditions aimed at breaking down JVO (Yugoslav Army in the Homeland) networks in eastern Bosnia, by burning down pro-chetnik villages and expelling their inhabitants. A secret-police type Commission for the Suppression of the Fifth Column was set up under the Serb member of the inner leadership, Aleksandar Ranković. An important, but failed, attempt was made to break through Bulgarian defences to southern Serbia.

Tito was again taken by surprise. On 25 May, the day after Churchill had announced that King Peter was about to drop Mihailović from the exiled government, the Germans carried out an airborne attack,

---

2   It came by British glider from Bari, as the Soviet generals were not keen on parachutes.

using SS mountain and 'Brandenburg' special units. The radio transmission apparatus and part of the archives were taken. Tito, his staff and the Allied missions barely escaped, but for the first time since he had taken the field in 1941, the communist leader lost control of, and was separated from, the bulk of his forces. Hitler believed that the news of the attack must have filtered through NDH contacts at the last moment; Tito thought that Churchill had revealed his hideout so that the Germans could liquidate him. A large-scale Anglo-American air support campaign saved the partisans. The Western Allies controlled the air space; the Germans did not have enough troops. Tito was on the move again, until the Russians, fearing for the coordinated control of the partisans, insisted that he should be air-lifted to Bari, thence to a secure base. On 3 June, he was evacuated by a Soviet-piloted American aircraft. The British were anxious not to have another Yugoslav exile in their care; Tito did not want to be a leader in exile. In the night of 7/8 June, he was taken by a British warship from Bari to Vis, an island 50 kms from the mainland, which the Germans had not recaptured and which had been turned into an Anglo-partisan supply base.

Churchill had accepted that Tito would be the dominant factor in postwar Yugoslavia, but he wanted to save the monarchy. Keeping the monarchy was a moral obligation to the young monarch, as well as an imagined way to moderate Tito's communism and safeguard British interests. It would facilitate the partisans' entry into Serbia, where they had little popular support. In January, the British Prime Minister had opened a personal correspondence with Tito, to ascertain whether the King could be accepted if Mihailović were dismissed. Tito demanded that his committee be recognised as the sole government; if that were accepted, some cooperation with King Peter could be envisaged, subject to the question of the monarchy being decided by the people when the whole country had been liberated. After Peter II's marriage to Princess Alexandra of Greece had been celebrated in London in March, pressure was increased on him to appoint a new government which would come to an understanding with Tito.[3] Šubašić, still formally the HSS-nominated Ban of Croatia with the government in exile, was suggested, and an impatient Churchill anticipated events. On 17 May he informed Tito that King Peter had dismissed the Purić cabinet (which included Mihailović) and was about to appoint Šubašić; on 24 May (the day before the German raid on Drvar) he told as much to the Commons. However, it was not until 1 June that Peter II finally gave in, and announced (without Purić having resigned) that he had asked Šubašić to form a government.

'England' remained a bogey for Tito. He feared a scheme to save Serbia for the chetniks, and prevent a linkup with the Red Army. He kept putting off the political settlement the British wanted to make with him. However, he took care not to risk losing their military help. He was making big requests to both the British and the Soviets as he was trying to establish a real army. From the Soviets he notably asked for uniforms for 100,000 men, uniforms for colonels and generals, a marshal's uniform for himself, and decorations. The escape from Drvar had been a serious blow to his pride, and he felt uncomfortable under British protection. Churchill now thought that he could arrange for King Peter and his new prime minister to go to Vis and settle with Tito. The King was but an instrument, and the Šubašić 'government' (of which he was sole minister for the time being) had been appointed simply to make such an agreement. Tito kept in touch with the Soviets, who cautioned him against Churchill. Šubašić went to Vis, with the British Ambassador, but without King Peter. He proposed a coalition government with Tito as war minister, and the monarch remaining as formal supreme commander,

---

3   Even though Churchill wanted to save King Peter, Sir Alan Lascelles, King George VI's Private Secretary, prevented the Yugoslav royal marriage from being performed in Buckingham Palace (as King George of Greece and Purić would have liked), because 'the British public would not be pleased at a Balkan wedding, with all its (to them) pagan ritual, being celebrated in so sacred a shrine of the Church of England [sic],' (Duff Hart-Davis, ed., *King's Counsellor. Abdication and War: The Diaries of Sir Alan Lascelles*, London, 2007: 207–8). The marriage was eventually performed at the residence of the Yugoslav ambassador in London, which served as King Peter's residence.

but then immediately accepted (much to the communists' surprise) Tito's counter-proposals with only a few stylistic changes. The 'Tito-Šubašić Agreement' of 16 August was hardly a compromise. Tito gave a written assurance that the issue of the monarchy would not be raised before the end of the war, and said that it was not his intention to impose a communist system. Šubašić recognised AVNOJ as the only legitimate authority on Yugoslav territory, and the NOV as the only legitimate fighting force. He would form a government of progressive elements who had not taken a stand against the NOP, to organise support abroad for the partisans. Tito put forward two names he wanted included. Both sides undertook to issue statements on the subject of their cooperation. On his return, Šubašić duly formed a small 'progressive' cabinet as agreed, and issued an appeal to the nation to unite around Tito.

This was not quite what the British had intended. They wanted a Yugoslav leader who could get all potential resisters together, and thus shorten the war by hindering the Germans' retreat. What if Tito were no more capable of it than Mihailović? They were worried by the inability of the partisans to get support in Serbia. Tito was invited to visit Sir Henry Maitland Wilson, the Allied Supreme Commander Mediterranean in Italy. He suspected a trap to spring King Peter on him; his entourage feared for his life. He turned down the invitation, with the excuse that, as President of the National Committee, he could only be invited by a government. Churchill then took the opportunity of a visit to Italy in August, to put his idea of a compromise directly to Tito, and repeated the invitation. Tito went reluctantly, on Soviet advice. Churchill told him he could expect no political recognition until he had come to an arrangement with the King, and that he was not being provided with arms to impose communism. Tito repeated his assurance that it was not his intention to impose communism, but he could not say so publicly so as not to give the impression that he was acting under duress. As for seeing King Peter, this was not the right moment. The meeting with Churchill had a great effect on Tito. It strengthened his self-confidence, and left him with the impression that the NOP had been accepted as the new régime in the making. On his return to Vis, he issued his counterpart to Šubašić's statement: the aim of the agreement was to strengthen the liberation struggle, and prevent traitors such as Mihailović from taking cover under the authority of a legitimate government. This was followed by getting the King to take measures to do just that, such as dismissing Mihailović from his command post, and appealing to all in Yugoslavia to rally round Tito.

From Vis, Tito again planned and directed operations. Serbia was his vital concern. German military strength in the Yugoslav lands, which had been reinforced between December 1943 and February 1944, had thereafter been much reduced again. In spite of that, and although the partisans concentrated on Serbia even at the cost of losing territory in Montenegro, their attempt in March-April had failed. Serbia was once again the centre of general attention as the German retreat from the Balkans had started. Both the Anglo-Americans and the Soviets were ready to give Tito full support to build up partisan strength there. The Soviets told him Serbia was the pivot on which turned the recognition of his movement at the head of Yugoslavia. In April, an SOE mission had come to the partisans in Serbia. Tito feared losing touch with developments if he stayed too long in Vis. On 18 September, he 'levanted' (to quote Churchill), in a Soviet plane, for Red Army headquarters in Romania.

Once the British had decided to sacrifice Mihailović to Tito, they needed to justify their decision. Wilson's request in December 1943, to destroy a number of rail bridges over the Ibar and Morava rivers in Serbia, was made with the conviction that Mihailović would not, or could not, carry it out.[4] His agreement caused consternation, and

---

4 The request occasioned another 'non-diplomatic' (and nostalgically francophile) outburst by Mihailović, on the occasion of a reception on the day of his family patron saint in December. Suspecting that he was being put to the test, he asked Armstrong whether the operations were really necessary; he argued that he needed more arms to carry them out, that the Germans would repair the damage within days and then execute hostages. An irritated Armstrong answered that Mihailović should realise how much of the sweat

the sabotage action was called off. He had ceased to be a bargaining counter in negotiations with Tito. Meanwhile, influenced by Topalović, he had accelerated the talks with the politicians, and accepted their demands. By then, most Yugoslavs were coming round to the idea of a restored Yugoslavia, based on a new order, even if they did not want a revolution. It was high time for Mihailović to meet the communists' challenge. He needed the firm and open commitment of party politicians to a programme that offered more than just a return to the *status quo ante*, in order to counter the image of militarism and nationalism, and remove the sinister shadow of the Šahovići chetnik congress in Montenegro held on 1 December 1941. He thus planned a national congress to be held on 1 December 1943 (again the anniversary of the unification of 1918), and worked hard at it with Topalović. Many ideas were mooted. On the one hand, politicians talked of renewing the old 'united opposition' alliance of the 1930s, of extending the federal concept so as to take into account the specificities of Bosnia-Herzegovina, Montenegro and Macedonia, and even of leaving the form of government to be decided after the war. On the other hand, there was talk of 'Serbdom', of 'unification of Serbia' and of 'Serbia's mission'. Preparations dragged on, so that the congress took place two months after AVNOJ II, when it was regarded as just a response to Tito's congress.

Mihalović's congress opened at Ba, a village not far from Ravna Gora, on 25 January 1944. Most of the 274 participants were from Serbia, with some from Montenegro and Bosnia, a few refugee Croats, one Slovene and one Muslim (six non-Serbs altogether). Because of their affiliations, they were deemed to represent the People's Radical, Democratic, Independent Democratic, Yugoslav National, Agrarian, Socialist and Republican parties, as well as various cultural, sport and other organisations, to signal the victory of the idea of multi-party democracy over a Serbian ultra-nationalism inimical to political

---

of British workers went into the manufacture of every single weapon sent to him. The French—Mihailović shot back—had been our only allies; they had not measured their sweat against our blood.

parties. The congress was also the expression of a reaction against the arbitrary behaviour of certain commanders, and the outcome of a showdown between Moljević (for the 'Ravna Gora Movement') and Topalović (for the parties lobby). The atmosphere on the eve of the meeting had been tense, with Mihailović coming out openly and unreservedly in favour of Topalović. In his opening address, he stressed the need for a return to normality through legality, and rejected talk of a transitional dictatorship and of collective retaliation. Topalović was elected president of the congress, which passed resolutions. Yugoslavia would be restored as a monarchical, constitutional, parliamentary and federal state, made up of three entities endowed with economic, social and cultural autonomy—Serbia, Croatia and Slovenia. Each in turn would provide forms of autonomy for the different communities within it. The changes would be implemented by a parliament freely elected after the full liberation and restoration of constitutional order. Until them, members of political parties and other organisations, including the Ravna Gora Movement, would act collectively, as part of the Yugoslav National Democratic Union, which was set up to federate them all, with an expanded Central National Committee to cooperate with the exiled government and the Allies. An appeal was made to the KPJ to join, while its unilateral action was deplored. It was all rhetorically strong on 'democracy', 'monarchy' and even 'federation', but vague on the territory of the federated units. The question of minorities within the three 'national' units was largely bypassed. The presumed party representatives were without party structures. The main resolution was dated Saint Sava's Day, 27 January, which seemed to give it a Serb imprint.

Although Mihailović had already been practically abandoned by the British, pro-Allied optimism had returned to Serbia. There was a return to Yugoslav feelings, even though it did not fit in with the plan sketched by AVNOJ II at Jajce. It boosted Mihailović, who appealed to, and again attempted to make contact with, Croats and Muslims. He even wrote to Krnjević, inviting him to his headquarters in Yugoslavia. The message was sent through the British, who did not even bother to pass it on. In spite of the failed specific British request, sabotage was resumed with the help of SOE operatives, on telephone, telegraph and railway lines. Various categories were once more threatened with being placed 'under the letter Z'—such as 'anti-Yugoslav' collaborators, informers, black marketers and looters. The head of Nedić's secretariat and his deputy at the Home Ministry (which Nedić had taken over in November 1943) were shot dead in Belgrade. The historian Dimitrije Djordjević—at the time a youth activist with the JVO—has called the period following the Ba congress in Serbia 'our swan song'.[5] The Central National Committee issued instructions to form local 'Ravna Gora committees' to oversee local government and take charge of propaganda. Propaganda was really their main activity. It promoted a new-formula Kingdom of Yugoslavia, federal, democratic and social, made up of three territorial units; it attacked the communists for dividing Serbs into Serbians, Bosnians, Herzegovinians, Montenegrins and Macedonians. It launched (or at the very least did not deny) rumours of landings and parachutings. Orders were issued not to make any arrangements with the occupation authorities, but to avoid action against them until further notice, to resist the call-up for service in collaborationist forces and to liquidate Ljotićite agents. The JVO command structure was formally divided into territorial divisions covering most of Yugoslavia. These included Montenegro under Djurišić and Dalmatia under Djujić, but no longer mentioned Jevdjević, who had been roundly, if not formally, condemned at Ba.

In the towns, which remained under German control, the population had mixed feelings, generally trying to get through the final stage of the war with as little trouble as possible. In rural Serbia, the Nedić administration, in so far as it survived, took orders from JVO commanders and Ravna Gora committees. The Germans so badly needed food imports that they came to use more carrot than stick to obtain deliveries. Peasants sold their produce to towns at inflated prices. They settled their debts in depreciated currency, or ignored

---

5   Dimitrije Djordjević, *Ožiljci i opomene*, I, Belgrade, 1994: 255.

them. Chetniks kept banditry at bay, protected villagers, and did not now make excessive exactions. They even paid in cash, for many people were coming from towns to offer their services and money—businessmen and industrialists, intellectuals and politicians, even collaborators in need of a pre-liberation alibi. They came partly out of optimism for the future, partly out of fear (of German reprisals, of Allied air raids, of communism). Industry was still geared to German military requirements and exports to the Reich. German occupation costs amounted to about forty per cent of Serbia's national income during the last year of occupation. In spite of that, and of continued large-scale plunder of the economy, Serbia was on the whole better off than the NDH, as there was less disruption to its territory until the summer of 1944. The number of refugees in Serbia in April was officially 241,000, but in fact 300,000-400,000 because of those who were not registered, and provided recruits for collaborationist forces, various chetniks and partisans.

The Germans reacted to the Ba congress by turning against chetniks with an operation conducted during February in northern Serbia, by SS and Brandenburg units, Bulgarian troops and SDK Volunteers, that killed over eighty guerrillas and captured 913. The latter included Perhinek, interrogated by the Gestapo (who were keen to know what Mihailović wanted to do with King Peter) before being sent to a prisoner camp in Germany. Police operations in towns, especially in Belgrade, resulted in arrests, executions and deportations to camps in Germany. Many delegates to the congress were among them. The aim was to disrupt the 'DM' organisation, weed out its agents in the collaborationist administration, and force native auxiliaries to cooperate in tracking down Mihailović himself, which caused a crisis in the Nedić government, most of whose ministers and SDS commanders were by that time fighting shy of blatantly unpopular action. Nedić denounced Ba as an anti-German manifestation, and again tried to resign. The Germans would not allow him to go; he lost whatever influence he still had, and Mihailović escaped capture. When the British mission was evacuated in May, Topalović went out with it to Bari, to plead with the Allies, to offer to place Mihailović's forces under Allied command, and to seek cooperation with Šubašić. He was able to see him before the Yugoslav prime minister went out to Vis, and it was he who suggested that King Peter be brought to some place in Yugoslavia which was not controlled by either of the contending forces, to act as a formal Supreme Commander. Mihailović, ever the francophile, also sent a message to General de Gaulle, asking him to help.

It is difficult to resolve the intricacy of events in Serbia in the spring and summer of 1944. The British loss of confidence in, and propaganda against, Mihailović (who in July still enjoyed the support of ninety per cent of the population according to German reports) played into the hands of German propaganda. Left without supplies, Mihailović's units were engaged in saving hundreds of Allied airmen from the crews of bombers shot over eastern Yugoslavia in the course of raids on positions mainly situated in Romania. When in April-May, a group of partisan divisions again attempted to get into Serbia, towards the Morava valley, all their opponents— Germans, Bulgarians, Serbian auxiliaries and Mihailović's chetniks—found themselves barring their entry and turning them back, not really in unison. They generally avoided fighting each other as they were fighting the partisans. The partisans too avoided fighting German and Bulgarian troops, who occasionally turned against chetniks, and there were clashes between the JVO and collaborationist units. Communist Party organisations were instructed on how to infiltrate German, collaborationist and chetnik formations, blame chetniks for sabotage action, and foment dissidence between them and Nedićites. It was Ljotić's Volunteers who were mainly responsible for stopping Tito's 'proletarians' at the Ibar valley. The collaborationists had a slightly more realistic appraisal of what was coming than Mihailović. Their régime would fall with Germany, but there was still a chance that the Western Allies would not allow a communist take-over. Wedged between the JVO and the German occupation authority, Nedić looked increasingly to Mihailović. He had obtained the release from captivity in Germany of a number of generals, including Miodrag Damjanović, to whom he offered the vacated position of head of his secretariat. Damjanović was a Mihailović sympathiser. He accepted, after consulting Mihailović, who thus obtained a confidant at the centre of the collaborationist structure. Nedić had also suggested to the Germans that the chetniks be legalised or amnestied, and that Mihailović be allowed to go abroad, or financed to stay inactive. Neubacher was still attempting to set up a Serb anti-communist front.

Serbia had not seen much of the partisans since 1941, and was rather confused by their reappearance. Their shock units were battle-tested and well-equipped, made up of young and enthusiastic Serbs from the NDH; they were endorsed by the Allies and by the King. Although the peasants were generally supportive of Mihailović, many were ready to see who would come out on top. The chetniks were so badly armed to resist the well-armed partisans' incursions, that some of Mihailović's officers (including Kalabić) met German officers to try and work out a meeting with Neubacher. Nedić seems to have picked up the idea. He suggested forming a Serbian army of 50,000 uniting all anti-communist fighters,[6] and eventually went on to organise an elaborate secret meeting with Mihailović. Of their probable meeting on 20 August, there is no evidence other than statements later made by them to their communist interrogators, and Neubacher's indirect testimony.[7] The meeting took place in a dark room. Nedić, who did all the talking, was not certain that he had actually talked to Mihailović, who was mostly silent. It appears that Nedić offered to obtain arms from the Germans and to place his SDS under Mihailović's command to fight the communists, in exchange for Mihailović to be represented in the Belgrade govern-

---

6   The SDS was then 25,000 strong; the Ljotić Volunteers had been strengthened to 10,000 (even to the point of obtaining the freedom of hostages who accepted to volunteer for service); the Germans estimated Mihailović's forces at 9,000 armed men.

7   Hermann Neubacher, *Sonderauftrag Südost, 1940-1945. Bericht eines fliegenden Diplomaten*, Göttingen, 1956: 164–5.

ment. Neubacher and the German generals were in favour. They put it to Hitler on 22 August, who immediately rejected the whole idea, on the grounds that 'even a certain communist danger is more acceptable', that it was an English plot to have a fifth column in Serbia, that all should be done to draw Nedić and Mihailović apart rather than together. Mihailović had reluctantly gone to the meeting, and did not like the proposals. The president of the collaborationist government and the outgoing war minister of the exiled government had tried to exploit each other's predicament. Mihailović had obtained as much equipment as Nedić's administration could yield. Nedić wanted Mihailović to take over; as Germany was on the verge of defeat and the Red Army approached, it seemed that Mihailović alone could save Serbia from communism and Nedić from the accusation of treason.

Mihailović's appointment as minister had been a constraint. He had not wanted it, but had then taken it too seriously. He felt that he was actually in command of various local leaders who declared their loyalty to him, and that he had to retain their loyalty, so that they would be available to secure the country for the legitimate government when the time came. Topalović's departure, followed by the loss of Mihailović's official positions, strengthened again the 'Ravnogorists' as Moljević eventually took over as chairman of the Central National Committee. When Šubašić expanded his cabinet in July, the Committee noted that the exiled government could not properly represent the country as it did not include any representatives of the parties in the Yugoslav National Democratic Union, and reserved for itself freedom of action. The Yugoslav Army in the Homeland (JVO) continued to call itself so, and Mihailović still occasionally used the title of minister.

The Reich was shaking. In July, Hitler had survived the attempt to kill him. Consequences were felt in the German command structure in the Balkans, as troop movements from Greece to the north started in late July. Worried about possible links of certain Serbian Orthodox Church leaders, albeit interned, with Mihailović and the British,

German security interrogated Patriarch Gavrilo and Bishop Nikolaj, and transferred them to Dachau concentration camp in September 1944, along with other 'important detainees' (*Ehrenhäfting*) from various countries. The two prelates were kept there until November, when Neuchbacher had them transferred to a hotel in the Bavarian Alps, and eventually to Vienna. Franz Neuhausen, Göring's plenipotentiary for Balkan economic affairs resident in Belgrade, was arrested for corruption.

A mission of the US Office of Strategic Services (OSS, the American version of SOE), led by Colonel Robert McDowell, came to Mihailović at the end of August and stayed until November, ostensibly to organise the evacuation of the airmen, in fact to see what was going on. It was an expression of independence by the OSS, backed by President Roosevelt, that did not change policy but influenced Mihailović at a critical moment. It effectively evacuated several hundred airmen in cooperation with Mihailović. It also served as a channel for German surrender proposals when, soon after his arrival, McDowell met a representative of Neubacher's. Did McDowell explore the possibility of an anticipated German capitulation to stop the Russians from entering Yugoslavia? Did he in any way encourage Mihailović to expect a change in his favour?

The arrival of Soviet troops on the eastern borders of Yugoslavia at the end of August 1944, and the speed of developments in Bulgaria as it switched sides in September, meant that the Germans could only hold on to their evacuation lines from the Balkans. To hinder that retreat, the Western Allies gave full support to Tito's new attempt to break into Serbia that had begun at the end of July with three of the best NOV divisions. Operation 'Ratweek' provided material help to the partisans' build-up there, as Allied bombers targeted the Belgrade-Zagreb, Belgrade-Skopje and Sava-Adriatic rail connections, and the bridges over the Danube. Under cover of 'Ratweek', the partisans carried the civil war into Serbia again, and established a base on the Kopaonik mountain between the Ibar and the Morava. Tito was intent on crushing the chetnik force and organisation; Mihailović strained all his resources to prevent the partisans from advancing into the heart of Serbia. Meanwhile, German troops continued their evacuation from Greece. They withdrew slowly, and fomented civil war as they withdrew.

Mihailović believed that the outcome of the war was about to be decided by Turkey going to war, followed at last by an Allied incursion in the Balkans. He called on all Serbs, Croats and Slovenes to remain faithful to King and Fatherland, for the final phase of the war, and the fight for the ideals of freedom, democracy and social justice. When the King issued a decree on 28 August 1944 dismissing him from his position of Chief of Staff of the Supreme Command in occupied Yugoslavia, Mihailović countered with a circular to his commanders, that he had received a personal communication from the monarch. King Peter had, he claimed, told him not to believe what was being communicated by Radio London, which was but part of a manoeuvre. The Anglo-Americans and the Soviets had agreed that they would not enter Yugoslavia, and that the country would be free to decide its own fate when the Germans had gone. The Western Allies' short-term aim was to overcome Russian distrust until Germany's final defeat, when they would turn in favour of democratic and anti-communist forces in Yugoslavia. From the end of May to August, Mihailović again had a direct channel of communication with sympathisers in exiled government services. What did they tell him? What did McDowell tell him? What did Mihailović, want to believe, and how did he interpret it? On 31 August, he signed an order of general mobilisation, made 'in the name of the King, with the approval of the Allies, and by virtue of the powers that had been vested' in him.

He realised that he was about to fight a decisive battle. With a general call-up, he hoped to ward off the partisans, and rid Serbia of occupation troops before the Red Army arrived. Instructions were given to his Belgrade underground command to prevent, by whatever means, the capital from falling into the hands of the communists. SDS cadres linked to Mihailović's organisation started going over openly. Whatever the number of men who responded to the call-up, it is reasonable to assume that no more than 40,000 could be armed, supplied and organised. There is evidence of enthusiastic young men going to join up, while evacuating German military lorries moved along the same roads in the opposite direction. There is also evidence of the JVO command having to resort to threats of prosecution after the war, in order to counter the effects of communist propaganda that the Anglo-Americans, and even the King, were backing the NOV. King Peter did indeed broadcast from London on 12 September calling all in Yugoslavia to rally round Tito, adding that the 'stigma of treason' would stick to those who did not do so. The mobilisation quickly turned sour, as the best equipped partisan units fought their way into Mihailović's home territory. Mihailović was losing control. For fear of being captured, he was forced to move around, his archives fell into partisan hands, and he became separated from the main body of his forces in Serbia.

The break-up of his JVO had started in mid-August, outside Serbia. Lukačević issued a proclamation in the name of commanders in eastern Bosnia, eastern Herzegovina and Sandžak, that they were no longer taking orders from the JVO Supreme Command, but from the King only, to form an independent national resistance to fight the occupiers and their collaborators. It may have been an idea brought back from London, where Lukačević had been to represent Mihailović at King Peter's wedding. In the belief of a British landing, he moved against a German-Croat division, attacked the Trebinje-Dubrovnik railway, captured some localities and made several hundred prisoners in September. He offered the partisans a non-aggression agreement, but received no answer. At the end of September, he was attacked and captured by them. After King Peter's broadcast, Ostojić and Baćović warned Mihailović that their men were losing the will to fight the communists. Albania with Kosovo was another line of retreat for the Germans before going through Montenegro and Sandžak to Bosnia. In September, chetniks attempted to hold territory behind Lake Skadar, in the hope of provoking an Allied intervention, and held talks with Albanian Catholic tribesmen, but there was not much they could do as the Germans gave more authority to an increasingly nationalist government in Tirana, that asked for the annexation of Sandžak. In February 1944, the SS Mountain Division 'Skanderbeg' was formed by the Germans, mostly from Kosovo Albanians, to serve in annexed territory. It took part in the round up and deportation of 280 Jews, and committed acts of violence against Serbs, but eventually melted through desertions. Serb refugees provided recruits for some 1,000 chetniks, under Djurić's command of central and southern Serbia This operated from Serbia although it also covered Yugoslav Macedonia and Kosovo. The communists were aware of the danger of Mihailović exploiting the discontent of Serbs in Kosovo, and even more so in northern Macedonia. They were successful in infiltrating the JVO in Djurić's area. Mihailović had him arrested in May for contacts with both partisans and Germans, but he escaped and defected to the partisans with many of his men.

It was from northern Montenegro that the partisans, supplied from Bari, were preparing their moves into Serbia. Djurišić's return to Sandžak had given new hope to the chetniks there and in Montenegro. He had obtained through Neubacher the initial release from captivity of 500 of his men, and some help from Nedić. In January and in March he was successful in barring the way to the partisans. In April, he attempted to join Lašić, but their link-up was foiled as the partisans attacked. Lašić's force was destroyed (Lašić was killed in an Allied bombardment in May), and Djurišić went back to Sandžak. After a visit to Belgrade in June, he returned to Montenegro, where he formed a 6,000-7,000 strong 'Montenegrin Volunteer Corps'. At the head of what was in fact a German auxiliary force, related on paper to Ljotić's Serbian Volunteer Corps (SDK), he also accepted once again Mihailović's nominal command. He justified it all by the need to fight the communists and to bring food to the near-starving province. For a while, he united all the remaining chetniks in Montenegro, and even managed to get Kolašin back again, but he was losing out, particularly from mid-September. Whatever his intentions, Mihailović had little or no attraction for non-Serbs, but he was still trying to reach out to them at that crucial moment. He did so through Mustafa Mulalić, a Muslim and prewar opposition JNS deputy who was vice-president of the Central National Committee, and also by sending General Djukić, his Belgrade-based nominal commander of the northern provinces, who was in touch with Croat personalities in Belgrade, together with Predavec, on a mission to Zagreb to contact Maček.

Ever since July 1944, Tito had been asking Stalin for more help. More suspicious of British intentions than ever, he feared a covert Western plan with Mihailović in Serbia. Eventually he requested a meeting with Stalin. He was flown to Soviet headquarters in Romania and thence to Moscow, after an absence of five years, for his first-ever face-to-face meeting with Stalin. He came to ask for the Red Army 'to help our units liberate Serbia and Belgrade'.[8] Judging from the account of Tito's conversation with Stalin given by Dedijer, and by what followed, they discussed the international recognition of the NOP and how the Red Army would come to help it in Serbia.[9] On 29 September, it was announced that the Supreme Staff of the Yugoslav NOV had agreed to a request by the Soviet High Command, for Soviet troops to cross Yugoslav territory bordering on Hungary in pursuit of retreating German troops.[10] In areas where Soviet troops

---

8   Speech on 8 August 1945, in Josip Broz Tito, *Govori i članci*, II, Zagreb, 1961: 10.

9   Vladimir Dedijer, *Tito Speaks. His Self Portrait and Struggle with Stalin*, London, 1953: 232-5; *Istoriya Velikoi otechestvennoi voiny Sovetskogo Soyuza, 1941-1945*, IV, Moscow, 1962: 417-20, quoted in Sava D. Bosnitch, 'The Significance of the Soviet Military Intervention in Yugoslavia 1944-1945, *Review published by the Study Centre for Jugoslav Affairs*, 8, London, 1969: 697.

10   On the same day, a number of Democratic Youth Movement activists suggested to Mihailović's commander in Belgrade, in view of the hopeless situation, to call on the Germans in Belgrade to lay down their arms, and evacuate, or be disarmed. The civil administration would then be taken over by representatives of the political parties. McDowell would be asked to take

operated, the civil authority would belong to the National Committee for Liberation. Tito's appeal for intervention was disguised as a Soviet request for permission to enter Yugoslav territory temporarily, so that no Western force could land without a similar consent from Tito's revolutionary government. Although Tito also had to agree to the participation of Bulgarian troops in operations on Yugoslav soil, he obtained much more than he had hoped for. Stalin undertook to send a tank corps and to equip a dozen NOV divisions. More help followed through Romania. The details were worked out at Marshal Tolbukhin's headquarters there, where Tito stopped for a fortnight on his way back, before returning to mainland Yugoslavia, just across the Danube.

The partisans' penetration into Mihailovićist Serbia in the summer of 1944 was a difficult conquest, in spite of Allied support, including the air bombardment of German-held towns. However, it hardly disrupted the ordered German evacuation. Mihailović's main force under his command had already been defeated when, on 6 October, what remained of Nedić's SDS, 6,500 officers and men, gathered at Jagodina, openly to join what still called itself the Yugoslav Army in the Homeland under the name of Serbian Shock Corps (*Srpski udarni korpus,* SUK). Three days earlier, Nedić's government had met for the last time, and left for Austria, where it continued to gesticulate formally as a government in hotels, in Vienna and later in the winter sports station of Kitzbühel, until the final capitulation of the Reich.[11] Nedić addressed memoranda to Neubacher, about coordinating the action of his government with that of the Reich against communism. By 25 May 1945, he even wrote to General Eisenhower, to explain that he had been a secret ally of Mihailović's, and to ask him to prevent the destruction of Serbia in the civil war.

---

command of liberated Belgrade. Even if that scenario failed and turned into a 'second Warsaw rising', it would still rehabilitate the JVO in the eyes of the Allies. The desperate plan was not even considered.

11 Nedić was turned over by the Allies to the Yugoslav authorities who made preparations for his trial. He is alleged to have committed suicide in February 1946 by throwing himself out of a third-floor window.

The German military had taken over its functions in Belgrade even before the Nedić government had left. Ljotić's SDK and the Russian Security Corps were evacuated with German forces.

When Soviet troops arrived from Romania and from Bulgaria, they found no partisans in that part of Serbia. For a brief period, they cooperated with Mihailović's units against retreating Germans, before disarming the chetniks. Mihailović sent a delegation to the Soviet command in Craiova, to offer the same plan that he had sent to the Allied Mediterranean command in Italy, but the Soviets took even less notice of it, and the delegation was arrested. As for Tito, he was able to get rid of almost exclusive reliance on the British: the honeymoon period with them was over. Churchill was indignant. On his way back, Tito cabled an explanation of his disappearance to the British mission. He had done it for state reasons, and 'since we are an independent state, I, as president and supreme commander, am not responsible to anyone outside my country for my actions'. In their advance into Serbia, the partisans were accompanied by a special People's Defence Corps whose task it was to fight 'internal enemies'. Furthermore, the Western Allies bombed towns in Serbia, including Belgrade, and the urban population suffered. An agreement had been reached with Tito about bombing sites in coordination with the partisan advance.

From April 1944, factories and aerodromes, oil installations, railway junctions and ports were bombed throughout Yugoslavia, from Maribor to Skopje. The number of victims is controversial. The Yugoslav government in exile and Mihailović, no less than Tito, had asked for air bombardments of special locations. Sometimes it was to boost morale, at other times to destroy it, but it was not the Yugoslavs who decided what should be bombed and when. Belgrade (particularly on Orthodox Easter Sunday in 1944, when people were coming out of churches), Podgorica (the principal city in Montenegro), Leskovac and Zadar (Zara) were the hardest hit. Belgrade was a central communications junction; Zara, then an Italian city, did not have important military installations. Various propaganda services said that the Allies had bombed their Serb friends at the request of the communists, or to make it harder for the communists to tackle post-war rehabilitation, or to send the inhabitants of towns out to the partisans. Often it was simply an inaccurate offloading of surplus bombs on returning from Romanian oil installations. Bulgarian troops were back as liberators, under Soviet command, to liberate territory they had occupied, under German command, causing strange fighting partnerships: Soviet troops and chetniks against Germans, Bulgarian troops and partisans against chetniks, partisans against chetniks and Germans.

Belgrade was a well-defended point on the Germans' withdrawal route. Tito's NOV on its own could not have freed it at that time without the Soviet contribution in tanks and heavy artillery. The Red Army took part in the campaign to free eastern and northern Serbia. The behaviour of the Red Army surprised the generally russophile population, and destroyed illusions. It surprised even the hero-worshipping communists as much as it impressed them with its might. Belgrade was liberated on 20 October 1944, after a week-long battle during which many perished. The number of those killed (German defenders, Yugoslav and Soviet liberators, and particularly 'people's enemies' liquidated by the new authorities) is again controversial. During most of that time, Tito was not in Yugoslavia. He landed at Vršac from Romania, and then went to Belgrade, on 27 October. Disowned by the Allies and his King, engaged against retreating Germans, attacked by partisans, Soviet and Bulgarian troops, Mihailović's movement collapsed, and he withdrew from Serbia. With his staff, McDowell and a force of a few hundred, he crossed the Drina into Bosnia, and retreated to the Majevica mountain, north of Tuzla. He still did not seem to realise the magnitude of his defeat, as he and some of his commanders talked of eventually heading for Sandžak.[12] Like Lukačević, he believed Allied troops were coming up from landing beaches. The belief was based on the 600 or

---

12 In December, in Moscow, Stalin was trying to make General de Gaulle believe that Mihailović had left Yugoslavia, and was hiding in Cairo.

so British commandos who had landed near Dubrovnik, to protect the artillery that the partisans had asked for. Mihailović managed to organise some Muslim units. He appointed General Matija Parac, a Croat who had briefly joined the Domobrans before withdrawing to Belgrade, to be commander of an as yet inexistent Croatian army within the JVO. Parac then left Belgrade for Croatia, with letters for Domobran officers.

The Long German Withdrawal from Macedonia to Slovenia

Until the autumn of 1943, the Yugoslav communists had had less success in Macedonia than any of the contending groups there. They faced bulgarophiles, serbophiles, a few remaining old IMRO revolutionaries and unorganised autonomists, between whom there was no unity. Anti-Serb, anti-Yugoslav, pro-Bulgarian or autonomist feelings were embedded in those urban educated who had carried the movement for recognition of a Macedonian individuality, but Macedonian nationalism was elusive. The KPJ was helped by the inflexibility of the traditional Serb approach, expressed by the JVO which did not even pretend to concede anything to Macedonian feelings, and which represented a Yugoslavia resented by Macedonians. The Yugoslav communists encouraged the population to think along 'Macedonian' lines, but for long misled it concerning the future status of the region. Most Bulgarians, including communists and pro-Bulgarian Macedonians, found it difficult to contemplate the loss of newly-acquired lands, but they were now on the defensive. The first NOV Macedonian brigade (700 strong) was formed in November 1943. The second session of AVNOJ had given Yugoslav Macedonians reasons to believe that a new Yugoslavia under the NOP might not be unacceptable, and Tito was cautious about openly overstepping (in the south-east, as opposed to the north-west) the territorial framework of the old Yugoslavia. The Serb element, strongest north of Skopje, supported the chetniks, and had been helped by the presence of SOE liaison officers, but the arrival of such a mission to the partisans also produced expectations of British help to the NOV in

Macedonia. Those missions, whatever else they achieved, attracted German troops to an imagined British intervention in the cross roads of the Balkans.

A renewed bulgarianisation campaign at the beginning of 1944 pushed more Serbs into the chetnik camp and brought Macedonian deserters from the Bulgarian army to the partisans, who expanded their activities, in particular to extend and to clear their liberated territory. The first large-scale German-Bulgarian anti-insurgent operations in Macedonia in the spring forced all armed men to retreat. The Yugoslav partisans, who had helped the Bulgarian partisans to organise in contiguous Bulgarian Macedonia, had to retreat, but without major losses, and not before they had broken up the JVO Vardar Corps. They maintained the greater part of their units, along with pockets of territory. With German and Bulgarian military power on the wane, the majority of the population, by a bandwagon effect, was coming to accept, with passive resignation, the KPJ programme of Macedonia as a unit in some sort of gathering of South Slav nationalities under Belgrade's aegis. As far back as September 1943, an action committee had been set up to organise an Anti-Fascist Council for the National Liberation of Macedonia, but preparations had been difficult. It was only on 2 August 1944 (the anniversary of the Ilinden, or St Elijah's day, rising of 1903) that delegates were brought together for a gathering at St Prohor monastery,[13] to define Macedonia as one of the equal units in Democratic Federated Yugoslavia, on the basis of the decisions of AVNOJ II, and to urge the population to join the NOV. The Macedonian communist party then announced that the KPJ accepted the border of prewar Yugoslavia as a working basis for further aggrandisement.

When Bulgaria switched sides in September, Hitler thought of the IMRO revolutionary Vancha Mihailov, to shore up the situation and cover the German retreat with a puppet 'independent' government of Macedonia. Outlawed before the war in both Yugoslavia

---

13 Sveti Prohor ended up in Serbia once the federated units of communist Yugoslavia were properly set up.

and Bulgaria, linked to Pavelić and living in Zagreb, he was flown to Skopje. He realised that he could do nothing, and returned to Zagreb after a few days. When the communist-led Fatherland Front took over the government in Sofia, army units were required to join Soviet and Yugoslav NOV forces in the war against Germany. Some from the new and occupied territories returned to Bulgaria; others were disarmed, by Germans, but also by partisans and chetniks. In fact, the once occupying and now liberating Bulgarian troops became the main fighters against retreating German armies, yet they and the partisans were generally held in check in Macedonia until the last Germans had left Greece. Niš was liberated in mid October, which blocked off German control of the Salonika-Belgrade rail line, and changed the line of retreat. The partisans' priority was taking over control, and cleaning out active opponents. German troops left Skopje by 13 November. By the middle of the month, 'Democratic Yugoslav' organs of authority had been established in Yugoslav Macedonia. Purges of the local communist organisation, the pull of the winners, and the alleged mutation of bulgarophiles into diligent supporters of the new Yugoslav communist order, ended Bulgarian influence in the Communist Party of Macedonia. Open expression of Macedonian nationalism was encouraged. Young men were mobilised to take part in continued fighting in the ranks of the NOV, and subjected to rigorous party indoctrination.

German forces thereafter had to go through Kosovo and Sandžak, through northern Albania and Montenegro, mostly on foot. The disruption of Bulgarian forces by the new Sofia government's sudden withdrawal of the old officer corps, and the help provided by the SS 'Skanderbeg' division before it was affected by mass desertion, helped maintain an orderly evacuation schedule. After Macedonia, part of the NOV was engaged against Albanian anti-communist forces, as the Yugoslav communists, patrons to Albanian communists, secured Kosovo for Yugoslavia again. The situation there was difficult. The region's Albanian population was antagonistic to anything Yugoslav. While the KPJ reinforced its influence over the Communist Party of

Albania, Vukmanović Tempo, Tito's representative for Macedonia and Kosovo, assured members of its leadership that frontiers had become anachronistic. General armed resistance to the partisans in Kosovo nevertheless continued until the end of 1944. Even more alarming was the refusal of ethnic Albanian recruits to be sent to the front: they wanted to stay and defend their homes from chetnik attacks. The Drenica revolt represented a force of some 8,000, and was not put down until March 1945.

Forced to leave Serbia, Mihailović wanted his forces to concentrate in south-eastern Serbia and head for Sandžak in the first instance, to link up with chetnik forces there and in Bosnia. McDowell was still with him. Djurišić wanted to go to Greece through Albania, but Mihailović told him to prepare for an Allied landing, the return of King Peter and the formation of a national government. Baćović asked whether it was true that Mihailović had agreed with Nedić and Ljotić not to attack the Germans; he stressed that it was necessary to go against them immediately, otherwise the population would turn against the chetniks as traitors. As for Ostojić, he told Mihailović that regrouping for action was out of the question, as they would all soon be left without troops; if the Western allies did not turn up, their only salvation was to place themselves under some Russian general. All semblance of co-ordinated action among chetnik commanders disappeared.

After their action through Serbia, Soviet forces moved into Hungary, leaving the NOV to tackle the Germans who, on leaving Belgrade, organised a defensive front which started along the Drava river (*Drau-Front*), was strongest in Srem between the Sava and the Danube (*Syrmien-Front*), and then stretched on through eastern Bosnia to the Adriatic (*Drina-Front*). They still had some 400,000 men on Yugoslav territory. Bitterly defended by the Germans, the Srem front was not broken until April 1945. Although it now recruited through all the liberated areas that it held, Tito's army was finding it difficult to switch to regular large-scale operations. Ethnic Albanian conscripts mutinied in Kosovo, and even in Macedonia there were mutineers who asked to be sent to liberate *Solun* (Salonika) rather than Srem. Over 250,000 were mobilised in Serbia. Most of them were sent to the Srem front without proper training, and tens of thousands died there in the course of the winter operations. The Organisation for the Protection of the People (OZNa, *Organizacija za zaštitu naroda*), set up in May 1944, had roving commissions which looked for chetniks, Ljotićites, Nedićites and various agents. Regular courts were not set up before December, but special military courts operated even after that. Those who had taken part in the occupation régime or fought with the JVO were dealt with summarily, often without trial or publicity, until the end of the war. Estimated numbers are all controversial. The most summary and brutal treatment was reserved for the ethnic Germans of Banat, of whom over 21,000 had served in the SS. The German authorities had in August decided the mass evacuation to the Reich of the Volksdeutsche of south-eastern Europe, but only started to move them out in October. According to official German data, the evacuation to the Reich of the German community in the NDH had been completed. Many also made their own way out, and many remained, to be transported to the Soviet Union as forced labour, dealt with by Yugoslav communist authorities, or expelled. The Soviet government opposed the expulsion of the Hungarian minority on the grounds that Hungary would be socialist.

The German attempt to make use of Serb anti-communist nationalism had frightened the ustashas, particularly as their control of the NDH shrank. Back in November 1943, the German SE Command had already noted that, outside the areas held by the partisans' 'Soviet state', the 'autonomous Serb areas', and those controlled by German forces, there was not much left for the ustashas. By 16 March 1944, SS General Ernst Fick wrote to Himmler that Pavelić, 'in terms of power, is but mayor of Zagreb, excluding the suburbs'.[14] German requirements

---

14 'Dr Ante Pawelitsch ist machtbereichsmäßig nur Bürgermeister von Agram, mit Ausnahme der Vororte' (quoted in Karl Hnilicka, *Das Ende auf dem Balkan 1944/45. Die militärische Räumung Jugoslaviens durch die deutsche*

rose while the economy's production capacity declined. Payments for German forces stationed in the NDH were one of the main causes of the increase in government expenditure, covered through loans from the State Bank or by printing notes. By the time of the collapse of the régime in May 1945, there had been a thirty-two-fold increase in the currency circulation since April 1941. As most of it ended up with peasants and partisans, urban dwellers experienced a great shortage of currency and suffered most from inflation. Black market food prices in Zagreb rose by 218 times between August 1939 and December 1944, which, Tomasevich notes, truly reflected the degree of inflation.[15] Agricultural production was disrupted by the large-scale atrocities against Serbs, the ever-growing guerrilla war, and the low prices given for compulsory deliveries. Inflation made it less and less attractive for peasants to produce a surplus for sale. Galloping inflation and deteriorating food supplies contributed to the steady decline of the popular base of the ustasha régime.

Hitler sent General Walter Warlimont, of the Wehrmacht's operations staff, to investigate, and report on, the situation in the last remaining satellite. On 9 March 1944, at a conference summoned by Hitler to receive his findings, Warlimont delivered a completely negative assessment of the ustasha régime: agriculture had collapsed, the transport situation was catastrophic, the combat value of NDH forces was negligible, and territories under partisan rule were better administered than under ustasha rule. Other reports followed in the same vein. Germany could barely afford the eleven divisions (only two of which were considered 'first rate') it still deemed necessary to keep in the NDH, to repel a possible Allied landing, and to keep open the main routes to the rear. The SS immediately and enthusiastically offered drastic solutions. These included: the sending of Pavelić and his government to the Reich for indoctrination; the removal of all the male population from twelve to seventy years of age, the best to be enrolled in the SS, and the rest to work in Germany;

Wehrmacht, Göttingen, 1970: 293).

15 Tomasevich, *War and Revolution[…].Occupation and Collaboration*, 703

the setting up of SS-sponsored and nazified military settlements to guard the coast and vital routes. Some of these were taken up in part. A 3 km-wide defensive strip was set up along the coast. The whole male population was indeed evacuated, at short notice, from certain villages and islands to secure locations in the hinterland. The operations were brutally carried out by SS units.

In April, after German soldiers had been killed in the Split hinterland, SE Command ordered reprisals. Perhaps as many as 2,000 executions were carried out. The NDH government at the time was addressing a string of complaints to the German authorities on a whole range of issues. These culminated in the note of 13 April, protesting against the reprisals, and demanding that the culprits (which it feigned at first to think were chetniks in German uniform) be punished. Ribbentrop had a fit of rage at such 'shameless arrogance'. He returned the note through the German legation in Zagreb, would no longer communicate with the Foreign Minister Stijepo Perić, and explicitly forbade the NDH government to address the Reich government in such a tone. Pavelić had to change his foreign minister, and an abject apology was sent. However, the Poglavnik had to accept the setting up of an operational zone along the whole coast, in which the German military would exercise supreme power. In October and December, similar zones were set up in Slavonia, Srem and Bosnia, along the front line. By way of compensation, Pavelić went on to strengthen again ustasha influence in the armed forces. General Navratil, who had favoured younger and more professional ex-Yugoslav officers, and was on friendly terms with Glaise, was replaced as Armed Forces Minister by Colonel Ante Vokić, a little-known 36-year old ustasha who had served in Sarajevo. Ustasha Headquarters submitted at the end of March a list of 129 officers to be removed, including the chief of the General Staff, General Prpić, and five other generals. Although Glaise protested that the army would be left without any properly qualified officers, the decision was taken to remove undesirable elements from the armed forces, and Prpić was retired.

Glaise had given up on the HSS. He realised that their preferred scenario was a neutral government of technicians to get Croatia out of the war, followed by an Allied occupation which would enable free elections, thus allowing the HSS to come into its own as the legitimate representative of the Croatian people. Ever since the withdrawal of Italy, HSS leaders in Zagreb had tried to get in touch with the Western Allies, in the belief that British interests in particular coincided with those of Croatia. They also banked on the Domobrans. Their most ambitious effort was to send out Colonel Babić. After long delays, he managed to get away in January 1944, not as originally intended to Istanbul with Tomašić, the HSS politician who had British contacts, but with an NDH military aircraft to Bari, with messages from Tomašić for Krnjević, and with documents showing the misdeeds of both partisans and chetniks. On arrival, he was interrogated, but the Allies were only interested in German forces. He was told that if he wanted to help his people and the Allies, he should go over to Tito, and was then kept in a prisoner-of-war camp, although he was allowed to meet Šubašić in June. HSS politicians in Zagreb had already let King Peter's new HSS prime minister know that General Ivan Tomašević, who commanded in north-western Croatia, was ready to turn against German forces at the appropriate time, but the British were not impressed. To the extent that they gave any advice, it was to come to an agreement with the NOP. There had been contacts with Mihailović that had led nowhere: he wanted to be acknowledged as commander of all Yugoslav forces, including the Domobrans, whereas Maček asked him to disown those chetnik groups who had killed innocent Croats. Realising that the partisans were becoming the winning side, Košutić had approached the NOP, starting from the position that his party was the legitimate representative of the Croatian people and thus an equal partner in any talks with the KPJ, which likewise had led nowhere.

The HSS as a political organisation no longer existed. Maček and his friends in the centre were stuck between a declining pro-ustasha tendency among one-time militants and a growing pro-partisan drift.

A group had already been set up in partisan territory, where it was being organised as a dissident HSS. Propaganda against those who collaborated with the occupier or with traitors at home and in exile, and even against Maček himself, had started again. Failing to establish any cooperation with the British, other than to be encouraged to turn to the NOP, Košutić went out again in September to Topusko in partisan territory, where he met Hebrang and Randolph Churchill. In May the NOP Territorial Council of National Liberation of Croatia had defined Croatia as one of the units of the new federal Yugoslavia. Košutić came with increased demands, for Croatia's right of self-determination, with its own government based on free elections, with its own diplomacy and armed force within a Yugoslav framework. For the time being, he asked for a merger on equal terms in Croatia between the NOP Territorial Council of National Liberation and the HSS, and between the NOV and the Domobrans. Not only were his demands all rejected, but he was arrested by the communists in October, and kept under arrest until 1946.

In the meanwhile a half-hearted attempt had been made from within the ustasha leadership to change sides before it was too late, based on the premise that the Western Allies would sponsor the survival of an independent Croatia. The ever-present possibility of an Allied landing would be the facilitator, and the Domobrans the executors. The idea came from Mladen Lorković, the Interior Minister, in association with Vokić, the new Minister for the Armed Forces. Lorković had already, at the time of Mussolini's fall, sought, and failed to establish, a link with the HSS personalities available in Zagreb—Farolfi, Tomašić and Košutić. He had then befriended Vokić, who had begun to probe senior Domobran officers. Lorković sought, but did not obtain, foreign contacts. However, the first step was to introduce serious reforms in the ustasha structure of government. Lorković, trusting in Pavelić's patriotism, kept him informed to a point, in the belief that he understood and approved. The Poglavnik feigned his support for a while, and then denounced them to Kasche, the German Minister in Zagreb, as seeking to abandon the German alliance, and placed the blame on Glaise, who had allegedly told them of his doubts about the successful outcome of the war.

On 30 August, some ten days after Pavelić had spoken to Kasche, there were perhaps as many as sixty arrests. Most of those arrested were subsequently released, some committed suicide or were liquidated. Lorković, Vokić and a dozen others (including Farolfi, Tomašić and several high-ranking officers) were kept in prison, charged with plotting to take Croatia to the enemy side. They were killed on Pavelić's orders just before Zagreb was evacuated in April 1945. It was announced that Lorković and Vokić had been dismissed. Pavelić did not want to give the 'coup' greater publicity. Košutić had been able to get away to partisan territory. General Marić was interned again. Lorković and Vokić may have renewed contacts with the HSS politicians, and, more probably, with some generals who, again, had communicated with Mihailović. The arrests had also eliminated any active HSS interim leadership in Zagreb. When he was shown Pavelić's accusations, an indignant Glaise left Zagreb to report to Field Marshal Wilhelm Keitel, chief of the Wehrmacht High Command, that he could not continue in his post. Keitel told Glaise that he could be happy that he 'would not have to witness the shameful end of that miserable state' (the NDH). It was subsequently announced that he had been transferred to the reserve. There was a delay in replacing him. SS General Hans Adolf Prützmann, who had been SS police head in the Ukraine, arrived in Zagreb as German Plenipotentiary General in December 1944.

As the importance of Croatia to the defence of the heartland of the Reich increased, any search for an alternative to Pavelić was given up. The Poglavnik had managed to get rid of Glaise. He still believed that the Reich would win the war, because it was manufacturing a new weapon which would be ready when the fallout came between the Anglo-Saxons and the Soviet Union. On his last visit to Hitler, on 18 September, he told the Führer that Croatia had gone through a period of crisis due to a weakening of morale among intellectuals, but that the faith of the people in the final victory remained.

Hitler having praised Croatia, whose government enjoyed his full confidence, Pavelić announced that he would merge the Domobrans with the Ustasha Militia, and return to an 'energetic' treatment of the Orthodox population. Kasche had won his battle with the Wehrmacht. The policy of supporting the ustashas was back with a vengeance. The German High Command instructed field commanders to give unconditional support to the ustasha course, and to wind down cooperation with chetniks. Commanders had come to use them after the collapse of Italy, in Herzegovina and in Dalmatia, to secure Italian-held areas, and then to harass the partisans. They regarded them as less unreliable than NDH troops, and did not want to alienate them too quickly as they were thought to be potentially dangerous in case of an Allied landing. In February 1944, a German report listed thirty-five different chetniks groups totalling some 23,000 men, of whom 5,800 were considered rebellious. The ustashas wanted them all disarmed, which General Rendulic said he would willingly do if the NDH could come up with the equivalent number of soldiers. Even Hitler, when he last received Pavelić, argued that it was better to have the chetniks fight alongside the Germans against the partisans, than alongside the partisans against the Germans.

The Germans had to use whatever manpower they could find. By the end of 1944 they had mobilised 25,000 ethnic Germans, most of them in the SS. They had decided to raise a second SS Muslim division. The territory entrusted to the Muslim SS units in Bosnia was practically excluded from the NDH. In the autumn, German troops started evacuating large tracts of territory, without even notifying the NDH authorities. By the end of the year, central and southern Dalmatia, eastern Herzegovina and eastern Bosnia had thus been taken over by the partisans. With Tito established in Belgrade, an atmosphere of gloom descended on Zagreb. Entire Domobran units went over to the NOV, encouraged by appeals and amnesties. 'Handschar' soldiers, Muslim 'Green Cadre' and other militias, and chetniks too were going over. The more obvious the coming defeat of Germany and the nearer the breakup of the NDH, the greater the number of

Croats who wanted to leave the sinking boat. The NOP now offered the best way out. Allied support caused many Croats to believe Tito would moderate his communism; in Croatia the NOP welcomed almost anyone who would cooperate. The seat of the German command in the Balkans was transferred to Zagreb. Hitler needed whatever remained of the NDH to ensure the passage of retreating German troops. Pavelić needed the presence of German troops to hold territory which he could no longer hold. In December, however, Himmler ordered that all Croat SS units be brought to Slovenia, to be sorted out according to categories and destinations, as Pavelić, with Hitler's blessing, put the ustashas in complete control of the NDH armed forces. But Germans again exchanged prisoners with the partisans, and ustashas made pragmatic local accommodations with partisans, who had agents infiltrated in ustasha organisations.

Of the whole of Yugoslavia in 1944, Slovenia under the overall rule of SS General Rösener was, perhaps, in the most paradoxical situation. The area was important for the communist leadership, because of the possibility of an Allied landing, and of relations with Italian communists. The Slovene Home Guard had risen to some 12,000 by September. It was more cohesive than the Italian MVAC had been. It was well organised, paid, armed and supplied by the Germans, nominally under Rupnik, collaborating with the occupation authorities, yet emotionally attached to the Allies, and with a single aim—to defeat the partisans. It helped the Allies by rescuing and assisting the airmen shot over Slovenia. It cooperated with various groups in the uplands who were loosely linked to the JVO. It was an open secret they would go over to the Allies and turn against the Germans at the 'right time'. Colonel Ivan Prezelj, Novak's deputy commander of JVO units and liaison officer with the Slovenian Alliance (SZ), had taken over command after Novak's withdrawal, and started to reorganise the JVO in Slovenia. Mihailović (although he no longer held any official position under the crown) had promoted him to Brigadier General. In his endeavour, Prezelj came up against many obstacles, from the Germans first and foremost, but also from the Slovene People's Party (SLjS) network. The SZ gave the Home Guard its moral support, but it remained underground, and kept in touch with the government in exile, with Mihailović and with the Vatican (through Bishop Rožman). It looked to the Anglo-Americans. Its policy was to wait for when they landed (the landing was now expected in Istria), to go over to them and turn against the Germans. German commanders, aware of the pro-Western leanings of the Home Guards, tightly controlled them, to thwart efforts to contact the Allies. Meanwhile, the partisans were their main enemy. To them and to most anti-communist Slovenes, the Tito-Šubašić Agreement at first seemed almost a guarantee that the communists would not be allowed to take over completely.

Concerned about the possibility of a British landing, the Germans had wanted to put an end to such duplicity. In April the Gestapo started making many arrests, of some fifty Home Guard officers linked to the JVO and of many underground participants in the takeover plan. Vauhnik managed to escape in time from Ljubljana, via Trieste, to Switzerland. Rupnik, who resisted a demand to cooperate in the formation of a Slovenian SS unit, had to accept that the Home Guard take an oath to fight with the SS, under the leadership of the Führer, against communists and their allies. A similar German-sponsored Home Guard was set up in the Adriatic Coastland. German action caused as much duplicity as it wanted to eliminate. The NOV was expanding. It attracted defectors from those Slovenes conscripted in the German armed forces in the annexed northern area, as well as a small proportion of Home Guard soldiers, but it fought the Home Guard rather than the Germans. Prisoner exchanges continued between JVO and German commanders. The fear of a British landing even led to a truce, in July 1944, between partisans and Germans in the coastland that alerted Home Guard and JVO to contemplate turning against the Germans, to the point where a worried Rösener had to assure Rupnik that the truce did not apply to the Province of Ljubljana.

The SZ also took a stand. In the autumn it set up a smaller and more cohesive National Committee for Slovenia which issued a statement on 29 October: since the Tito-Šubašić arrangements had changed the legitimate basis of the Yugoslav government, the Committee assumed power over Slovenia, and aimed for the unification of all Slovene territory in an autonomous Slovenia in a federal Kingdom of Yugoslavia. It went on to make plans over the winter—to gather all Slovene members of the last pre-war Yugoslav legislature, proclaim a provisional government for Slovenia within a federal Yugoslavia, invite King Peter to Ljubljana, take over the Home Guard, and call on the Western Allies to send troops from northern Italy. The optimistic plans were all based on the assumption of Western Allied support, and on its magical power to put everything right.

Deception plans had worked. Everyone in Yugoslavia believed that the Western Allies would land in the Balkans. Even after the Normandy landings, and as the Allies slowly moved up Italy, rumours continued to reverberate of Churchill's alarm at the advance of the Soviet armies and at what Tito was up to, of the British leader's disappointment with the Tito-Šubašić Agreement he had sponsored, and of Anglo-American differences in Italy. They fed the fears of some and the wishful thinking of others. In May, in order to prevent things getting any worse and to prevent possible Soviet intervention in Greece, the idea had been put by the British to the Soviet government of a temporary division of spheres of action in the Balkans. In October, after the successful British offensive against the German Gothic Line in Italy, Churchill went to see Stalin in Moscow to reach an agreement on sharing influence in the control of events in the Balkans for the duration of the conflict. On Yugoslavia they 'went 50-50'. On that basis it was agreed to recommend jointly to Tito and Šubašić the constitution of a united government. Back in liberated Belgrade from Tolbukhin's headquarters in Romania, with the Soviet Order of Suvorov on his new marshal's uniform, Tito and Šubašić, who had joined him from London, made a second agreement on 1 November 1944. Pending a plebiscite to decide on the future form of government after the complete liberation of the country, the King would remain abroad, and delegate the exercise of the royal prerogative to a regency council appointed in agreement with Tito. A joint government would be set up, from Šubašić's cabinet and Tito's committee, to supervise arrangements for a plebiscite. Five weeks later, they agreed to drop the plebiscite in favour of elections to a constituent assembly, which would decide the organisation of the post-war régime. On 11 November, Serbia had also been given an Anti-Fascist Council.

The Germans had believed that Soviet forces would, after Belgrade, continue to push further into Yugoslavia, towards Zagreb. When, at the end of November, they realised that this would not be the case, they felt they had a respite on the front they had established. They also understood that a majority of Yugoslavs had come to consider Tito and the NOP as liberators who enjoyed the support not only of the Soviet Union but of the Western Allies—particularly the British—and of the King. For some, as in Slovenia, it was evidence that the British would not allow Yugoslavia to become completely communist. For others, such as Mihailović, it was evidence of a clever deception game that he understood. Deception of one kind or another and rumours had fanned the flames of civil war more than they had drawn German troops away from other theatres, and the civil wars allowed them to continue their orderly retreat once they had had to leave Serbia.

The End: The Final Withdrawal of the Germans and the Communist Takeover

King Peter had at first refused to accept the new agreements concluded in Belgrade on 1 November 1944 between his prime minister and Tito, on the grounds that Šubašić had simply subscribed to giving power in advance to one party before the final decision by popular vote. He gave way after Churchill had told the Commons on 18 January 1945 that 'if we were so unfortunate as not to be able to obtain the consent of King Peter, the matter would have, in fact, to go ahead, his assent being presumed', and by mid-February Šubašić had definitely left London for Belgrade. A few days earlier at Yalta, Churchill, Roosevelt and Stalin had also recommended that the arrangement be put into effect immediately, and that AVNOJ be enlarged to include those members of the last pre-war parliament who had not compromised themselves with the enemy. Another fortnight elapsed before a final agreement was reached on the composition of the regency council and of the united provisional government. More British pressure got the King to appoint the regents, who, on 7 March, on the proposal of the presidency of AVNOJ, entrusted Marshal Tito with the formation of the new government. Composed of twenty-three communists, two fellow-travellers and three 'Londoners' (including Šubašić as foreign minister), this government was granted formal recognition by the Allies.

For the sake of its international position, the KPJ leadership had made transient formal concessions to satisfy the Western Allies. With that, the new structure that was being set up in liberated territory under its control received formal sanction. Tito was still fearful that the West might intervene militarily, and make things difficult for him, hence the peremptory demand in January for the withdrawal of the small British commando force that had been sent the previous October on the southern Adriatic coast in answer to a partisan request for artillery to hamper the German withdrawal from Montenegro. Acknowledged as Yugoslavia's prime minister, Tito went to Moscow in April to sign a twenty-year treaty with the Soviet Union. On his return, he openly emphasised the Soviet connection.

Meanwhile a defeated Mihailović disbanded the mass of his recently-acquired recruits and withdrew from Serbia. Estimates of the numbers who remained with the JVO vary from several thousands to tens of thousands, depending on who is included. There were military units, some organised others less so, and there were civilian refugees including women and children. There was tension and bad coordination between General Trifunović's older JVO formations from Serbia and the new Serbian Shock Corps (formerly Serbian

State Guard). The idea was to take control of a territory that was not on the path of the expected Soviet advance, gather and reorganise there, to await the Allies; there was no agreement on where that could be. Mihailović himself had crossed the Drina with his staff, McDowell and a small force, whereas the main body of his troops was heading south for initial regrouping in south-east Bosnia. He was now asking for US support; he was dreaming of French support. He hoped, just as Tito feared, that the Western Allies would turn up, since the Soviets had come. The presence of that British force between the Neretva river and Dubrovnik influenced chetniks commanders—particularly Djurišić who was planning to hold a free territory in the Montenegrin hinterland. Mihailović realised that the small British unit was not the prelude to the hoped-for Western intervention, and that his area in northern Bosnia was of no real interest to the Allies, but it could provide more food, and was more central to his 'Yugoslav' plans. When McDowell was evacuated on 1 November 1944, he was instructed to offer Mihailović the opportunity to leave with him. Mihailović refused, as he wanted to remain until the expected change of Western Allied policy.[16]

On 3 January 1945 he issued orders for all to regroup on the Ozren heights where he was, in north-central Bosnia, west of the river Bosna. He appealed to Domobrans, to Muslim militiamen and to 'chetniks' to rally to the JVO. He planned Croatian and Slovenian armies, and even a Muslim corps, under his overall command, and designated as commanders, officers who had been with him and whom he promoted to the rank of general, although he no longer had the authority to do so, and they had no troops. He tried hard to prevent the pillage of Croat and Muslim villages, and contacts with Germans. However, all was fast deteriorating. Many of the combatants were worn out, selling their weapons and ammunition to, and

---

16 Captain Nicholas Lalich stayed on to complete the work of the US Air Crew Rescue. He left on 27 December, by which time the unit had evacuated 432 Americans and more than one hundred other Allied personnel from chetnik territory (Roberts, *Tito, Mihailović and the Allies*, 282).

pillaging, the local population. Many of the Montenegrins did not see the point of gathering in northern Bosnia. Ljotić had sent an emissary to ask them to come to Slovenia; he reminded them that, as the Montenegrin Volunteer Corps, they were formally associated with the Serbian Volunteer Corps. When the fall of Grahovo opened the way into Montenegro for the partisans from Herzegovina, Djurišić had to withdraw. As the Germans completed their evacuation across Montenegro, and the partisans started a new round of pitiless civil war, Metropolitan Joanikije of Montenegro asked Djurišić to come and help him leave with about sixty clergy who feared the return of the partisans (as many again of the clergy had sided with the partisans). Djurišić was able to break through the encirclement of Cetinje before the partisans entered the town on 13 November 1944. He then led a long trek to the north to join Mihailović, across Sandžak and Bosnia, with at least 15,000 combatants and civilian refugees, including the clergy and members of the Cetinje collaborationist administration, joining en route with Ostojić's Herzegovinians and others. As they were attacked by partisans and ustashas, bombed by the Allies, battling against the cold, hunger, sickness and rumours, the commanders expressed their anger at contradictory and changing orders, and their resentment against a discredited Mihailović.

Djurišić at that stage stuck to Mihailović's instructions, and continued to resist Ljotić's calls to join his force in Slovenia. To be precise, 'Slovenia' turned out to be Italy's post-1918 north-eastern territories which were dubbed 'Venezia Giulia' when the Italian army took control of them at the end of the First World War. When his depleted force met Mihailović's, Djurišić discovered that the JVO was disintegrating, and that it had no effective plan, even though it had temporarily managed to stabilize a front in the area between the rivers Bosna, Sava and Drina. Jevdjević and Djujić had not come to Bosnia, but gone to Slovenia. The 5,000-strong SUK (ex-SDS) had broken up. Some of its members had returned to Serbia, attracted by the news of Tito's amnesty. The rest had left Mihailović to try and reach Slovenia. Winter weather, attacks by partisans and ustashas, lack of food, the rising number of sick and wounded, disagreements between their commanders, and the help of sympathetic Domobran officers, had induced the 3,000 or so who remained, to give themselves up, and ask the Germans for transport to cross the NDH. They were disarmed, and taken by train under German escort (to protect them from ustashas), eventually to Vienna. Many stayed there as workers. About 1,500 were relocated to Istria, to join the concentration of Ljotić's volunteers and others.

Djurišić demanded that they should all transfer to Slovenia. Mihailović's response was severe, hierarchical, and disciplinarian: he, as overall commander, took military decisions, and the Central National Committee took political decisions. When Djurišić and other commanders nevertheless decided to go west, Mihailović accused them of disobedience and even of treason. The tension was so high that it was feared the two sides would come to blows. Djurišić looked for help from anyone to get through the NDH with his sick and wounded—even from Sekula Drljević, the Montenegrin separatist who was in Zagreb with Pavelić, and who wanted to set up his own Montenegrin 'army'. Mystery surrounds the liquidation of Djurišić. He tried to bypass Drljević, who got Pavelić to stop him. Ljotić tried to help him fight his way to Slovenia. Rupnik and Bishop Rožman intervened with the Germans, who were instructed to stick with the ustashas. On 12 April, Djurišić's Montenegrin force was destroyed in battle by much stronger ustashas at Lijevča Polje, north of Banjaluka by the river Sava. Some saved themselves by going over to Drljević; others were destroyed by the partisans. Djurišić and a nucleus of about thirty were captured and killed by the ustashas.

The driving force behind the scheme for a concentration of anticommunist forces in the Julian area was Ljotić. Back in October 1944, some 4,000 members of his SDK (Serbian Volunteer Corps) had been transported there under German protection, for use against bands and generally to safeguard the southern approaches to the railways in the area between the river Isonzo (Soča) and Fiume (Rijeka). Neubacher had been unable to secure safe passage for the Serbian

Volunteers from the ustasha government. They had been smuggled through the NDH along with evacuated ethnic Germans. Jevdjević's 2,000 chetniks and Djujić's 6,000, with accompanying unarmed refugees, had since also made their way there from Lika and northern Dalmatia, suffering losses en route from ustasha attacks. Ljotić and the independent chetnik leaders in Istria were keen for Mihailović and his force to join them. They needed him to organise them all into an anti-communist force acceptable to the Allies, not realising that his patronage could no longer help. Ljotić obtained from Neubacher (now in Vienna, and still charge of 'South-Eastern' affairs) that Patriarch Gavrilo and Bishop Nikolaj be allowed to visit the anti-communists units in March. However, Mihailović was opposed to the formation of such a gathering on the north-western coast. It was too heterogeneous; it was compromised by the patronage of SS General Globocnik in Trieste; fighting one's way through ustasha-controlled territory was dangerous. Furthermore, he was being fed communist disinformation of a swell against the new régime in Serbia, and of bogus chetnik groups, to stop him from going west. This also led him to reject advice from some members of the Central National Committee to try and reach an accommodation with the new communist régime.

He would return to Serbia, where people were waiting for an opportune moment to rise against the new order; the rising would then certainly be followed by a Western intervention. Nevertheless, since most chetnik personalities still with him were in favour of the Istrian plan, he no longer rejected Ljotić's overtures entirely. That part of the littoral was a convenient area for meeting the Allies coming from Italy, for contact between Slovene anti-communists and the Western Allies, and for freed Yugoslav prisoners of war to make their way to after the collapse of the Reich. He had hopes that the latter would change the character of the disparate anti-communist conglomerate. Mihailović authorised the departure of all who wanted to go. He sent General Damjanović to coordinate those efforts and take over formal command as chief of a detached staff of the Supreme Command. The departure caused further tension between those who left and those who remained. Many left; most of them were destroyed on the way by ustashas, partisans, sickness and hunger; few arrived.

The Germans continued their retreat relatively undisturbed. Having lost the easier withdrawal route through Serbia, they fought to hold the Srem front in order to secure the more difficult passage through Kosovo, Sandžak and Bosnia. They even scored a series of temporary successes against the People's Liberation Army. They left Mostar on 22 February. They did not leave Sarajevo until 15 April. Sarajevo had assumed a last-moment strategic position on the only remaining withdrawal route, and was held at substantial cost. This enabled ustasha Colonel Vjekoslav Maks Luburić to set up a special Criminal War Tribunal for a final round of terror. Meanwhile, in early March the Germans moved troops from southern Bosnia to support an unsuccessful counter-offensive in Hungary, which enabled the NOV to score some successes by attacking the Germans' weakened positions. Although strengthened by Allied aid, a secure rear and mass conscription in areas under their control, the one-time partisans found it difficult to switch to regular warfare, particularly in the open country west of Belgrade, where the Germans held their own until April in spite of all the raw and untrained conscripts the NOV hurled in a bloody war of attrition against the *Syrmien-Front*.

Behind the German front, and parallel to the German evacuation, a three-cornered fight continued in Bosnia—of ustashas, chetniks and partisans. The latter still faced much opposition from all communities. As they advanced, they used the opportunities offered by liberation to take revenge on opponents, almost all of whom could be labelled 'collaborators'. Chetnik influence was still present in areas of northern and eastern Bosnia and northern Herzegovina. Tito's orders were to pursue chetniks without respite and 'eradicate' them. Communist rigidity had pushed Croats to the HSS, which was trying to make a comeback and hoping to share power with the NOP. During that time, the Germans were confused as to what the chetniks were up to. They were interested in the chetniks' help against the NOV; at the very least they needed to ensure their neutrality. Chetniks were turning against them or going over to the partisans, which helps to explain certain soundings to Mihailović, to see what his intentions were and to ask him to pass on to Allied headquarters in Italy another offer of surrender. On 6 April 1945, on the occasion of the anniversary of the German attack on Yugoslavia in 1941, Mihailović addressed a message to 'Serbs, Croats and Slovenes', issued 'in the Yugoslav mountains' on behalf of the Central National Committee of the Kingdom of Yugoslavia and of its listed components (the political parties, the Ravna Gora Movement, Yugoslav-minded Croats and Muslims, various other political organisations). A week later, he and his remaining forces left north-central Bosnia for a long march back to Serbia.

The long-drawn out liberation of western Yugoslavia caused more victims among the population. The breakthrough of the Srem front on 12 April was, in Djilas's words, 'the greatest and bloodiest battle our army ever fought', and it would not have been possible had it not been for Soviet instructors and arms.[17] By the time General Peko Dapčević's NOV units had reached Zagreb, they had perhaps lost as many as 36,000 dead. Pavelić's belief in last-minute salvation notwithstanding, the ustasha régime was considering the end. There were by then over 400,000 refugees in Zagreb. Domobranstvo and Ustasha Militia were merged and placed under the command of high-ranking ustashas, the draft age was lowered to seventeen, and the population generally squeezed to provide as much military personnel as possible, all bolstered by indoctrination and the execution of deserters. By the beginning of 1945 the newly-merged Croatian Armed Forces numbered 150,000 (with slightly more ustashas than Domobrans). Ustashised as they were, they resisted well the NOV, whose best troops were rushed to Istria rather than towards Zagreb. The Yugoslav communist leadership was frightened by rumours of all sorts—of Mihailović's moves, of chetniks going to meet the Anglo-Americans, of plots in the NDH government, of collaborationist and

---

17 Djilas, *Wartime*, 440.

anti-communist groups receiving support from the West. Priority was given to closing off the northern borders, and staking territorial claims, before the Western Allies could act.

The ustasha leadership also believed in a turn in the fortunes of the war. As it made plans to evacuate temporarily in order to be able to continue, there was a renewal of anti-Serb terror and even of confrontation with Germany. A sharp note from Ribbentrop at the end of 1944 forced Pavelić to allow the unhindered passage of Djujić's chetniks from northern Dalmatia to Istria, but in March 1945 élite ustasha units were withdrawn from the Srem front to destroy Djurišić's exhausted chetniks trying to make their way across the northern NDH. Help was enlisted from the Catholic Church for a propaganda exercise in defence of Croatian independence aimed at foreign audiences. Archbishop Stepinac obliged, but in his own terms. In a Lenten sermon, he said that the Croatian people would reject any extreme left- or right-wing régime that did not take into account its more than millenarian Catholic tradition. To a partisan emissary who came to warn him to watch his words now that the war was about to end, he answered that he needed permission from neither ustashas nor partisans to say what he had to say. A bishops' conference was convened at the urging and with the help of the government, that also had a hand in drafting the pastoral letter issued on 24 March. Those bishops from territory still under ustasha control (five out of twelve) gathered in Zagreb and issued an outpouring of resentment against interwar Yugoslavia, and of self-justification. They condemned communism, urged allegiance to the Croatian state where the law applied equally to all. In a strange echo of the bishops' call, a decree-law was issued in the very last days of the NDH to nullify all measures that differentiated between subjects on the basis of race.

There were mysterious contacts in Zagreb during March and April 1945. According to Predavec,[18] McDowell had, before leaving, said

---

18 Author's interviews with Predavec, September 1977. Cf. statements by Mihailović at his trial, and Gen. Djukić's reminiscences in *Srpska zastava*,

he was going as political adviser to the US fifth Army in Italy. He had advised Mihailović to send part of his army to Slovenia, and to set up a joint body from his Central National Committee, the HSS leadership and the National Committee for Slovenia. This would create a sufficiently strong 'other Yugoslavia' for the fifth Army to encourage talks with 'Tito's Yugoslavia' to end the civil war. Predavec was sent in April 1945, to explain the 'McDowell plan' to Maček. On arriving in Zagreb, he and General Djukić who was accompanying him, were detected and taken to see Pavelić. The Poglavnik told them that Maček had no support, and that they had better come to some agreement with him. As Predavec tried to let Mihailović know that he had been uncovered, Pavelić passed a message to Maček through a Domobran general. Maček, still under house arrest, rightly feared a trap and did not respond. Other emissaries and alleged emissaries of Mihailović's turned up in Zagreb—to contact HSS personalities and Domobran officers, with a fake letter for Pavelić, or to tell the German command to hand over its weapons to the JVO.

At the end of April, the final German withdrawal started, and the NOV rolled up the anarchic NDH. Zagreb became a transit point for various armed formations and the scene of daily executions. All sorts of people fled the city in a scramble for safety—not only ustashas and Domobrans, but masses of civilians, including Maček, all trying to reach Austria and the protection of the Western Allies before Soviet forces and the NOV cut off their retreat routes. The ustasha leaders debated whether to concentrate all available forces in Lika, establish contact with the Western Allies and lay down arms under honourable conditions, or turn to guerrilla warfare, all in anticipation of a split between the Allies. They sent emissaries to Field Marshal Alexander to argue the case for the continued existence of an independent Croatian state, and to say that they wanted to continue their national struggle under the aegis of the Allies. The messengers were intercepted and shot by the partisans, or interned by the Allies. General Löhr, who had returned on 25 March to his former position

---

33-36, Buenos Aires, 1955.

as Commander-in-Chief SE, still had command over NDH troops whom he needed to act as a rearguard for the German withdrawal. On 5 May, the NDH government left Zagreb, followed by Pavelić. Before leaving, he wanted a formal act of handing over power, and approached Stepinac to become some sort of regent. The archbishop refused, and suggested Maček who, having been freed, had also just left. Stepinac remained in Zagreb. He went to see the German commander to persuade him not to blow up the bridge over the Sava and the electricity generating plant, and ustasha Colonel Luburić, back from Sarajevo, not to offer armed resistance. The withdrawal was completed by the time partisan troops entered the city on 9 May. Löhr had finally handed over command of NDH armed forces to Pavelić when they were already moving through Slovenia. Berlin had fallen on 2 May, and on 9 May the terms for a general German surrender were ratified there, but in Yugoslavia German forces held out until 15 May, reluctant to surrender to 'irregulars'.

The ustasha leaders without Pavelić reached Austria, but were caught by a NOV liaison group with British troops, and delivered to the Yugoslav government. Pavelić, who no longer communicated with the troops, avoided capture and, through Croat Catholic networks managed to make his way to Argentina. There is as yet no scholarly study of what happened to NDH troops.[19] Some did cross from Slovenia into Austria at the village of Bleiburg, at the head of a 45-65 km column much of which was still in Yugoslavia. They were told that they would have to surrender to the Yugoslav army, and were given an ultimatum by the partisans to do so. Tomasevich estimates at 116,000 the number of NDH military personnel who fell into partisan hands on both sides of the border. The Croatian demographer Vladimir Žerjavić estimates that 60,000 were then killed.[20]

---

19 See however Tomasevich's reconstruction, *War and Revolution [...] Occupation and Collaboration*, 757-61, and Nicholas Bethell, on the basis of British army reports, *The Last Secret*, London, 1974.

20 Vladimir Žerjavić in Marko Grčić ed., *Bleiburg. Otvoreni dossier*, Zagreb, 1990: 227-32.

Predavec and Djukić at the end of April made their way from Zagreb to Ljubljana, where they found a surreal situation. Over the winter, the Gestapo had arrested about 150 officers, priests and others suspected of working for the Allies against the Germans. Predavec told the National Committee of Slovenia of the 'McDowell plan', but its members were afraid to commit themselves, as they did not know enough about it, and had no agreement with Croats. They had hoped that Allied forces would come from Italy, and prevent a communist takeover. Although still nominally under German command, the Slovene Home Guard had begun to cooperate with the Serb anti-communist forces that had come to the coast. On 28 April, Rupnik and Rožman met a representative of the National Committee, and Rožman appealed through the Vatican to the Allied Mediterranean Command to send troops. Predavec was invited to attend the 'secret' meeting of the Slovenian assembly of pre-war members of parliament and of representatives of the two major parties, called together on 5 May to proclaim a united Slovenia in the Federal Kingdom of Yugoslavia. He described this illusory 'revolution of the bourgeoisie', with speeches, addresses to King Peter and the Allies, an appeal to the partisans to stop the fratricidal war, the dismissal of Rupnik, printed proclamations and special editions of newspapers, which General Rösener forthwith confiscated. The Germans were still in Ljubljana and refusing to hand over to the Home Guard, renamed Slovenian National Army and declared to be part of Mihailović's JVO. There was no plan to defend Ljubljana from the partisans. Germans, ustashas, Domobrans, the Cossack Cavalry Corps and sundry anti-communists were all withdrawing through Slovenia towards the Austrian border, with the NOV in pursuit. Rupnik went, to be handed over to Yugoslav authorities in 1946, when he was sentenced to death and executed. Bishop Rožman with some 200 clergy and seminarians also went into exile, and did not return.

There had been talk of a linkup between Damjanović and a Slovenian force to form a 'Slovenian front'. There had been more unrealistic talk of an anti-communist alliance between that front and

Mihailović's force in northern Bosnia, separated by the remaining NDH armed forces. Even in Slovenia, Rupnik had been reluctant to hand over control of the Home Guard before the Western Allies had actually arrived. On learning that the Damjanović force was no more, the newly-named Slovenian National Army also headed for Austria, with some units of Ljotić's Volunteers who were in Slovenia and various chetniks. They crossed the border on 11 May, and were in their turn disarmed and encamped by the British near the village of Viktring. They were sent back under the impression that they were bound for Italy, only to find the partisans waiting to shoot them over mass open graves. Most of them were liquidated; others were taken to Kočevski Rog in southern Slovenia, to be killed; more died on marches to detention camps—an estimated 24,000 all told according to Žerjavić's calculations. The communists feared Western-supported anti-communist forces, and even suspected that the British were returning them as a fifth column to undermine the fledgling communist régime. To organise the repatriation of large numbers of anti-communist Yugoslavs, who had come over the border to Austria to seek British protection, was part of the 'damage limitation and tidying up' that Heather Williams sees as SOE's final rôle in Europe, as the war came to an end, and the Cold War began to look just as dangerous.[21] NOV operations against fleeing enemy troops were ruthless and bloody. Believing that the British would show class solidarity with refugees trying to escape from communism, fearing that they would enlist the anti-communists for future use against the new régime, Yugoslavia's communist leaders were surprised that British forces in Austria did nothing of the sort. In pursuing its enemies, Tito's army wanted to establish territorial claims, and this expansionism caused concern. In Austrian Carinthia, where the Western Allies won the race, the refugees were a burden to the British, and they were a danger in so far as they attracted pursuing troops. To repatriate them, and shut one's eyes on the consequences was, perhaps, an easy way to get rid of the burden and the danger.

---

21 Williams, *Parachutes, Patriots and Partisans*, 241.

In Italian Istria, the Western Allies lost the race for Trieste, as the Yugoslav partisans were in the port city one day ahead of the New Zealanders. They entered Trieste a week before entering Zagreb or Ljubljana. Tito was anxious to secure the coast against a landing by Western forces, and to get rid of anti-communists who could be supported by the new invaders. The NOV held Trieste for forty-two days from 1 May before it had to withdraw under pressure. Damjanović's nominally JVO force was in the area, unintegrated, and somehow remote-controlled by Ljotić with German money. The Volunteers were the least unreliable from the Germans' point of view, but Ljotić was killed in a road accident. In fact, each group heeded only its own commander. Jevdjević and Djujić controlled their own chetniks. There were á few survivors from Djurišić's Montenegrins, and some SDS soldiers. There were also the weak contingents of the just-constituted 'Croatian army' and 'Slovenian army', made up of Domobran deserters, Slovene chetniks and wayward Home Guards. Mihailović's hoped-for freed prisoners of war did not turn up, for there was no longer a JVO force in the region for them to go to by the time they were freed. Even so, Mihailović had given orders, should they turn up, to join Djujić, who was, after all, the most dependable choice (*'ipak nam je najsigurniji'*). On 5 May, Damjanović's men crossed the Isonzo (Soča); they surrendered to the British at Palmanova, north-west of Trieste, and were disarmed and interned as surrendering combatants in the Yugoslav civil war. They were not returned to the Yugoslav authorities. Mihailović's remote patronage had probably saved them.

✻

After the formation of Tito's provisional government, the Peoples' Liberation Army became the Yugoslav Peoples' Army[22] and AVNOJ

---

22 The old revolutionary appellation 'Peoples' Liberation Army' used the Serbo-Croatian word *vojska* for 'army', whereas the new one adopted the Russian *armija* in imitation of the Soviet terminology.

turned itself into the Provisional National Assembly. This was done on the occasion of a third and last session, held in Belgrade in August 1945, when 318 delegates co-opted another 118, of whom thirty-six former members of the last pre-war parliament were deemed worthy of joining them. The provisional parliament proceeded to adopt laws to protect the territorial integrity and the revolutionary achievements of Democratic Federative Yugoslavia. In the federated units gradually set up by the KPJ, the territorial people's liberation committees simply became governments.

The Second World War continued in Yugoslavia for a whole week after it had stopped elsewhere in Europe. In their final operations, the armed forces under the control of the KPJ exercised vengeance against all its enemies through massive liquidations and extra-legal settlements of accounts. The OZNa political police carried out executions according to its criteria that were often local and inconsistent. Tito himself, at a meeting of the Central Committee at the end of 1945, cried out: 'Enough of all these death sentences and of all this killing; the death sentence no longer has any effect; no one fears death any more'. Montenegro in particular was scorched, demolished, fought over and bombed; government representatives had to be escorted by truckloads of soldiers and secret-police agents. The German ethnic minority suffered massively. Thousands of Italians in regions reached by the NOV were tortured, shot or pushed to death in the pitfalls of the Karst; tens of thousands were forced to flee. All the armed units formed, armed, fed or simply tolerated by the occupying forces to fight communists had fled or been destroyed in flight. No anti-communist front had been set up in western Yugoslavia. No Western intervention had taken place. Only Mihailović remained.

On 13 April 1945 he set out from northern Bosnia with his remaining followers (estimated numbers vary between 8,000 and 12,000) on a 280 km-long march back to Serbia, to start everything again as in April 1941, this time against the new communist order. They started by going west, to give ustashas and partisans the impression that they too were heading for Slovenia. They broke through ustasha barriers after suffering losses, and turned south into the mountains of Bosnia. The communists soon found out the manoeuvre. Pressing in from east, north and west, the NOV harassed his columns. Mihailović was able to regroup his forces in Travnik before setting off again for Herzegovina. During the first half of May, his units, already decimated by dissension and typhus, with the sick and wounded, and no transport, went through all that Tito's partisans had gone through, two years earlier, in those same mountains of northern Herzegovina. Between the Neretva and the Drina, they were entrapped. On 10 May, on the Jezerica tributary of the Neretva, while descending the sheer cliff bank and crossing the river, they faced a concentrated attack by special partisan forces, as aeroplanes circled above them by night. Djilas relates how they fought with despair, knowing that they were already condemned to death. Most of them were killed in battle or after they had been captured. Not many prisoners were taken. Those who broke away to make their separate way into Serbia were eventually caught and liquidated by the end of the year. Mihailović escaped with 1,000-2,000 who gradually dispersed as they were too exhausted to cross the Drina, where fresh NOV troops were massed. Mihailović himself with a handful of men managed to move on from mountain to mountain, protected by groups of chetniks and by village sympathisers, but fed with spurious radio messages from Serbia. The communist leadership wanted to catch him alive in order to stage a full-scale political trial. Trapped and wounded, he was eventually captured in March 1946. For sixteen years, the elaborate circumstances of his capture were kept secret. He was tried along with twenty-three other co-defendants—his own advisers and commanders, commanders and functionaries of the collaborationist administration and forces in Serbia, pre-war politicians, and (*in absentia*) members and functionaries of the exiled government. Mihailović was sentenced to death, executed and buried in great secrecy in July.

The last federated unit to be formally set up was Serbia, in August 1945, because of the military government that had to be imposed on Vojvodina (October 1944-February 1945) and on Kosovo and

Metohija (February-June 1945). In Vojvodina, this was due to the deportation of ethnic Germans, the subsequent question of abandoned and confiscated land, and preparations for resettlement. The re-establishment of control over Kosovo by the new communist government of Yugoslavia was practically a full-scale reconquest, in spite of the presence of Albanian communist partisans operating with the NOV. The last German troops had withdrawn by late November 1944, but only the remaining Serbs greeted liberation with relief. Yet in March 1945 the new authorities prevented the return of pre-war settlers to their previous holdings in order not to complicate further an already difficult situation. Equipped by the Germans before leaving, anti-communist Albanian groups rallied people frightened at the prospect of a victorious return of vindictive Serbs. In spite of the mobilisation of all males between sixteen and sixty sent out to fight—from Srem to Istria, what started as guerrilla quickly turned to general revolt. When Tito introduced military government in February, he admitted to 20,000 insurgents whose aim was to detach the region from Yugoslavia so as to create a greater Albania, impede the functioning of a people's government, and create centres of attraction to be used by imperialist forces. The rebellion was not put down until March, by using 40,000 troops who treated all Albanians as Axis collaborators.

In the transitional revolutionary period, all legal acts of occupation or collaborationist administrations were declared null and void and pre-war legislation was ignored if it was contrary to the rulings of AVNOJ and the achievements of the Peoples' Liberation Struggle. The Provisional Assembly ratified all AVNOJ legislation, set up people's courts, confiscated the assets of real or alleged collaborators, war profiteers and enemies of the people, introduced a new land reform, control of the press, and withdrew citizenship from certain categories of refugees. It legislated on elections to the Constituent Assembly. It gave the vote to all men and women over eighteen and everybody regardless of age who had fought with the partisans. It disenfranchised all deemed to have collaborated with enemies and occupiers, all who had adhered to 'fascist' organisations, and all who had been condemned to the loss of political rights. For the elections, a People's Front was set up in August 1945, as a coming together with the KPJ of various partisan organisations and of individuals of non-communist background willing to collaborate with the new régime.

There was no confrontation. The other parties had no organisation. Those leaders who had returned from exile were unable to organise their followers or run a campaign. They could only resign, withdraw and boycott. The government ran the election as a plebiscite for Tito and the People's Front, and against the monarchy. The whole network of the partisan administration was mobilised to secure an impressive result. It was reinforced by the visible presence of a large KPJ-controlled army, and the visible and invisible presence of the OZNa, which was turning into a political police patterned after that of the USSR. An unredeemable oppositional five per cent of the electorate was out of the way, having gone into exile or been deprived of the vote. With the reins of power firmly in the hands of the KPJ, a single list of candidates presented by the People's Front and headed by Tito, no opposition to speak of, and following a terror-backed campaign, to stay at home and not vote required courage. On 11 November 1945, eighty-eight per cent of the electorate voted, and the Front received over ninety per cent of the ballots cast. The Constituent Assembly met on 29 November (the anniversary of the Jajce AVNOJ decisions in 1943). It immediately abolished by acclamation the monarchy, proclaimed the Peoples' Federal Republic of Yugoslavia, and on 31 January 1946 unanimously approved a draft constitution modelled on Stalin's Soviet constitution of 1936.

CONCLUSION
THE DEATH AND REBIRTH
OF YUGOSLAVIA

Hitler's Germany and Mussolini's Italy, their ideologies and their occupation policies all denied the historical justification of Yugoslavia. There was no place in their New Order for a state called Yugoslavia. They supported, encouraged and abetted sectional nationalisms and local differences.

By the time that Yugoslavia had been destroyed, all Balkan governments were in fact part of the New Order—those who, having aligned themselves with the conquerors, were determined to make the best of it; those who had been brought to power by them; and those who had been put in place to restore the administration amid the ruins of defeat. They all had at least one thing in common—they promoted varieties of an ideological national-pastoralism that glorified simple rural life against the cosmopolitanism associated with democracy and communism. They all encouraged a return to native roots under German overlordship. Defeat had come too quickly, and the situation was extremely unstable. Italian commanders in particular felt as though the enemy had not really been defeated. The Axis partners, who were the two supreme occupation authorities, were in constant friction from the beginning, even if Yugoslavia remained a sideshow to decisive campaigns waged elsewhere. Mussolini wanted to establish Italy's predominance over the Balkan approaches to the Adriatic; for Hitler, the Balkans were strategically important only in so far as the peninsula held important communication lines and mineral deposits. The Nazi leadership was not prepared to accept Italy's claim to equality, except formally and on sufferance. The Reich had to continue the war while holding on to what it controlled in many different ways that looked more like a 'new disorder' than anything in the nature of a 'new order'.

What, anyhow, was the intended New Order? It seems to have been the exercise of permanent German hegemony over Europe. What German plans were made for the Balkans[1] reveal a future of toil, subsistence standards of living and political impotence. Their purpose was to provide the Reich with the material means to pursue the war, and then to ensure the continued oppression of the non-Germanic subject populations. The economic historian Adam Tooze[2] has shown that the Germany that went to war in 1939 was in fact economically weak, starved of reserves and foreign currency, reduced to scarcity management. Occupied territories, mainly in the east, were looted for raw materials, food and labour. There was no real plan for a post-war New Order. The need to hold and, if possible, to develop communication lines and the sources of essential raw materials, added to Hitler's low opinion of the Slavs (even those who tried to pass off as not being real Slavs), were all that mattered. In terms of economics, German occupation policy in Yugoslavia was to maximise control (and minimise cost) for the benefit of the Reich's war machine, with total disregard to the needs of the population. This was not done without contradictions, however. Food had at times to be imported to provide minimal feeding for the natives, so that production destined for Germany could be carried on. The all-essential transport system was fatally damaged, not only by sabotage, but by military action, by removal and, finally, by systematic destruction. By the end of the war, Yugoslavia's production capacity had been all but destroyed by war damage, dislocation, chaos, rampant inflation and loss of trained personnel.

The conquerors had destroyed the state and existing authority. They had set its components against each other, yet they did not

---

1   See, for instance, Dietrich Orlow, *The Nazis in the Balkans. A Case Study of Totalitarian Politics*, Pittsburgh, 1968.

2   Adam Tooze, *The Wages of Destruction. The Making and Breaking of the Nazi Economy*, London, 2006.

have sufficient strength and time to build an alternative system. They attempted to enforce a brutal peace without the means to impose it. The outcome was near-anarchy and an ideal situation for the propagation of a revolutionary war. It left the traditional élites bereft of power, and gave ample scope to the communists' organising ability. The native imitators that the occupiers had fostered—the ustashas—also thrived in the chaotic disruption of order, but with a passionate, imprecise and irrational violence that undermined whatever the Axis occupiers might have wanted to achieve. They shocked the German military, and even more so the Italian military. They fed the insurgency. They increased the need for the Axis occupiers, and in particular for the Wehrmacht, to intervene as 'technocrats of violence'[3] to create some order in a land bereft of it. Klaus Schmider has described the Wehrmacht's anti-insurgent operations as a 'wave-like' process of trial and error that alternated between more or less severe tactics, tied to different commanders, units and areas.[4] Because of insufficient numbers, equipment and training of the troops at their disposal, German commanders generally preferred the encirclement-and-destruction method, concentrating force on defined spaces for a certain period of time. In the process, they further maximised its use by expanding their targets. If formally they insisted on a connexion between the perpetrators of anti-German violence and the victims of reprisals, the levels of insurgency and the limits of German manpower and time extended the criteria of guilt—from captured armed insurgents to relatives, supporters, sympathisers, fellow-villagers, and even all civilians present within the operational areas.

Italy was the awkward junior partner of the Axis. The rhetoric of the régime presented the war as one to create a new man—a fascist man, dynamic, virile and heroic. However, by the time he went to war, Mussolini had not yet been able to get rid, or to create fascist versions, of Italy's inherited monarchy or of the army. The latter's fas-

3   Gumz, 'Wermacht Perceptions of Mass Violence', 1029.

4   Klaus Schmider, *Partisanenkrieg in Jugoslawien, 1941–1944*, Hamburg, 2002.

cism was *epidermico*.[5] Its rôle in Yugoslavia was more irredentist than fascist, unless simply playing a rôle next to Germany was deemed to be dynamically 'fascist'. Its rank and file did not understand what it was doing there. Antoine Sidoti dedicates his *Le Monténégro et l'Italie durant la Seconde guerre mondiale* (Paris, 2003) 'A mon père, qui n'a jamais compris pourquoi on l'avait envoyé de l'autre côté de l'Adriatique …'. From the day in April 1941 when they accepted for repatriation all those listed by the British Minister in Belgrade as alleged diplomats, who included SOE and other agents, the Italians were half-hearted. They found themselves ill-suited to deal with sabotage to communication lines, attacks on small units and individuals, the sight of dead or mutilated comrades, and eventually Italian prisoners killed because they could not be fed by insurgents. Out of frustration, they often reacted with instant reprisals, the taking and shooting of hostages, the burning of houses, the confiscation of property, internment. However, anecdotal evidence contradicts much of the bombastic orders to execute and burn, issued at the beginning of operations, rarely carried out to the letter, and whose application was recorded in official reports at the end of operations. Italians blamed Germans for policies that stimulated revolts. They mistrusted German strategic objectives, and hampered major anti-insurgent operations. Germans blamed Italians for failing to obtain results with their more 'political' policies, yet allowed them to occupy most of the territory. Eventually, by their withdrawal from the war, the Italians left the partisan's Liberation Army a rich inheritance of weapons, ammunition and equipment. They all but destroyed the chetnik and other anti-communist armed groups they had supported in their zone, and thereby created a void for the partisans to fill.

By the time Hitler attacked the Soviet Union, Yugoslavia had been well and truly conquered, destroyed, partitioned, 'revisioned' and subjugated. Even thought it had been broken up as a state, and apparently put to death even as an idea, it survived as a nominal legal

---

5   As described by Giorgio Bocca, *Storia d'Italia nella guerra fascista, 1940–1943*, Bari, 1973: 99.

entity in the Allied camp, where it was upheld by its government in exile, acknowledged and supported by Britain, the US and the USSR, as well as by the forces of resistance in their different ways in the dismembered country. Yugoslavia's social structures had been predominantly 'bourgeois' topped, however small the bourgeoisies. Although the old élites were dazed, divided and demoralised by the collapse, not many among them believed in the ultimate triumph of the Reich, and many continued to put their faith in the Western Allies. The occupiers and their ideological collaborators had done their best to marginalise and discredit them. Even though not many on the traditional right took to fascism, most of them were obsessed with the danger posed by the enemy within, which could be communism as it could be radical 'greater-Croat' or 'greater-Serb' nationalism. Their order had already largely been destroyed by nazi-fascism. It was, in the course of the war, increasingly threatened with extinction by communism. However, at ground level, those peasants who felt that the past had been destroyed, that the present was catastrophic, and that there was no future in the German-dominated New Order, could be tempted by the hope of a really new order provided by the Peoples' Liberation Movement. The occupiers had more than prepared the ground for the communists.

The KPJ under Tito adopted and used the concept of 'national liberation', which became the predicate of their movement, of their army and of their authority—*Narodnooslobodilački pokret* (NOP), *Narodnooslobodilačka vojska* (NOV), etc. The meaning of the ubiquitous *narodno* could vary according to context. It could be 'national'; it could be 'people's' in the singular, when relating to the general population; and it could be 'peoples'' in the plural, when referring to the multiple nations of Yugoslavia. The communist leadership turned 'national liberation' into an instrument of liberation from unwanted integrating, sectional or unitarist pan-Yugoslav, nationalism, as well as an instrument of social upheaval and political conquest, in the course of the many-faceted strife that raged under foreign rule. It was able to turn the poorest and most miserable peasants—those of the food-deficit areas, those who had suffered most in the NDH, and who were for the most part Serbs in the early years of the war—into a revolutionary army. Naïve expectations of the Soviets' arrival in 1941, induced expectations of an Anglo-American landing later in the war, and finally real expectations of the arrival of the Red Army in 1944, aroused resistance, and rivalries within the resistance. The KPJ established an overall unified strategy under Tito which enabled it to exploit various situations, and practice different tactics, while showing a single face to the outside world.

The chetnik movement, by contrast, 'was a disaster'—in the words of its not unsympathetic historian Lucien Karchmar.[6] It was not really a movement at all, but an amorphous phenomenon that had emerged from the breakup of the Yugoslav army. It subsequently acquired some sort of a form by the will of one man, General Mihailović, who gave it a name, that of Yugoslav Army in the Homeland, and who set up contacts with local Serb insurgent bands in Bosnia, Herzegovina, Montenegro and Croatia. Because it was not structured, because it claimed to be a regular army, because it was for ever waiting for the right moment, except when it acted to prove its existence, it was generally unsuccessful as a guerrilla movement. The different Serbs had never been integrated into a nation. In 1941, when the common state was shattered, they were more disintegrated than ever. They were joined only by the fact that they were treated collectively as vanquished foe. The different risings in 1941 were thus certainly Serb, but they were local, fragmented and diverse. They were not even a rising against a 'new order'. They were disjointed risings against a 'new disorder'.

Whereas Serbs were treated as vanquished foe, Croats were to be somehow brought into the New Order, and thus had no immediate reason to resist. The political party that had come to represent a majority of them, in and out of parliament, the Croat Peasant Party (HSS) was after April 1941 effectively leaderless, split and waiting for the storm to pass. By not adding his personal political prestige to

---

6 Karchmar, *Draža Mihailović*, 923.

the Yugoslav government in exile, Maček had contributed to reducing its standing. Those who had supported the HSS only because of its stand against Yugoslav centralism, and even more so those who had joined it after it had become the governing party in Zagreb and a party in government in Belgrade had generally rallied the ustashas, eagerly or reticently. Other supporters were passive. As the war moved towards its end, what political objective did HSS leaders have for after the war? It seems that they were ready to accept any one of several possibilities, as long as it emerged in the form of a genuinely negotiated agreement between the freely-elected representatives of national communities. In the final analysis, it seems that what they wanted more than anything else was a truly free election, to prevent, with Allied help, a communist takeover. They were also more and more passive, especially once the ustashas and the communists had eliminated the remaining active members of the HSS leadership in Croatia. Otherwise, there was among Croats diffuse and increasing opposition to ustasha terror—from those who considered it counterproductive, from those who wanted to save friends and neighbours, from those whose beliefs were incompatible with the official creed, from those who belonged to marginalised groups, from those who had links with or had spent time in other parts of Yugoslavia.

Resistance movements were anyhow more or less than just *resistance* movements. The seizure, or recovery, of political power at the time, or in anticipation, of liberation, was at least as important as, if not more important than, resistance to the occupier. It was definitely more important at times when the Yugoslav contestants for power within and after the resistance envisaged the defeat of the Axis. The British did not always seem to realise (or did not want to know) that Mihailović, Tito or the interim HSS leadership in Zagreb were not in the service of British war aims. Similarly, those same leaders did not accept that the British were not fighting a world war in order to prevent a communist takeover of Yugoslavia or a restoration of the pre-war political régime. It must be said that the Yugoslavs did not realise (and that the British did not explain it to them) that

Yugoslavia was never more than a sideshow in the overall context of the war. Intimately linked to resistance and the struggle for power was the existential horror of what people had gone through in some areas, and the distorted and surreal horror transmitted to others who heard the tales of those for whom 'life had lost all meaning apart from survival'.[7]

After the 1941 rising in Serbia had been put down, the KPJ-led partisans moved west, beyond the horizon of their military rivals in Serbia, who believed that the communist adventure had failed, especially after the partisans had been expelled from Montenegro. In those western regions where Serbs could not afford to stand on the sidelines, the partisans seemed to offer better opportunities than did chetniks of taking revenge on their oppressors. The communists managed to side with the majority in areas where Serbs had been oppressed, while defending the Serbs who had been oppressed. They first concentrated upon the victimised, and then forced the undecided to take sides. They provoked attacks on villages where there was no resistance. They pushed their rivals into prejudicial arrangements with collaborators and occupiers. Beyond Mihailović's horizon, the partisan army was thus resurrected in Bosnia in the summer of 1942, and turned into a mobile force that could take in other Yugoslavs than Serbs. Meanwhile in Serbia, Mihailović's organisation did organise a genuine resistance movement, which made a real effort to assist the Allied cause in the summer of 1942. More generally, with his Yugoslav Army in the Homeland (JVO), he went on trying to muddle through until the expected Allied landing. He muddled through with silences and misunderstandings, with false orders and falsified orders, with wishful thinking and lack of realism, fighting against the occupiers (with sabotage and deception), against the ustashas, but first and foremost against the communists. He also tried to unite against the communists all the 'national' (meaning non-fascist and at least formally pro-Yugoslav) conservative forces. In doing so, he had to deal with Croats and Slovenes who had their own agenda. He

---

7   Djilas, *Wartime*, 148.

found it even more difficult to deal with Muslims, as most of his real, nominal and potential followers no longer wanted to have them in their midst. He did not control JVO commanders. Even less did he control self-appointed political advisers.

Partitioned and occupied Yugoslavia was a land of contrasts and contradictions. Between territories, and within territories. Between city-dwellers and villagers, between insurgents who tried to achieve realistic results and insurgents who devised blueprints, between the autochthonous population that tried to protect its livelihood and the many refugees who were ready recruits for all armed groups. Such contrasts and contradictions help us to understand why and how whole regions went over to the partisans, and whole regions again resisted them.

No anticommunist front was possible. Mihailović did not have a political strategy compatible with that of the Great Allies. He had poor judgment as well as poor information. He was ill-served by his government and by most of those who acknowledged his command. He was eventually denounced by his King. He was generally out of his depth. His beliefs, that a transition could take place between the pre-war order and a slightly improved post-war régime, or that the Western Allies would eventually come round to his views, or that peasants could not truly be attracted to the partisans, or that his King could not really let him down, did not change. If anything, they were reinforced in the darkness of defeat. This was even more the case with fascists. The ustashas fought with suicidal fury in the spring of 1945, as they had never done before, in the belief that Hitler's secret weapons or magical powers would stave off defeat, or hold the Soviet advance until a clash occurred between the Allies. The Ljotićites of Serbia were not tempted to collaborate with Mihailović until the very end, indirectly, on the north-western fringes and almost outside Yugoslavia. They, and a few of the more moderate ustashas before them, believed that they could be accepted by the Allies on the strength of their anti-communism. Serbian and other non-fascist collaborators and semi-collaborators believed that democrats and communists had been only short-term partners in the ideological war against nazi-fascism, and that the war was about to start again between democrats and communists. They viewed their collaboration and semi-collaboration with Germans as no worse than British and American collaboration with the Soviets.

Some of the military aspects of Tito's leadership were dubious. As a general, he often could not see the wood from the trees; he too was ill informed; he gave contradictory orders; he made glaring mistakes; he would not be criticised. However, he usually managed to recover his balance, so that his entourage looked up to him as an inspired strategist. He was a political leader and an organiser. He was not an adept of terror for its own sake, but he accepted it as an effective weapon if integrated in an overall plan. He tied a popular resistance movement to the cause of world communism led by the Soviet Union under Stalin. In the course of the struggle against foreign occupiers and the communists' native opponents, he forged a new power. The KPJ did not so much resolve Yugoslavia's 'national question', as prove that it was the only group capable of coming out on the surface and of ruling in spite of it. Its contradictions were neutralised by a determined authority able to develop strong local roots while remaining essentially Yugoslav in its outlook. Indeed, part of its strength lay in the way in which the partisans harnessed local feelings to their cause. In spite of the popularity that it had gained, the communist-led NOP met strong regional opposition at the time of liberation. Liberation was also at times a conquest by the NOP. In Serbia, by the Serb partisans from the west, who moved into the land as in a Balkan Vendée; in Croatia too, by the landless Serb peasants who moved into towns as in enemy nests. Even when the snowball effect worked in favour of the winning partisans, they fought a class war against 'kulaks' and 'bourgeois', or an ethnic war against Germans, Italians and Albanians. They exploited and manipulated nationalism to attract, to detract and to attack.

The Peoples' Liberation Army completed the cycle of massacres started by the ustashas in 1941, by doing away in the last days of the war with more opponents who had retreated into Austria, only to be returned by the British. They were the combatants of native units armed by the occupation authorities and their camp followers, including many Ljotićite Volunteers and various chetniks, alongside the much more numerous NDH Domobrans and ustashas and the Slovene Home Guards. They had sought a solution of Yugoslavia's national question in separation and in a return to an imagined past under the umbrella of the Axis. They had linked their fate and their solution to a permanent victory of the Axis. They were defeated along with the Axis, in the 'new disorder', in the civil war, in the revolution, in the collapse of the Reich. No sooner was the defeat of the Reich and of its hangers-on envisaged, than the belief in the possibility of a renewed Yugoslavia returned. This was achieved by the KPJ, with all the contradictions attending its realisation.

Yugoslavia suffered tremendous human and material losses, probably greater than in any other European country, except the Soviet Union and Poland. There were military operations over a large part of the territory throughout the period 1941-1945, when insurgents were rarely treated according to international rules, and when Serbs were generally considered as subhumans. Belgrade was savagely bombed on the first days of the invasion. There were mass executions of hostages, of insurgents, of sympathisers and of bystanders. There were acts of reprisals by all the combatants in the cause of liberation and revolution. The civil war practiced 'ethnic cleansing' by partially destroying settlements and terrorising inhabitants in order to induce minorities to leave. Not much was achieved of German plans to reorganise the Yugoslav space and its population, or of Italian plans of completing the 'redemption' of 'unredeemed' lands and of setting up a string of satellite kingdoms. Those Croats and Serbs who wanted to 'nationalise' the separate Serbo-Croat-speaking Muslim community into Croats or Serbs, or to get them out of their midst in one way or another also failed. All these tragic failures and the suffering that they caused led to the renewal of Yugoslavia, not as it had been before 1941, but according to the ideological plan of the Communist

Party of Yugoslavia under Tito. He and his lieutenants were both 'Yugoslav' and internationalist. They too wanted to create a 'new man'; their ambitions went beyond Yugoslavia. The KPJ ultimately failed to build on its capital of domestic and international goodwill. The postwar régime hid the complexities of the 1941-1945 period under its red carpet, to facilitate a return to the peaceful cohabitation of populations under the worthy slogan of 'brotherhood and unity', but also to enable continued one-party rule based on the one-sided, single-track and simplified version of the Peoples' Liberation War which was its founding myth. Mihailovic's Yugoslav Army in the Homeland and the followers of King Peter II had failed dismally by 1945, but Tito's Liberation Movement and the KPJ were no less dismal failures by 1991. The legacy today of the civil war fought during the Second World War and of the decades of communist one-party rule founded on its wartime success, is a mess of myths, idealised and sanitised, that has distorted and continues to distort the story of the death and rebirth of Yugoslavia during the years 1941-1945.

DRAMATIS PERSONAE

AĆIMOVIĆ, MILAN, head of German-appointed Commissioners' Administration in Serbia, then home minister in Nedić government.

ALEXANDER, SIR HAROLD, British general, later field marshal and Supreme Allied Commander Mediterranean.

AMBROSIO, VITTORIO, Italian general, Commander Second Army, Commander-in-Chief Armed Forces Slovenia and Dalmatia (Supersloda), later Chief Army General Staff.

ARMELLINI, QUIRINO, Italian general, commander XVIIIth Army Corps (Split).

ARMSTRONG, CHARLES, British brigadier, head liaison mission to Mihailović.

AVŠIČ, JAKA, Yugoslav army colonel, Mihailović's representative in Slovenia, went over to partisans.

BABIĆ, IVAN, NDH lieutenant-colonel, close to the HSS.

BAĆOVIĆ, PETAR, Yugoslav army major, JVO commander Herzegovina and E and C Bosnia.

BADER, PAUL, German Plenipotentiary General in Serbia.

BADOGLIO, PIETRO, Italian marshal, Head of Government after Mussolini deposed.

BAILEY, S.W., British colonel, head of SOE mission to Mihailović.

BAKARIĆ, VLADIMIR, political commissar NOV Staff and KPJ secretary in Croatia.

BARBASETTI DI PRUN, CURIO, Italian general, Military Governor of Montenegro.

BASTIANINI, GIUSEPPE, Italian Governor of Dalmatia.

BÖHME, FRANZ, German Plenipotentiary General in Serbia.

BOTTAI, GIUSEPPE, Italian education minister,

BUĆ, STJEPAN, Croat National-Socialist ideologue.

BUDAK, MILE, NDH education and religious affairs minister.

CHURCHILL, RANDOLPH, British major, liaison officer with partisans, son of Prime Minister Churchill.

CHURCHILL, WINSTON, British prime minister.

CIANO, COUNT GALEAZZO, Italian foreign minister.

CINCAR-MARKOVIĆ, ALEKSANDAR, Yugoslav foreign minister.

CVETKOVIC, DRAGIŠA, Yugoslav prime minister (president of Council of Ministers).

DAMJANOVIĆ, MIODRAG, Yugoslav army general, *chef de cabinet* to Nedić, later Chief of Detached Staff of Mihailović's Supreme Command in Istria.

DANGIĆ, JEZDIMIR, Yugoslav gendarmerie major, chetnik commander in E Bosnia.

DAPČEVIĆ, PEKO, NOV general, commander Second Proletarian Division, later commander First Army.

DEAKIN, F.W.D., British captain, first head of SOE mission to Tito.

DRLJEVIĆ, SEKULA, Montenegrin independentist linked to ustashas.

DJILAS, MILOVAN, member of KPJ inner leadership.

DJUJIĆ, MOMČILO, Serbian Orthodox priest, chetnik commander in Tromedja area of NDH.

DJUKANOVIĆ, BLAŽO, Yugoslav army general, Ban of Zetska (Cetinje), later nominal commander 'nationalist' forces in Italian-occupied Montenegro.

DJUKIĆ, SVETOMIR, Yugoslav army general, JVO commander 'northern territories'.

DJURIĆ, RADOSLAV, Yugoslav army major, JVO commander S Serbia, went over to partisans.

DJURIŠIĆ, PAVLE, Yugoslav army captain, chetnik commander in Montenegro.

EREMIĆ, JOCO, partisan commander Kordun area of Croatia, went over to chetniks.

FAROLFI, IVANKO, HSS acting secretary in wartime Zagreb.

FICK, ERNST, SS general in Croatia.

FILIPOVIĆ, SULEJMAN, NDH colonel, went over to partisans.

FRANCETIĆ, JURE, commander ustasha Black Legion.

GAMBARA, GASTONE, Italian general, commander XIth Army Corps (Ljubljana).

GAVRILO, Patriarch of the Serbian Orthodox Church.

GERMOGEN, bishop of Russian Orthodox Church Abroad, Pavelić-appointed head of Croatian Orthodox Church.

GIUNTA, FRANCESCO, Italian Governor of Dalmatia.

GLAISE VON HORSTENAU, EDMUND, German Plenipotentiary General in NDH.

GRAZIOLI, EMILIO, Italian High Commissioner of Ljubljana Province.

GRDJIĆ, RADMILO, Serb 'nationalist' personality of Italian zone of NDH.

HADŽIEFENDIĆ, MUHAMED, commander 'Muslim Volunteer Legion' militia in Bosnia.

HEBRANG, ANDRIJA, KPJ secretary of Central Committee for Croatia.

HIMMLER, HEINRICH, *Reichsführer* SS.

HITLER, ADOLF, German Chancellor and Fuhrer.

HUSSEINI, AMIN EL-, former Mufti of Jerusalem acting as recruiter of Muslim volunteers for the German forces.

IVKOVIĆ, BRANISLAV, Democratic Party politician.

JACOMONI DI SAN SAVINO, FRANCESCO, Italian King's Lieutenant of Albania.

JEVDJEVIĆ, DOBROSLAV, chetnik leader in Herzegovina.

JOANIKIJE, Serbian Orthodox Metropolitan of Montenegro.

JONES, WILLIAM, British major, liaison officer with partisans.

JOSIF, Serbian Orthodox Metropolitan of Skoplje (Skopje), acting head of the Serbian Orthodox Church.

JOVANOVIĆ, SLOBODAN, deputy prime minister and later prime minister, Yugoslav governments in exile.

KALABIĆ, NIKOLA, Yugoslav army captain, JVO commander in Serbia.

KALAFATOVIĆ, DANILO, Yugoslav army general, chief of Supreme Command Staff at time of capitulation.

KAMMERHOFER, KONSTANTIN, SS general, Himmler's plenipotentiary in NDH.

KARDELJ, EDVARD, Tito's lieutenant in Slovenia, member of NOV Supreme Staff.

KASCHE, SIEGFRIED, German minister in Zagreb.

KEITEL, WILHELM, German field marshal, chief of Armed Forces High Command.

KOCBEK, EDVARD, Slovene Christian Socialist politician who joined OF.

KOLIŠEVSKI, LAZAR, head of KPJ organisation for Macedonia.

KOŠUTIĆ, AUGUST, HSS deputy leader.

KREK, MIHA, leader of the SLjS, minister in Yugoslav government in exile.

KRNJEVIĆ, JURAJ, HSS secretary-general, deputy prime minister Yugoslav government in exile.

KULENOVIĆ, DŽAFER, leader of the JMO.

KULOVEC, FRAN, Roman Catholic priest, leader of the SLjS.

KUNTZE, WALTER, German general, Commander-in-Chief Armed Forces South-East (*Wehrmachtsbefehlshaber Südost*).

KVATERNIK, EUGEN DIDO, director of NDH Public Order and Security, son of Slavko Kvaternik.

KVATERNIK, SLAVKO, NDH marshal.

LAŠIĆ, DJORDJE, Yugoslav army major, chetnik commander in Montenegro.

LIST, WILHELM, German field marshal, Commander-in-Chief Armed Forces South-East.

LÖHR, ALEXANDER, German general, Commander-in-Chief Armed Forces South-East.

LORKOVIĆ, MLADEN, NDH home minister.

LUBURIĆ, VJEKOSLAV MAKS, ustasha colonel.

LUKAČEVIĆ, VOJISLAV, Yugoslav army major, JVO commander.

LÜTERS, RUDOLF, German general, commander German troops in NDH.

LJOTIĆ, DIMITRIJE, leader of Zbor movement.

MACLEAN, FITZROY, British brigadier, head of liaison mission to Tito.

MAČEK, VLADKO, leader of the HSS.

MANDIĆ, NIKOLA, president of NDH government.

MARIĆ, AUGUST, Yugoslav army general, then NDH general.

McDOWELL, ROBERT, US colonel, head of OSS mission to Mihailović.

MENTASTI, LUIGI, Italian general, commander XIVth Army Corps (Montenegro).

MEYSZNER, AUGUST, SS general, German SS and police chief in Serbia.

MICHAEL OF MONTENEGRO, Prince, presumed claimant to the throne of Montenegro.

MIHAILOV, IVAN VANCHA, leader of IMRO, linked to ustashas.

MIHAILOVIĆ, DRAGOLJUB DRAŽA, Yugoslav army colonel, later general, war minister in government in exile and chief of Supreme Command Staff in homeland.

MIKUŽ, METOD, Roman Catholic priest who joined partisans end 1941.

Miljković, Husnija Huska, commander 'Muslim Army' militia in Bosnia.

Milovanović Pećanac, Kosta, head of veteran chetniks association to 1941, then chetnik commander in southern Serbia.

Mišić, Alojzije, Roman Catholic Bishop of Mostar.

Moljević, Stevan, civilian political adviser to Mihailović.

Mulalić, Mustafa, JMO politician, vice-president of Central National Committee after Ba Congress.

Musakadić, Fehim, Yugoslav army major, Muslim officer with Mihailović.

Mussolini, Benito, Italian Duce and Head of Government.

Natlačen, Marko, Ban of Dravska (Ljubljana), member of Italian-appointed Consultative Council Ljubljana Province.

Navratil, Friedrich, NDH general, armed forces minister.

Nedić, Milan, Yugoslav army general, German-appointed minister-president of Serbian government.

Neubacher, Hermann, German Special Foreign Affairs Plenipotentiary for South-East.

Neuhausen, Franz, German Plenipotentiary for Economic Affairs, Belgrade.

Nikolaj, Serbian Orthodox Bishop of Žiča.

Novak, Karel, Yugoslav army major, Mihailović's representative in Slovenia.

Ostojić, Zaharije, Yugoslav army major, officer on Mihailović's staff, arrived with first SOE mission.

Ott, Hans, German Abwehr officer who negotiated with partisans and chetniks.

Oxilia, Giovanni Battista, Italian general, commander 'Venezia' Division (Montenegro).

Pandža, Muhamed, commander 'Muslim Liberation Army' militia in Bosnia.

Parac, Matija, Yugoslav army general, Mihailović-appointed commander of 'Croat Army' of JVO.

Pariani, Alberto, Italian general, King's Lieutenant of Albania.

Paul of Yugoslavia, Prince, regent of Yugoslavia to 1941.

Pavelić, Ante, ustasha *Poglavnik*.

PERHINEK, RUDOLF, Yugoslav army captain, Slovene officer on Mihailović's staff.

PERIĆ, STIJEPO, NDH foreign minister.

PETER II, King of Yugoslavia.

PHLEPS, ARTHUR, SS general, commander SS 'Prinz Eugen' division.

PIÈCHE, GIUSEPPE, *carabinieri* general on a mission for Italian foreign ministry.

PIJADE, MOŠA, member KPJ leadership, organiser of 1941 revolt in Montenegro.

PIRZIO BIROLI, ALESSANDRO, Italian general, Military Governor of Montenegro.

POPOVAC, ISMET, Bosnian Muslim personality with Mihailović.

POPOVIĆ, KOČA, NOV general.

POPOVIĆ, KRSTO, commander of Montenegrin Green militia.

PREDAVEC, VLADIMIR, member of Central National Committee after Ba Congress, son of HSS politician Josip Predavec.

PREZELJ, IVAN, Yugoslav army colonel, Mihailović-promoted general and JVO commander in Slovenia.

PRPIĆ, IVAN, NDH general and chief of General Staff.

PRÜTZMANN, HANS ADOLF, SS general, German Plenipotentiary General in NDH.

PUCELJ, IVAN, Slovene politician, member of Italian-appointed Consultative Council of Ljubljana Province.

PURIĆ, BOŽIDAR, Yugoslav diplomat, later prime minister Yugoslav government in exile.

RAINER, FRIEDRICH, *Gauleiter* of Carinthia, head of Adriatic Coastland Operational Zone.

RANKOVIĆ, ALEKSANDAR, member NOV Supreme Staff and KPJ inner leadership.

RENDULIC, LOTHAR, German general, commander Second Panzer Army (NDH and Serbia).

RIBBENTROP, JOACHIM VON, German foreign minister.

ROATTA, MARIO, Italian general, Commander-in-Chief Armed Forces Slovenia and Dalmatia.

ROBOTTI, MARIO, Italian general, commander XIth Army Corps (Slovenia), later Commander-in-Chief Armed Forces Slovenia and Dalmatia.

RONCAGLIA, ETTORE, Italian general, commander XIVth Army Corps (Montenegro).

ROOSEVELT, F.D., President of the United States.

RÖSENER, ERWEIN, SS general in Slovenia.

ROŽMAN, GREGORIJ, Roman Catholic Bishop of Ljubljana.

RUPNIK, LEON, Yugoslav army general, Italian-appointed Mayor of Ljubljana, later German-appointed Head of Ljubljana Province.

SIMOVIĆ, DUŠAN, Yugoslav army general, prime minister (president of Council of Ministers).

SPOLETO, AIMONE DI SAVOIA AOSTA DUKE OF, Italian 'King-Designate' of Croatia.

STALIN, IOSIF DJUGASHVILI, general secretary Soviet Communist Party and chairman of USSR government.

STANIŠIĆ, BAJO, Yugoslav army colonel, chetnik commander in Montenegro.

STEPINAC, ALOJZIJE, Roman Catholic Archbishop of Zagreb.

STILINOVIĆ, MARIJAN, delegate of NOV Supreme Staff for negotiations with Glaise von Horstenau.

STRECKER, ARTHUR, German major who negotiated with partisans.

ŠARIĆ, IVAN, Roman Catholic Archbishop of Vrhbosna (Sarajevo).

ŠATOROV ŠARLO, METODIJE, head KPJ regional committee Macedonia.

ŠUBAŠIĆ, IVAN, HSS politician, Ban of Croatia, later prime minister Yugoslav government in exile.

TITO, JOSIP BROZ, general secretary KPJ, supreme commander and marshal NOV.

TODOROVIĆ, BOŠKO, Yugoslav army major, JVO commander in Herzegovina.

TODOROVIĆ, ŽARKO, Yugoslav army major, JVO commander of Belgrade and 'northern territories'.

TOLBUKHIN, FYODOR, Soviet marshal and commander Third Ukrainian Front.

TOMAŠEVIĆ, IVAN, NDH general and divisional commander.

TOMAŠIĆ, LJUDEVIT, member of HSS leadership in wartime Zagreb.

TOPALOVIĆ, ŽIVKO, leader Socialist Party of Yugoslavia, president Ba Congress.

TOPČIĆ, NEDŽAD, commander 'Muslim Green Cadre' militia in Bosnia.

TRIFUNOVIĆ, MIROSLAV, Yugoslav army general, JVO commander of Serbia under Mihailović.

TRIFUNOVIĆ BIRČANIN, ILIJA, chetnik commander nominally in charge of Bosnia, Herzegovina, Lika and Dalmatia, resident in Split.

TURNER, HARALD, head of administrative staff, German Military Command Serbia.

VASIĆ, DRAGIŠA, civilian political adviser to Mihailović.

VAUHNIK, VLADIMIR, Yugoslav army colonel, military attaché in Berlin to 1941, later head of an intelligence network in occupied Yugoslavia.

VELEBIT, VLADIMIR, Tito's negotiator with Germans in 1943, later liaison officer with British mission.

VICTOR EMMANUEL III, King of Italy.

VOKIĆ, ANTE, NDH colonel, armed forces minister.

VUČKOVIĆ, ZVONIMIR, Yugoslav army captain, JVO commander in Serbia.

WARLIMONT, WALTER, German general on an investigating mission in NDH.

VUKMANOVIĆ TEMPO, SVETOZAR, member NOV Supreme Staff, delegate for Macedonia and Kosovo.

WEICHS, MAXIMILIAN FREIHERR VON, German field marshal, Commander-in-Chief Armed Forces South-East.

WILSON, SIR HENRY MAITLAND, British general, Supreme Allied Commander Mediterranean.

ŽUJOVIĆ, MLADEN, Mihailović's delegate in Split in 1943.

CHRONOLOGY

1939

May   *German–Italian Pact of Steel signed.*

June   Prince Paul's state visit to Germany.

August   *Nazi–Soviet Pact signed.*
Cvetković-Maček Agreement; setting up of Banovina of Croatia.

September   *Germany and USSR invade Poland. France and UK declare war on Germany.*

1940

June   *Italy declares war on France; France signs armistice; De Gaulle's 18 June appeal from London.*

September   *Italians invade Egypt from Libya. Tripartite Pact between Germany, Italy and Japan.*

October   *Italy invades Greece.*

November   *Hungary and Romania join Tripartite Pact.*
Yugoslav foreign minister visits Hitler.

December   *Hitler issues Directive 22 for invasion of USSR.*

1941

February   *British capture Benghazi. Rommel arrives in Libya.*
Yugoslav prime minister and foreign minister visit Hitler.

March   *Bulgaria joins Tripartite Pact.*
Prince Paul visits Hitler; Yugoslavia joins Tripartite Pact; coup d'Etat ends regency; General Simović forms all-party government.

April   *British enter Addis Ababa.*

Germany and Italy attack Yugoslavia; Independent State of Croatia (NDH) proclaimed under Pavelić; King Peter and the government leave Yugoslavia; Yugoslav armed forces capitulate after 12 days; Vienna arrangement on division of spoils; Serbia declared war zone again, with reprisals order.

May   Germans appoint a Commissioners' Administration in occupied Serbia. KPJ leadership meets in Zagreb to prepare to seize power in alliance with USSR; Tito and Central Committee move to Belgrade; Mihailović arrives at Ravna Gora. Rome Agreements between Italy and the NHD.

June   German General in Zagreb reports: 'The ustashas have gone raving mad'. Serb rebellion starts in eastern Herzegovina. KPJ manifesto to prepare for armed action.

July   KPJ issues call to arms. Declaration on the Restoration of Montenegro, general uprising against Italian rule.

August   Germans appoint Nedić as president of a Serbian Government; Mihailović's officers and Tito's communist partisans go into action.

September Italian troops reoccupy Zone 2 of the NDH. Mihailović establishes radio link with London; Tito leaves Belgrade, and meets Mihailović. KPJ leadership decides to stimulate risings all over Yugoslavia, and sets up Supreme Staff. SOE mission lands in Montenegro.

October   Italian troops move into Zone 3; Pavelić has Maček arrested. Insurgency in Serbia, Germans go into counteraction; Tito and Mihailović meet again, civil strife starts between chetniks and partisans in Serbia. Direct Italian military rule in Montenegro.

November Meeting between Abwehr and Mihailović; BBC announces that Mihailović is commander of Yugoslav forces in the homeland; Tito leaves Serbia.

December *Japanese attack Pearl Harbour; USA declare war on Japan.*

Mihailović escapes capture by Germans; German and NDH bounties offered for him; Tito escapes capture by Italians; he moves to Bosnia.

1942

January   Jovanović prime minister of Yugoslav government in exile, with Mihailović as war minister. Tito arrives in Foča, eastern Bosnia; German action against partisan concentration in area; Germans plan 'Trio' operations. Italians declare Ljubljana Province an 'operational area'; Ljubljana disarmed.

February   Chetnik revolt against partisans in Montenegro; first agreements between Italian and chetnik commanders.

March   Slovenian non-communist parties set up Slovenian Alliance (SZ).

April   *Anglo–Soviet Treaty signed.*

May   Mihailović leaves Serbia for northern Montenegro; Tito evacuates Foča.

June   *Tobruk falls to Rommel.*
Mihailović chief of staff of Yugoslav Supreme Command. Italians legalize Voluntary Anti-Communist Militia (MVAC). Tito decides on 'march across Bosnia'.

July   *First battle of El Alamein begins.*
Djukanović acknowledged by chetnik commanders and Italians as overall commander of native armed formations in Montenegro. German 'battle without mercy' against partisan concentration in north-west Bosnia. Main chetnik leaders from Italian zone meet Mihailović at Avtovac. New cycle of operations by Italians in Slovenia; Rupnik appointed Mayor of Ljubljana. Muslim organizations in Sarajevo call for an end to religious discord.

August   *Dieppe raid. Churchill attends Moscow Conference.*

September Mihailović sabotages communication lines through Serbia. Pavelić visits Hitler.

November *Allied landings in French North Africa.*

Mihailović announces campaign of civil disobedience in Serbia; renewed German repression. Partisans capture Bihać and hold meeting of Anti-Fascist Council of the Peoples' Liberation of Yugoslavia (AVNOJ).

December Šahovići conference of young chetnik 'intellectuals' of Montenegro. Bailey arrives at Mihailović's headquarters. Mihailović plans a 'march on Bosnia'. Hitler issues Directive 47 for cycle of anti-insurgent operations known as 'Weiss' and 'Schwarz'

1943

January *Casablanca Conference. British troops enter Tripoli.*
Partisans lose Bihać.

February *German forces capitulate at Stalingrad.*
Tito's forces reach river Neretva; Battle of Neretva; Mihailović's 'christening speech'.

March Negotiations in Zagreb between Tito's emissaries and German military. Hitler entrusts SS with powers to ensure pacification of NDH. Mihailović contacts party politicians in Belgrade.

April SOE missions arrive to partisans in eastern Bosnia. Tito's main operational force breaks through into 'chetnik state' in Montenegro. Hitler receives Pavelić.

May *Axis forces capitulate in North Africa.*
German forces move into Italian Montenegro; they capture and disarm Djurišić and his chetniks; Mihailović returns to Serbia. Deakin mission dropped to Tito. Germans attack Tito and his force, who extricate themselves by crossing Sutjeska gorge. Italians offer rewards for capture of Tito and Mihailović. SOE mission to partisans in Slovenia.

June   *French Committee for National Liberation formed in Algiers. Formal dissolution of Comintern.*

Pavelić sets up a Croatian Orthodox Church. Italians arrest Žujović, Mihailović's delegate in Split.

July   *Allied forces land in Sicily. Mussolini resigns and is arrested. Badoglio becomes Italian prime minister.*

Germans offer rewards for capture of Mihailović and Tito.

August   All-party Yugoslav government in exile gives way to Purić's small cabinet of civil servants; Mihailović retained. Jajce, taken by partisans, becomes Tito's 'capital'.

September *Allies land on Italian mainland; Italian armistice; Germans occupy Rome.*

Italian units in Yugoslavia disintegrate as a result of 8 September announcement of armistice; the bulk of their weaponry goes to Tito's forces. Maclean at Tito's headquarters. Armstrong at Mihailović's encourages renewed action, which is then attributed to partisans. Gestapo capture most of Mihailović's underground personnel in Belgrade. Partisans capture Turjak castle from Slovene MVAC and kill many of its adherents. Germans appoint Rupnik head of Ljubljana Province; he sets up Slovene Home Guard.

October *Foreign Ministers' Moscow Conference.*

Maclean reports on Yugoslavia to Churchill in Cairo. Bulk of chetnik forces in Montenegro destroyed by partisans. Archbishop Stepinac denounces 'injustice and violence committed in the name of theories of class, race or nationality'.

November *Red Army captures Kharkov. First part of Cairo Conference. Tehran Conference.*

Neubacher appointed to Belgrade with the task of guiding national anti-communist forces; Djurišić reappears to rally remains of chetniks in Montenegro. Second session of AVNOJ at Jajce sets up Federative Peoples' Yugoslavia, with a provisional government in all but name; Tito given rank of Marshal.

December *Second part of Cairo Conference. Eisenhower named supreme commander for Normandy landings.*
Hitler rejects Neubacher's proposals for making use of Serb anti-communist forces.

1944
January *Red Army crosses prewar Polish border. Leningrad siege ends. Allied landings at Anzio.*
New round of German anti-insurgent operations in NDH; Tito, forced out of Jajce, settles in Drvar; Soviet mission arrives. Churchill opens a personal correspondence with Tito. Mihailović holds a 'national congress' at Ba in Serbia under chairmanship of Socialist leader Topalović.

February *First and second battle of Monte Cassino.*
Germans conduct operations against chetniks in Serbia.

March *Third battle of Monte Cassino.*
SS general estimates that Pavelić, 'in terms of power, is but mayor of Zagreb, excluding the suburbs'.

April Muslim personalities from Sarajevo present a memorandum of grievances to NDH prime minister; NDH protests against German reprisals; defection of Kordun partisan commander to chetniks. SOE mission to partisans in Serbia; partisans fail to break into Serbia. Beginning of Allied air bombardment of targets in Yugoslavia. Germans arrest more officers in Slovenia.

May *Fourth battle of Monte Cassino.*
Tito escapes capture by Germans. Churchill announces change of Yugoslav government in exile; British mission to Mihailović evacuated.

June *US troops enter Rome. Allies land in Normandy.*
King Peter announces appointment of Šubašić as prime minister. Tito evacuated to Bari.

July   *Red Army captures Minsk, Wilno, Lwów and Brest-Lito-
vsk.*
Tito asks Stalin for more help; operation 'Ratweek' to
help Tito's new attempt to break into Serbia.

August   *Warsaw rising begins. Allies enter Florence. Allied landings
in southern France. Red Army attacks Romania; Romania
accepts armistice terms and declares war on Germany. Ger-
mans surrender in Paris.*
Tito-Šubašić Agreement signed on Vis; Tito meets
Churchill in Italy. Probable secret meeting of Nedić
with Mihailović; Hitler rejects idea of an approach to
Mihailović; break-up of Mihailović's forces begins; Mc-
Dowell's US OSS mission comes to Mihailović; King
Peter dismisses Mihailović from his command position.
Soviet troops reach Yugoslav border; Mihailović orders
general mobilization.

September   *USSR enters Bulgaria; Bulgaria surrenders and declares war
on Germany.*
King Peter calls on all in Yugoslavia to rally round Tito.
Tito 'levants' from Vis for a meeting with Stalin in
Moscow, to ask for help to liberate Serbia and Belgrade.
Pavelić's last visit to Hitler.

October   *Warsaw rising ends. Red Army enters Hungary. Germans
decide to evacuate Greece. 'Tolstoy' Conference in Moscow.
British enter Athens. Aachen falls to US troops.*
Red Army enters Yugoslavia; Nedić government leaves
for Austria; Belgrade liberated; Tito returns; Mihailović
withdraws from Serbia.

November   German troops leave Skopje. Partisans enter Cetinje.
Second Tito-Šubašić agreement signed in Belgrade.
McDowell evacuated. German troops withdrawn from
Kosovo.

1945

January   *Red Army takes Warsaw.*
Mihailović orders his forces to regroup in north-central Bosnia. Churchill announces that he intends to 'presume' King Peter's assent to Tito-Šubašić agreement.

February   *Yalta Conference.*
Germans leave Mostar. Tito introduces military rule in Kosovo to put down rebellion.

March   *US Third Army crosses Rhine. Red Army enters Austria. US Fifth Army takes Bologna.*
King Peter appoints regency council; Tito forms new government.

April   *Soviet and US troops meet at Torgau. Germans sign surrender terms for their troops in Italy. Hitler commits suicide.*
Mihailović leaves north-central Bosnia to return to Serbia. Tito in Moscow signs treaty with USSR. Djurišić's Montenegrin chetnik force destroyed by ustashas as they try to cross NDH. Srem front broken; Germans leave Sarajevo. Mihailović emissaries in Zagreb.

May   *Red Army takes Berlin. Germany surrenders unconditionally.*
NDH government leaves Zagreb; Slovene pre-war members of parliament proclaim a united Slovenia in the Federal Kingdom of Yugoslavia. Tito's troops reach Trieste and hold it for 42 days. Partisans enter Zagreb and Ljubljana. Mihailović's force destroyed in Bosnia.

August   AVNOJ meets for a third session in Belgrade, and turns itself into a provisional parliament. People's Front set up for general elections.

November   People's Front receives 90% of ballots cast. Constituent Assembly proclaims Peoples' Republic of Yugoslavia.

BIBLIOGRAPHY

What follows is a catalogue of the sources I have used in order to write this book. It is *not* an exhaustive list of sources, published and unpublished, for the history of the Second World War in Yugoslavia.

Unpublished Documents

National Archives (Public Records Office), Kew:
Foreign Office papers: FO 371 (General Correspondence, Southern European Department); FO 536 (Embassy and Consular Archives-Yugoslavia Correspondence); FO 898 (Political Warfare Executive).
War Cabinet papers: CAB 65 (War Cabinet Minutes); CAB 66 (War Cabinet Memorandum WP & CP Series); FO 67 (War Cabinet Memorandum WP [G] Series).

Archivio storico dello Stato maggiore dell'Esercito, Rome:
Fondo M 3: Documenti restituiti dagli alleati alla fine della seconda guerra mondiale – II Armata; divisioni italiane in Jugoslavia.
Fondo H 3, SIM: Notiziari stati esteri, bolletini seconda guerra mondiale – Jugoslavia.
Fondo L 13: Documentazione acquisita dal 1968 – Jugoslavia.
Fondo N 1-11: Diari storici della seconda guerra mondiale – Jugoslavia.

Žujović, Mladen: Memorandum for Ambassador Stevenson, 8 December 1944.

Interviews and Correspondence

Interviews and correspondence (with occasional access to private letters and diaries indicated as '+ D') with the following:

Julian Amery (April 1974), Ivan Babić (December 1977), Milan Bandović (January 1973, April 1974, September 1975), Mrgud Bojanić (January-March 1974, December 1977, November 1979), Peter Boughey (October-November 1976), Professor Franco Catalano (June 1971), Stephen Clissold (April 1974), Kosta Cukić (Zoukitch, November-December 1973, July 1974), Milovan Djilas (February 1990), Joco Eremić (December 1973, May 1974), Nenad Grisogono (November 1971, January-April 1974, January 1977, September 1977, +D), Radmilo Grdjić (August 1973, January 1974), D.T. Hudson (November 1983, January 1984), Radovan Ivanišević (June-August 1974, June 1975), Lazar Janić (July-September 1978, September 1979), Ilija Jukić (October-December 1974), Živan Knežević (February 1977, January 1984, +D), Stevo Kosanović (December 1973, January 1974), Robert Lethbridge (April 1975), Salvatore Loi (September 1972, February 1973), Michael Lees (November 1986, April 1987), Guido Lucich-Rocchi (February-May 1974, +D), Rusko Matulić (December 1972, May 1974, January 1978, December 1978, January 1979), Vaso Miljuš (May 1972, November 1973, +D), James Millar (April 1974), Armando Moroni (January 1974, May 1974), Rudolf Perhinek (December 1978, August 1980), Vladimir Perić (Peritch, April-July 1974, May 1981, +D), Mane Pešut (September 1973, May 1981), Ambassador Detalmo Pirzio Biroli (February 1981, +D), Vladimir Predavec (September 1971), Borivoje Radulović (May 1974, January 1975), Mihailo Radusinović (October 1973, June 1974), Stanislav Rapotec (September-November 1973, May 1974, October 1977, July 1980, March 1982), Miloš Saičić (August 1975), General Umberto Salvatores (December 1973, +D), Professor Hugh Seton-Watson (May 1974, July 1977, October 1977, January 1981, May 1981), Ljubo Sirc (April 1974), Angelo Varalli (February 1974, October 1974), Zvonimir Vučković (November 1981, March 1985).

Unpublished Doctoral Theses

Brashaw, Nicholas C., 'Signals Intelligence, the British and the War in Yugoslavia, 1941-1944', University of Southampton, 2001.

Fattig, Richard Cavill, 'Reprisals. The German Army and the Execution of Hostages during the Second World War', University of California, San Diego, 1980.

Ford, Thomas Kirkwood, Jr, 'Pawns and Powerbrokers. OSS and the Yugoslav Resistance during the Second World War', University of Mississippi, 1980.

Kay, Margaret Anne, 'The British Attitude to the Yugoslav Government-in-Exile, 1941-1945', University of Southampton, 1986.

Palmer, Peter, 'The Communists and the Roman Catholic Church in Yugoslavia, 1941-1946', Oxford University, 2000.

Scrase, Gavin M., 'Britain, the Balkans, and the Politics of the Wartime Alliance. Great-Power Collaboration and the Pre-Percentages Agreement of May 1944', University of Southampton, 1997.

Published Documents

Actes et documents du Saint Siège relatifs à la seconde guerre mondiale, Pierre Blet et al., ed., Vatican City, 1 (1965), 4 (1967), 5 (1969), 6 (1972), 7 (1973).

Akten zur deutschen auswärtigen Politik, 1918-1945, E 1941-1945, Göttingen, 1969-1979.

Das Ende auf dem Balkan, 1944/45. Die militärische Räumung Jugoslawiens durch die deutsche Wehrmacht, Karl Hnilicka, ed., Göttingen, 1970.

Documenti diplomatici italiani, IX, 1939-1943, Rome, 1960-1987.

Hitlers Weisungen für die Kriegsführung, 1939-1945. Dokumente des Oberkommandos der Wehrmacht, Walter Hubatsch, ed., Frankfurt am Main, 1983.

Kriegstagebuch des Oberkommandos der Wehrmacht, 1940-1945, Hans-Adolf Jacobsen et al., ed., Frankfurt am Main & Munich, 1961-1969.

Jugoslovenska demokratska narodna zajednica, *Odluke Svetosavskog kongresa u slobodnim srpskim planinama* (printed in the 'free Serbian mountains'), 1944.

La vicenda italo-croata nei documenti di Aimone di Savoia, 1941-1943, Gian Nicola Amoretti, ed., Rapallo, 1979.

Memorijalni centar 'Josip Broz Tito' & Arhiv Josipa Broza Tita, *Zapisnici NKOJa i Privremene vlade DFJ, 1943-1945*, Branko Petranović & Ljiljana Marković, ed., Belgrade, 1991.

Mihailović, Dragoljub, *Izdajnik i ratni zločinac Draža Mihailović pred sudom*, Belgrade, 1946, is the first (selected) edition of the stenographic minutes of the Mihailović trial. Also available in English as *The Trial of Dragoljub-Draža Mihailović*, Belgrade, 1946. The full version, *Ne osećam se krivim. Draža Mihailović pred sudom. Stenografske beleške sa sudjenja vodji četničkog pokreta*, Jovan Kesar & Dragoje Lukić, ed. were published in Belgrade, 1990.

Mihailović, Dragoljub, *Dragoljub M. Mihailović. Rat i mir Djenerala. Izabrani ratni spisi*, Milan Vesović et al., ed., Belgrade, 1998.

Petranović, Branko & Nikola Žutić, ed., *27. mart 1941. Tematska zbirka dokumenata*, Belgrade, 1990.

Službene novine Kraljevine Jugoslavije, Belgrade to 1941, London 1941-1945.

Stato maggiore dell'Esercito, Ufficio storico, *Le operazioni delle unità italiane nel settembre-ottobre 1943*, General Mario Torsiello, ed., Rome, 1975.

—— *Le operazioni delle unità italiane in Jugoslavia, 1941-1943*, Salvatore Loi, ed., Rome, 1978.

—— *Verbali delle riunioni tenute dal Capo di Stato maggiore generale*, volume IV, covering period 1 January–7 September 1943, published in Rome in 1985.

—— *Dalmazia. Una cronaca per la storia*, Oddone Talpo, ed., Rome, 1941 (1985), 1942 (1990), 1943-1944 (1994).

—— *I rapporti fra Alleati e Italiani nella cobelligeranza*, Salvatore Loi, ed., Rome, 1986.

—— *Diario storico del Comando supremo*, III, IV & V (1941), Rome, 1989-1992.

Zakoni, zakonske odredbe, naredbe i t.d. Nezavisne Države Hrvatske, I-XXXVIII, A. Mataić, ed., Zagreb, 1941-1943.

Zbornik dokumenata i podataka o narodnooslobodilačkom ratu jugoslovenskih naroda, I-XIV, Belgrade, 1949-1983.

Published Books and Articles

Afrić, Vjeko, *U danima odluka i dilema*, Belgrade, 1970.

Alexander, Stella, *The Triple Myth. A Life of Archbishop Alojzije Stepinac*, New York, 1987.

Almuli, Jaša, *Živi i mrtvi. Razgovori sa Jevrejima*, 2nd ed., Belgrade, 2002.

Amery, Julian, *Approach March. A Venture in Autobiography*, London, 1973.

Anfuso, Filippo, *Roma Berlino Salò, 1936-1945*, Milan, 1950.

Antonić, Zdravko, *Ustanak u istočnoj i centralnoj Bosni 1941*, Belgrade,1973.

Arsenijević, Drago, *Un voyage oublié*, Paris, 1976.

Babić, Ivan, 'Moja misija kod Saveznika 1944', in *Hrvatska revija, jubilarni zbornik 1951-1975*, Munich & Barcelona, 1976.

Baird, Jay W., *The Mythical World of Nazi War Propaganda, 1939-1945*, Minneapolis, MN, 1974.

Bajt, Aleksandar, *Bermanov dosije*, Belgrade, 2006.

Bartolini, Alfonso, *Storia della resistenza italiana all'estero*, Padua, 1965.

Bassi, Maurizio, *Due anni fra le bande di Tito*, Bologna, 1950.

Basta, Milan, *Agonija i slom Nezavisne Države Hrvatske*, Belgrade, 1971.

—— *Rat je završen 7 dana kasnije*, 4th ed., Belgrade, 1982.

Bedeschi, Giulio (ed.), *Fronte jugoslavo-balcanico. C'ero anch'io*, Milan, 1985.

Benigar, Aleksa, *Alojzije Stepinac, hrvatski cardinal*, Rome, 1974.

Biondich, Mark, 'Religion and Nation in Wartime Croatia. Reflections on the Ustaša Policy of Forced Religious Conversion, 1941-1942', in *Slavonic and East European Review*, 83/1, 2005.

Bjelajac, Mile S., *Generali i admirali Kraljevine Jugoslavije, 1918-1941*, Belgrade, 2004.

Bjelajac, Slavko N., *Memoirs of Colonel Slavko N. Bjelajac, 1941-1948*, Estapona (Malaga), 1984.

Boban, Ljubo, *Maček i politika Hrvatske seljačke stranke, 1928-1941*, Zagreb, 1974.

Bocca, Giorgio, *Storia d'Italia nella guerra fascista, 1940-1943*, Bari, 1973.

Bojić, Mirko, *Jugoslovenski narodni pokret "Zbor", 1935-1945. Jedan kritički prilaz*, Belgrade, 1995.

Bolta, Bogdan L., *Gračačka četnička brigade, 1941-1945*, Sydney, 1987.

Borković, Milan, *Komunistička partija Jugoslavije u Srbiji, 1941-1945*, Belgrade, 1974.

—— *Kontrarevolucija u Srbiji. Kvilinška uprava, 1941-1944*, Belgrade, 1979.

303

Bošković, Branko N., *Narodnooslobodilačka borba u Ibarskom bazenu*, Priština/Prishtinë, 1968.

Bottai, Giuseppe, *Diario, 1935-1944*. Milan, 1994.

Božović, Jovan, *Ovdje Prva proleterska*, Belgrade, 1964.

Brajović, Petar, Jovan Marjanović & Franjo Tudjman (ed.), *Les Systèmes d'occupation en Yougoslavie, 1941-1945*, Belgrade & Zagreb, 1963.

Brignoli, Pietro, *Santa messa per i miei fucilati. Le spietate rappresaglie italiane contro i partigiani in Croazia dal diario di un cappellano*, Milan, 1973.

Broszat, Martin & Ladislaus Hory, *Der Kroatische Ustascha Staat, 1941-1945*, Stuttgart, 1964.

Browning, Christopher R., 'Wehrmacht Reprisal Policy and the Mass Murder of Jews in Serbia', in *Militärgeschichte Mitteilungen*, I, 1983.

Broz Tito, Josip, *Autobiografska kazivanja*, Cetinje, Skopje, Belgrade & Ljubljana, 1982.

Carnier, Pier Arrigo, *Le sterminio mancato. La dominazione nazista nel Veneto orientale, 1943-1945*, Milan, 1982.

Cavalli, Fiorello, *Il processo dell'arcivescovo di Zagabria*, Rome, 1947.

Ceriana Mayneri, Carlo, *Parla un comandante di truppe*, Milan, 1947.

Ceva, Lucio, *La condotta italiana della guerra. Cavallero e il Comando supremo, 1941-1942*, Milan,1975.

Ciano, Galeazzo, *Diario, 1937-1943*, Renzo De Felice, ed., Milan, 1980.

Clissold, Stephen, *Whirlwind. An Account of Marshal Tito's Rise to Power*, London, 1949.

Cenčić, Vjenceslav, *Enigma Kopinič*, Belgrade, 1983.

Colić, Mladen, *Takozvana Nezavisna Država Hrvatska 1941*, Belgrade, 1973.

Colotti, Enzo, Teodoro Sala & Giorgio Vaccarino, *L'Italia nell'Europa danubiana durante la seconda guerra mondiale*, Milan, 1967.

Comité d'histoire de la Seconde Guerre mondiale, *La Guerre en Méditerranée, 1939-1945. Actes du Colloque international tenu à Paris du 8 au 11 avril 1969*, Paris, 1971.

Cvijić, Vlastimir, *Dnevnik žigosanog*, Paris, 1988.

Ćirković, Sima M., *The Serbs*, Oxford, 2004.

Čulinović, Ferdo, *Okupatorksa podjela Jugoslavije*, Belgrade, 1970.

Dapčević, Peko, *Kako smo vodili rat*, Belgrade, 1975.

——*Od Pirineja do Cetinja*, Belgrade 1981.

Davidson, Basil, *Partisan Picture*, Bedford, 1946.

—— *Special Operations Europe. Scenes from the Anti-Nazi War*. London, 1980.

Deakin, F.W.D., *The Embattled Mountain*, London, 1971.

Dedijer, Vladimir, *Dnevnik*, 1ˢᵗ ed., Belgrade, 1945-1950.

——*Josip Broz Tito. Prilozi za biografiju*. Belgrade, 1953. *Tito Speaks. His Self-Portrait and Struggle with Stalin*, London 1953.

—— *Novi Prilozi za biografiju Josipa Broza Tita*, II, Rijeka & Belgrade, 1981.

De Felice, Renzo (ed.), *L'Italia tra tedeschi e alleati. La politica estera fascista e la seconda guerra mondiale*, Bologna, 1973.

De Lorenzis, Ugo, *Dal primo all'ultimo giorno. Ricordi di guerra, 1939-1945*, Milan, 1971.

Deroc, Milan, *British Special Operations Explored. Yugoslavia in Turmoil, 1941-1943, and the British Response*, New York, 1988.

Dimitrov, Georgi, *The Diary of Georgi Dimitrov, 1933-1949* (ed. by Ivo Banac), New Haven CT & London, 2003.

Djilas, Milovan, *Land without Justice*, New York, 1958.

—— *Wartime*, London, 1977.

Djordjević, Dimitrije, *Ožiljci i opomene*, Belgrade, 1994, 1995 & 2000.

Djordjević, Miodrag J., *Aprilski nemačko-jugoslovenski rat 1941*, Berne, 1966.

Djurić, Veljko Dj., *Ustaše i pravoslavlje. Hrvatska pravoslavna crkva*, Belgrade, 1989.

Doder, Milenko, *Kopinič bez enigme*, Zagreb, 1986.

Donia, Robert J., *Sarajevo. A Biography*, London, 2006.

Dujmović, Sonja, 'Srpsko gradjanstvo Bosne i Hercegovine prema Sporazumu Cvetković-Maček', in *Tokovi istorije*, 1-2, 2005.

Dulić, Tomislav, *Utopias of Nation. Local Mass Killings in Bosnia and Herzegovina, 1941-1942*, Uppsala, 2005.

Erak, Tomislav & Slavko Grubičić, ed., *Šibenik ustaničke 1941. Sjećanja na dogadjaje iz grada i okoline*, Šibenik, 1971.

Favagrossa, Carlo, *Perchè perdemmo la guerra. Mussolini e la produzione bellica*. Milan, 1948.

Fricke, Gert, *Kroatien 1941-1944. Der "Unabhängige Staat" in der Sicht des Deutschen Bevollmächtigten Generals in Agram, Glaise v. Horstenau,* Freiburg, 1972.

Gestro, Stefano, *L'armata stracciona. L'epopea della divisione "Garibaldi" in Montenegro, 1943-1945,* Bologna, 1964.

—— *La divisione italiana partigiana "Garibaldi". Montenegro 1943-1945,* Milan, 1982.

Glaise von Horstenau, Edmund, *Ein General im Zwielicht. Die Erinnerungen Edmund Glaises von Horstenau* Peter Broucek, ed., Vienna, Cologne & Graz, 1988.

Glen, Alexander, *Footholds against a Whirlwind,* London, 1975.

Glišić, Venceslav, *Teror i zločini nacističke Nemačke u okupiranoj Srbiji, 1941-1944,* Belgrade, 1970.

Godeša, Bojan, *Kdor ni znami je proti nam. Slovenski izobraženci med okupatorji, Osvobodilno fronto in protirevolucionarnim taborom,* Ljubljana, 1995.

—— *Slovensko nacionalno vprašanje med drugo svetovno vojno,* Ljubljana, 2006.

Goldstein, Slavko, ed., *Jews in Yugoslavia,* Zagreb, 1988.

Gorla, Giuseppe, *L'Italia nella seconda guerra mondiale. Diario di un milanese, ministro del Re nel governo di Mussolini,* Milan, 1959.

Grčić, Marko, ed., *Bleiburg. Otvoreni dossier,* Zagreb, 1990.

Gumz, Jonathan E., 'Wehrmacht Perceptions of Mass Violence in Croatia, 1941-1942', in *The Historical Journal,* 44, 4, 2001.

Gutman, Yisrael & Efraim Zuroff, eds., *Rescue Attempts during the Holocaust. Proceedings of the Second Yad Vashem International Historical Conference (April 1974),* Jerusalem, 1977.

Hadri, Ali, ed., *Kosova-Kosovo, 1941-1945,* Prishtinë/Priština, 1975.

Hametz, Maura, *Making Trieste Italian, 1918-1954,* London, 2005.

Hamilton-Hill, Donald, *SOE Assignment,* London, 1973.

Harriman, Helga H., *Slovenia under Nazi Occupation, 1941-1945,* New York & Washington, 1977.

Hilberg, Raul, *The Destruction of the European Jews,* 3rd ed., New Haven CT & London, 2005.

Hinsley, F.H. et al., *British Intelligence in the Second World War. Its Influence in Strategy and Operations,* London, 1979-1981.

Höttl, Wilhelm, *The Secret Front. The Story of Nazi Political Espionage*, London, 1953.

Howard, Michael, *British Intelligence in the Second World War. Strategic Deception*. Cambridge, 1990.

Hurem, Rasim, *Kriza NOPa u Bosni i Hercegovini krajem 1941. i početkom 1942*, Sarajevo, 1972.

Hussard, Jean, *Vu en Yougoslavie, 1939-1944*, Yverdon, 1944.

Ilić, Predrag, *Srpska pravoslavna crkava i tajna Dahaua. Mit i istina o zatočeništvu patrijarha Gavrila i episkopa Nikolaja Velimirovića u Dahau*, Belgrade, 2006.

Imlay, Talbot C., 'A Reassessment of Anglo-French Strategy during the Phoney War, 1939-1940', in *English Historical Review*, CXIX/481, 2004.

Inks, James M., *Eight Bailed Out*, New York, 1954.

International Conference on the History of Resistance Movements, *Les Systèmes d'occupation en Yougoslavie, 1941-1945*, Belgrade, 1963.

Ivanković-Vonta, Zvonko, *Hebrang*, Zagreb, 1988.

Jakšić, Mato, *Dubrovnik. Sjećanja*. Belgrade, 1966.

Jakšić, Pavle, *Nad uspomenama*, Belgrade, 1990.

Janojlić, Dragoljub, *Lošinjska zamka*, Smederevska Palanka, 2003.

Janjetović, Zoran, *Between Hitler and Tito. The Disappearance of the Vojvodina Germans*, Belgrade, 2000.

Jareb, Jere, *Pola stoljeća hrvatske politike*, Buenos Aires, 1960.

Jelić, Ivan, *Hrvatska u ratu i revoluciji, 1941-1945*, Zagreb, 1978.

Jelić-Butić, Fikreta, *Ustaše i Nezavisna Država Hrvatska, 1941-1945*, Zagreb, 1977.

────── *Hrvatska seljačka stranka*, Zagreb, 1983.

Johnson, Stowers, *Agents Extraordinary*, London, 1975.

Joksimović, Milorad T., *Iz minulih dana. Gradja za istoriju Drugog svetsksog rata*, Hamilton (Ontario), 1974.

Jovanić, Djoko, ed., *Lika u NOB 1941. Zbornik*, Belgrade, 1963.

Jovanović, Žarko S., *Seljaštvo u Srbiji u Drugom svetskom ratu, 1941-1945*, Belgrade, 1995.

Jurišić, Želimir Bob, *Ivo Andrić u Berlinu, 1939-1941*, Sarajevo 1989.

Kačarević, Bora, *U službi otadžbine*, Windsor (Ontario), 1993.

Kačavenda, Petar, *Nemci u Jugoslaviji, 1918-1945*, Belgrade, 1991.

Kalabić, Radovan, ed., *Ravnogorska istorija*, Belgrade, 1992.

Karapandžić, Bor. M., *Gradjanski rat u Srbiji, 1941-1945*, Cleveland OH, 1958.

Karchmar, Lucien, *Draža Mihailović and the Rise of the Chetnik Movement, 1941-1942*, New York, 1987.

Kardelj, Edvard, *Sećanja. Borba za priznanje i nezavisnost nove Jugoslavije, 1944-1957*, Ljubljana & Belgrade, 1980.

Kazimirović, Vasa, *NDH u svetlu nemačkih dokumenata i dnevnika Gleza fon Horstenau, 1941-1944*, Belgrade, 1987.

Kečkemet, Duško, *Židovi u povijesti Splita*, Split, 1971.

Kiszling, Rudolf, *Die Kroaten. Der Schicksalsweg eines Südslawenvolkes*, Graz & Cologne, 1956.

Knežević, Radoje L., *Rat 1941. i Kraljev izlazak iz zemlje* , Windsor (Ontario), 1958.

——— ed., *Knjiga o Draži*, Windsor (Ontario), 1956.

Knežević, Živan L. *27. mart 1941*, New York, 1979.

Kocbek, Edvard, *Tovarišija*, Ljubljana, 1949.

——— *Dokument*, Ljubljana,1967.

Kočović, Bogoljub, *Žrtve Drugog svetskog rata u Jugoslaviji*, London 1985, and subsequent editions Sarajevo & Belgrade.

Koljanin, Milan, *Nemački logor na Beogradskom sajmištu*, Belgrade, 1992.

Konjhodžić, Mahmud, *Od Kupe do mora*, Zagreb, 1963.

Košutić, Ivan, *Hrvatsko domobranstvo u Drugom svetskom ratu*, Zagreb, 1992.

Kovačić, Matija, *Od Radića do Pavelića*, Munich & Barcelona, 1970.

Krakov, Stanislav, *General Milan Nedić*, Munich, 1963-1968.

Krizman, Bogdan, *Ante Pavelić i ustaše*, Zagreb, 1978.

——— *Ustaše i Treći Reich*, Zagreb, 1983.

——— *NDH izmedju Hitlera i Mussolinija*, 2nd ed., Zagreb, 1983.

——— *Pavelić u bjekstvu*, Zagreb, 1986.

Kulić, Dimitrije, *Bugarska okupacija, 1941-1944*, Niš, 1970.

Kvaternik, Eugen Dido, *Sjećanja i zapažanja. Prilozi za hrvatsku povijest*, Jere Jareb, ed., Zagreb, 1995.

Lašić-Vasojević, Milija M., *Enemies on All Sides. The Fall of Yugoslavia*, Washington, 1976.

Lawrence, Christie, *Irregular Adventure*, London, 1947.

Lees, Michael, *Special Operations Executed in Serbia and Italy*, London, 1986.

—— *The Rape of Serbia. The British Role in Tito's Grab for Power, 1943-1944*, San Diego, New York & London, 1990.

Lekić, Radovan, *Andrijevički srez, 1941-1944. Prilog istoriji NOB Crne Gore*, Cetinje, 1961.

Leković, Mišo, *Martovski pregovori*, Belgrade, 1985.

Leontić, Boro, *Split 1941*, Belgrade, 1960.

Lukić, Milisav, *Grebići. Ratni dnevnik, 1942-1944*, Belgrade, 1972.

Maclean, Fitzroy, *Eastern Approaches*, London, 1949.

—— *The Heretic. The Life and Times of Josip Broz Tito*, New York, 1957.

—— *Disputed Barricade. The Life and Times of Josip Broz Tito, Marshal of Yugoslavia*, London, 1957.

Makedonska akademija na naukite i umetnostite, *Simpozium. Razvojot i karakteristikite na narodnoosloboditelnata voja i na revoluciijata vo Makedonija (Skopje 9-10.12.1971)*, Skopje, 1973.

Malcolm, Noel, *Kosovo. A Short History*, London, 1998.

Manoschek, Walter, *"Serbien ist judenfrei". Militärische Besatzungspolitik und Judenvernichtung in Serbien, 1941/2*, Munich, 1993.

Marjanović, Jovan, *Draža Mihailović izmedju Britanaca i Nemaca*, Zagreb, 1979.

Martin, David, *Ally Betrayed. The Uncensored Story of Tito and Mihailovich*, New York, 1946.

McConville, Michael, *A Small War in the Balkans. British Military Involvement in Wartime Yugoslavia, 1941-1945*, London 1986.

Milazzo, Matteo J., *The Chetnik Movement and the Yugoslav Resistance*, Baltimore & London, 1975.

Milošević, Slobodan, *Izbeglice i preseljenja na teritoriji okupirane Jugoslavije, 1941-1945*, Belgrade, 1981.

Milovanović Lune, Miodrag, *Nedovršeni dnevnik*, Belgrade, 1968.

Minić, Mihailo P., *Rasute kosti, 1941-1945*, Detroit, 1965.

Ministero della Difesa. Ufficio storico SM dell'Esercito, *Otto settembre 1943. L'Armistizio italiano 40 anni dopo. Atti dell Convegno internazionale, Milano 7-8.9.1983*, Aldo A. Mola & Romain H. Rainero, ed., Rome, 1985.

Mladenović, Miloš, *Lažni idoli i varljivi ideali*, London, (I)1965, (II)1983.

Montemaggi, Amedeo, *Linea Gotica 1944. La "Battaglia di Rimini" e lo sbarco in Grecia decisivi per l'Europa orientale e il Mediterraneo*, Rimini 2002.

—— *Linea Gottica 1944. Scontri di civiltà*, Rimini, 2006.

Morača, Pero, ed., *The Third Reich and Yugoslavia, 1933-1945*, Belgrade, 1977.

Mužić, Ivan, *Pavelić i Stepinac*, Split, 1991.

Nadj, Kosta, *Ratne uspomene*, Zagreb, 1979.

Nenadović, Aleksandar, *Razgovori s Kočom*, 2nd ed., Zagreb, 1989.

Nenezić, Dragan, *Italijanski okupacioni sistem u Jugoslaviji, 1941-1943*, Belgrade, 1999.

Neubacher, Hermann, *Sonderauftrag Südost, 1940-1945. Bericht eines fliegenden Diplomaten*, Göttingen,1956.

Nikolić, Kosta, *Istorija ravnogorskog pokreta, 1941-1945*, Belgrade, 1999.

—— *Strah i nada u Srbiji, 1941-1944. Svakodnevni život pod okupacijom*, Belgrade, 2002.

Nikolić, Vinko, *Pred vratima domovine*, Munich, 1967.

Nikoliš, Gojko, *Memoari. Korijen, stablo, pavetina*, 3d ed., Zagreb 1981.

Novak, Bogdan C., *Trieste, 1941-1943. The Ethnic, Political, and Ideological Struggle*, Chicago, 1970.

O'Kney, Louis, *What Prince Freedom?* New York, 1972.

Orlow, Dietrich, *The Nazis in the Balkans. A Case Study of Totalitarian Politics*, Pittsburgh, 1968.

Orović, Savo, *Ratni dnevnik, 1941-1945*, Belgrade, 1972.

Pahor, Boris, *Zgodba o reki, kripti in dvorljivem golubu*, Maribor 2006.

Pajović, Radoje, 'Politička akcije Sekule Drljevića i njegova saradnja sa ustaškim vodjstvom i njemačkim poslanstvom u Zagrebu, 1943-1945', in *Časopis za suvremenu povijest*, 3/1, 1975.

—— *Kontrarevolucija u Crnoj Gori. Četnički i federalistički pokret, 1941-1945*, Cetinje, 1977.

Palmer, Stephen E., Jr & Robert R. King, *Yugoslav Communism and the Macedonian Question*, Hamden, CT, 1971.

Parežanin, Ratko, *Drugi svetski rat i Dimitrije V. Ljotić*, Munich, 1971.

310

Pavlović, Momčilo & Veroljub Trajković, 'Savezničko bombardovanje Leskovca 6. septembra 1944', in *Leskovački zbornik*, 1995.

Pavlowitch, Stevan K., *Yugoslavia*, London, 1971.

―― *Unconventional Perceptions of Yugoslavia, 1940–1945*, New York, 1985.

―― *Yugoslavia's Great Dictator Tito. A Reassessment*, London, 1992.

―― *A History of the Balkans, 1804–1945*, London, 1999.

―― *Serbia. The History behind the Name*, London, 2002.

Pešelj, Branko, *U vrtlogu hrvatske politike. Sjećanja i pogledi*, Zurich 1989.

Pešut, Mane M., *Revolucija u Lici, 1941–1945*, Bielefeld, 1966.

Petranović, Branko, *Revolucija i kontrarevolucija u Jugoslaviji, 1941–1945*, Belgrade, 1983.

―― *Srbija u drugom svetskom ratu, 1939–1945*, Belgrade, 1992.

―― *Strategija Draže Mihailovića, 1941–1945*, Belgrade, 2000.

―― & Sava Dautović, *Jugoslovenska revolucija i SSSR*, Belgrade, 1988.

Petrović, Dragoljub, *Jugoslavija u antifašističkom ratu 1941–1945. pred sudom istorije*, Belgrade, 2001.

Petrović-Njegoš, Mihailo, *Iz mojih memoara*, Windsor (Ontario), 1961.

Piccini, Umberto, *Una pagina strappata*, Rome, 1983.

Piemontese, Giuseppe, *Ventinove mesi di occupazione italiana nella provincia di Lubiana. Considerazioni e documenti*, Ljubljana, 1946.

Pillon, Giorgio, *Spie per l'Italia. Come fecero la guerra gli 007 dei nostri servizi segreti*, Rome, 1968.

Plazina, Stanojlo S., *Sa jelice planule varnice. Prilog za istoriju narodnog ustanka Ravnogorskog pokreta u Dragočevu*, Melbourne, 1974.

Plećaš, Nedjelko B., *Ratne godine 1941–1945*, Columbus, OH, 1983.

Plećaš-Nitonja, Nikola, *Požar u Krajini*, Chicago, 1975.

Popović, Branko, ed., *Djelo Milovana Djilasa*, Podgorica, 2003.

Popović, Koča, *Dnevnik. Beleške. Dokumenti*, Belgrade, 1988.

Prcela, John & Stanko Guldescu, ed., *Operation Slaughterhouse. Eyewitness Accounts of Postwar Massacres in Yugoslavia*, Philadelphia, 1970.

Pulić, Nikola, *Sinovi Orjune*, Zagreb, 1971.

Radić, Radmila, *Verom protiv vere. Država i verske zajednice u Srbiji, 1945–1953*, I, Belgrade, 1995.

—— *Život u vremenima: Gavrilo Dožić* (*1881-1950*), Belgrade, 2006.

Radonjić, Borivoje I., *Sećanja iz rata, revolucije i kazamata*, Belgrade, 2006.

Redžić, Enver, *Muslimansko autonomaštvo i 13. SS divizija. Autonomija Bosne i Hercegovine i Hitlerov Treći Rajh*, Sarajevo, 1987.

—— *Bosnia and Herzegovina in the Second World War*, London, 2005.

Rešetić, Ivan, ed., *Lika u NOBu 1942. Zbornik*, Belgrade, 1971.

Ribbentrop, Joachim von, *The Ribbentrop Memoirs* (trans. Oliver Watson), London, 1954.

Ribar, Ivan, *Uspomene iz Narodnooslobodilačke borbe*, Belgrade, 1961.

Ristić, Dragiša N., *Yugoslavia's Revolution of 1941*, University Park, PA & London, 1966.

Ristović, Milan D., *Nemački "Novi poredak" u jugoistočna Evropa, 1940/41-1944/45. Planovi o budućnosti i praksa*, Belgrade, 1991.

Ritchie, Sebastian, *Our Man in Yugoslavia. The Story of a Secret Service Operative*, London, 2004.

Roatta, Mario, *Otto milioni di baionette. L'esercito italiano in guerra, 1940-1944*, Milan, 1946.

Roberts, Walter R., *Tito, Mihailović and the Allies, 1941-1945*, 3rd ed., Durham, NC, 1987.

Rodogno, Davide, *Il nuovo ordine mediterraneo. Le politiche di occupazione dell'Italia fascista in Europa, 1940-1943*, Turin, 2003.

Rojnica, Ivo, *Susreti i doživljaji, 1938-1945*, Munich, 1969.

Romano, Jaša, *Jevreji Jugoslavije, 1941-1945. Žrtve genocida i učesnici Narodnooslobodilačkog rata*, Belgrade, 1980.

Rootham, Jasper, *Miss Fire. The Chronicle of a British Mission to Mihailovich, 1943-1944*, London, 1946.

Rossi, Francesco, *Come arrivammo all'armistizio*, Milan, 1946.

Russo, Alfio, *Rivoluzione in Jugoslavia*, Rome, 1944.

Saje, Franček, *Belogardizem*, 2nd ed., Ljubljana, 1952.

Scotti, Giacomo, *Ventimila caduti. Gli italiani in Jugoslavia dal 1943 al 1945*, Milan, 1970.

—— *Il battaglione degli "Straccioni". I militari italiani nelle brigate jugoslave, 1943-1945*, Milan, 1974.

—— *"Bono Taliano". Gli italiani in Jugoslavia, 1941-1943*, Milan, 1977.

——— *I "disertori". Le scelte dei militari italiani sul fronte jugoslavo prima dell'8 settembre*, Milan, 1980.

——— & Luciano Viazzi, *L'inutile vittoria. La tragica esperienza delle truppe italiane in Montenegro, 1941-1942*, Milan, 1989.

Schmider, Klaus, *Partisanenkrieg in Jugoslawien, 1941-1944*, Hamburg, 2002.

Seitz, Albert B., *Mihailović Hoax or Hero?* Columbus, OH, 1953.

Shoup, Paul, *Communism and the Yugoslav National Question*, New York & London, 1968.

Sidoti, Antoine, *Le Monténégro et l'Italie durant la Seconde guerre mondiale. Histoire, mythes et réalités*, Paris, 2003.

——— *Partisans et tchetniks en Yougoslavie durant la Seconde guerre mondiale. Idéologie et mythogenèse*, Paris, 2004.

Simoni, Leonardo, *Berlino Ambasciata d'Italia, 1939-1943*, Rome, 1946.

Sinovčić, Marko, *NDH u svietlu dokumenata*, Buenos Aires, 1950.

Sirc, Ljubo, *Between Hitler and Tito. Nazi Occupation and Communist Oppression*. London, 1989.

Smodlaka, Josip, *Partizanski dnevnik*, Belgrade, 1972.

Stanković, Djordje, 'Savezničko bombardovanje Nezavisne Države Hrvatske, 1943-1945', in *Tokovi istorije*, 1-4, 2001.

Stefanović, Mladen, *Zbor Dimitrija Ljotića, 1941-1945*, Belgrade, 1984.

Steinberg, Jonathan, *All or Nothing. The Axis and the Holocaust, 1941-1943*, London, 1990.

Stenton, Michael, *Radio London and Resistance in Occupied Europe. British Political Warfare, 1939-1943*, Oxford, 2000.

Stevanović, Dragomir S., *Sura grobnica. "Prihvatni logor Zemun", 1942-1944*, London, 1967.

——— *Agonija slobode*, Windsor (Ontario), 1970.

Sugar, Peter, ed., *Native Fascism in the Successor States, 1918-1945*, Santa Barbara, CA, 1971.

Sweet-Escott, Bickham, *Baker Street Irregular*, London, 1965.

Šegrt, Vlado, *Ratne uspomene*, Belgrade, 1964.

Šehić, Nusret, ed., *Migracije i Bosna i Hercegovina*, Sarajevo, 1990.

Šibl, Ivan, *Iz ilegalnog Zagreba 1941*, Zagreb, 1965.

Šuljak, Dinko, *Tražio sam Radićevu Hrvatsku*, Barcelona & Munich, 1988.

Terzić, Milan, 'Jugoslovenska kraljevska vlada, general Draža Mihailović i savezničko bombardovanje ciljeva u Jugoslaviji, 1942-44.g.'. in *Tokovi istorije*, 1-2, 2005.

Terzić, Velimir, *Slom Kraljevine Jugoslavije 1941. Uzroci i posledice poraza*, Belgrade & Titograd, 1982.

Timofejev, Aleksej, 'General Krejter o budućnosti ruske emigracije u Rusiji', in *Tokovi istorije*, 4/2006, 2006.

Tito, Josip Broz, *Vojno delo*, I 1941-1945, Belgrade, 1982.

Todorovich, Boris J., *Last Words. A Memoir of World War II and the Yugoslav Tragedy*, New York, 1989.

Tolstoy, Nikolai, *The Minister and the Massacres*, London, 1986.

Tomasevich, Jozo, *War and Revolution in Yugoslavia, 1941-1945. The Chetniks*, Stanford, CA, 1975.

—— *War and Revolution in Yugoslavia, 1941-1945. Occupation and Collaboration*, Stanford, CA, 2001.

Topalović, Živko, *Pokreti narodnog otpora u Jugoslaviji, 1941-1945*, Paris, 1958.

—— *Kako su komunisti dograbili vlast u Jugoslaviji*, London, 1964.

—— *Borba za budućnost Jugoslavije*, London, 1967.

—— *Srbija pod Dražom*, London, 1968.

—— *Jugoslavija. Žrtvovani saveznik*, London, 1970.

—— *Draža Mihajlović i engleska vojna misija*, Paris, 1980.

Tošić, Desimir, *Crkva, država i društvo*, Belgrade, 2005.

Trew, Simon, *Britain, Mihailović and the Chetniks, 1941-1942*, Basingstoke & London, 1998.

Trifković, Srdja, *Ustaša. Croatian Separatism and Croatian Politics, 1929-1945*, London, 1998.

Tripković, Djoko, *Beograd pod bombama*, Belgrade, 1999.

Trucco, Giovanni, *Nell'ombra di Tito*, Milan, 1954.

Umiltà, Carlo, *Jugoslavia e Albania. Memorie di un diplomatico*, Milan, 1947.

van Crefeld, Martin L., *Hitler's Strategy 1940-1941. The Balkan Clue*, 1973.

Vauhnik, Vladimir, *Nevidna fronta. Spomini*, Buenos Aires, 1965.

Velebit, Vladimir, *Sećanja*, Zagreb, 1983.

—— *Vladimir Velebit svjedok istorije (Razgovore vodila i knjigu priredila Mira Šuvar)*, Zagreb, 2001.

—— *Tajne i zamke Drugog svjetskog rata*, Zagreb, 2002.

Višnjić, Čedomir, *Partizansko ljetovanje. Hrvatska i Srbi, 1945-1950*, Zagreb, 2003.

—— *Kordunaški proces*, Zagreb, 2004.

Vrančić, Vjekoslav, *Hochverrat. Die Zweite Italienische Armee im Kroatischen Küstengebiet*, Zagreb, 1943.

—— *Branili smo državu. Uspomene, osvrti, doživljaji*, Barcelona & Munich, 1985.

Vučetić, Stevan J., *Gradjanski rat u Crnoj Gori, 1941-1945*, Detroit, MI, 1947.

Vučković, Zvonimir, *Sećanja iz rata*, London, 1980 & 1984.

White, Leigh, *The Long Balkan Night*, New York, 1944.

Williams, Heather, *Parachutes, Patriots and Partisans. The Special Operations Executive and Yugoslavia, 1941-1945*, London, 2003.

Wuescht, Johann, *Jugoslawien und das Dritte Reich. Eine dokumentierte Geschichte der deutsch-jugoslawischen Beziehungen von 1933 bis 1945*, Stuttgart, 1969.

Yovitchitch, Lena A., *Within Closed Frontiers. A Woman in Wartime Yugoslavia*, London, 1956.

Zaccone, Umberto, *Guerra partigiana in Montenegro*, Turin, 1966.

Zanussi, Giacomo, *Guerra e catastrofe d'Italia*, Rome, 1945.

Žerjavić, Vladimir, *Gubici stanovništva Jugoslavije u drugom svjetskom ratu*, Zagreb, 1989.

Researched and written in Southampton, London, Paris, Milan, Bologna, Florence, Rome and Belgrade 1971–2006

INDEX

N.B. 'Yugoslavia' and 'Second World War' are not entered. Serbo-Croatian and Slovenian letters are listed as follows: Č and Ć after C, Dj after D, Lj after L, Š after S and Ž after Z.